Ted Walker is a poet, travel writer, autobiographer, short story writer and radio and television comedy dramatist. He lives and works in his native Sussex.

IN SPAIN

Ted Walker

CORGI BOOKS

IN SPAIN

A CORGI BOOK   0 552 99343 3

Originally published in Great Britain by
Martin Secker & Warburg Ltd.

PRINTING HISTORY
Secker & Warburg edition published 1987
Corgi edition published 1989

This book is set in 10/11pt Mallard

Corgi Books are published by Transworld Publishers Ltd.,
61-63 Uxbridge Road, Ealing, London W5 5SA, in Australia by
Transworld Publishers (Australia) Pty. Ltd., 15-23 Helles
Avenue, Moorebank, NSW 2170, and in New Zealand by
Transworld Publishers (N.Z.) Ltd., Cnr. Moselle and Waipareira
Avenues, Henderson, Auckland.

Made and printed in Great Britain by
The Guernsey Press Co. Ltd., Guernsey, Channel Islands

ACKNOWLEDGEMENTS

I should like to thank the Society of Authors and New England College for their assistance before and during the writing of this book.

FOR MY GRANDCHILDREN
JONATHAN AND RUTH

LA CORUÑA
PRINCIPADO DE ASTURIAS
OVIEDO
SANTANDER
CANTABRI
LUGO
GALICIA
PONTEVEDRA
ORENSE
LEÓN
BURGOS
PALENCIA
VALLADOLID
ZAMORA
CASTILLA Y
SALAMANCA
SEGOVIA
ÁVILA
MADRID
MADRI
PORTUGAL
TOLEDO
CÁCERES
CASTILLA - L
EXTREMADURA
CIUDAD RE
BADAJOZ
CÓRDOBA
JAÉ
ANDALUCÍA
SEVILLA
HUELVA
GRAN
MÁLAGA
CÁDIZ

CHAPTER ONE

The warmish maytime air of Santander, away from the water-front, carried mingled scents no visitor to Spain disremembers: fresh bread and over-ripe melons, shellfish, chopped onion, red meats being cooked in sauces containing bitter dark chocolate. I had time to kill while waiting for the Madrid train. Up alleys, after leaving my luggage at the station, I smelled the beginnings of slow-to-simmer soups and stews, newly-crushed garlic heads releasing juice into hot olive oil; and the fragrances of late breakfasts: pungent coffee, newly-fried *churros*, the smoke of black tobacco.

Outside the Imago supermarket there sat in his filthy rags a skeletal little boy of maybe six or seven. Round his neck he wore a notice, pencil scrawl on a bit of cardboard box: *I am Paco. My father is out of work. I need 50 pesetas to eat. Help me, for the love of God.* There were forty-five pesetas in his tray. Making up the price of his meal with a duro, I noticed that the leg I'd thought he was sitting on had been amputated. Further along the same prosperous shopping street, an ancient woman in widow's black sat in the gutter against a parked car. Her skirts and the tassels of her shawl trailed in a puddle of dirty water. She supported her begging claw with her other hand, keeping it pointed at you as you passed and forcing you to look at her in the eye. Unlike Paco, she had no tray; if you gave to her, you had no option but to place the coin carefully into her horny palm.

At once I saw dozens more beggars, all parading and exploit-ing, with exquisite professionalism, their various abjectness: great age, mutilation, disfigurement, plain indigence. Straight from a canvas by Goya they confronted me with hideous, twisted faces, shrivelled arms, huge strawberry marks a deep shade of sepia. One of them had the whole side of his face and neck a continuous passage of scar-tissue the artificial

11

colour of some new plastic; another, a warty nose the size of a lemon. Some of the older men – amputees and those with old wounds to display – would perhaps have been survivors of the Civil War. A much younger, wrecked creature, with no legs and only one flipper-like arm, propelled himself at a startling lick on a kind of skateboard. In Britain he would have been concealed from the public gaze with welfare and genteel tact. In Spain, you participated in his existence – just as (such being the promiscuous nature of street life where the weather is hot) you couldn't help getting, through open doors and windows, whiffs of other people's dinners and snatches of their domestic rows. When I took a few quick steps to escape, he paddled himself alongside, loudly demanding money. I sensed how deeply etched on my face must have been the guilt by which he knew I should feel forced to give; and with a hot onrush of anxiety I wondered how many more beggars – hundreds, thousands, tens of thousands – inhabited other streets and alleyways the length and breadth of Spain, lying in wait. In and out of smart fashion-houses, well-dressed shoppers came and went impassively past the human detritus. When accosted, a few gave the odd coin or two; but most spoke a few quiet words and went on their way unmolested. I listened for whatever it was they murmured: a ritual phrase like a response in a catechism. I learned it; and found the courage and callousness to say to my persecutor, 'Que Dios te ampare.' Straightaway and without rancour, he left me and navigated back to his favourite pitch.

I practised my know-how along the opposite side of the street. 'May God succour you,' I said: twice, three times, four times, the words were a charm.

Now I saw blind lottery ticket sellers at their stations every twenty yards or so in the shade of shop doorways or under awnings. Not beggars, these: but for certain using something of the beggar's art. Some made the most of blank sockets; others tilted heads at angles sighted people seldom adopt, so that the white of an eye might pathetically glisten, faintest blue of a peeled egg. Then there were the gipsies, for whom begging was a craft more itinerant than stationary. A family of ten was working the wide, busy pavement, trawling like a fleet of canny fishermen who know where the shoals will swim.

There was something cheering, I thought, about the candour

and breezy confidence with which these gipsies closed upon their prey. The others were there still: the disabled, the obviously suffering, those whose evident pain and misery made you wince and grit your teeth. Could I pass all of them by with no more to offer than a mindless phrase? How could I not give, at least to some? Within half an hour of arriving in the country that was to be my home for three months, I was being drawn by pity into the lives of perfect strangers: no bad thing perhaps for one such as I, only too prone to *self* pity. Which was worse: to be wilfully impervious, or to give in to a chronic, soft, bleeding-heart liberal sentimentality which would have me distributing single pesetas to as many as asked? How should I deal with genuine hard-luck cases; how resist the pleadings of undernourished urchins? It was a problem immediately made even more complex when I saw Paco's father, a snappy dresser, scoop up the contents of his son's full tray and head for the nearest bar.

'When you've lived here as long as I have, you don't notice them any more,' said the young, bearded Englishman in the train an hour later. We were talking not about beggars but about the countless heaps of hardcore, tiles and bricks you saw lying about in odd corners of yards and vacant lots long after a new building had been put up, or an old one repaired. Nobody ever seemed to clear up afterwards: it was as though the materials were deliberately left so that, next time a roof needed patching or a wall needed making good, they'd already be to hand.

By now we had left behind the lush, watery Cantabrian dairy pastures for the uncompromising terrains of Old Castile: high country whose scattered, dusty villages looked as though they were all collapsing upon themselves out of exhaustion. My companion worked for the British Council in Madrid. He had just put his wife on the ferry so that she could go home to England to have her baby. I looked from the window and felt at once daunted and exhilarated by the landscape. It was vast, and it was noble. If you looked very carefully, you could usually descry at least one human being in what at first had seemed an emptiness: a figure in the far distance leading a mule; a peasant woman, hoe at the slope, walking towards some distant but not yet visible habitation; or perhaps a rock chaos strewn over a flat-topped prominence would turn out

13

to be, on further inspection, a flock of sheep whose shepherd would rise to his feet and stand foursquare to watch us pass.

We went to the refreshment car for a bottle of beer and to watch the approach of Ávila. The view of this city from the train is one of the great sights of Europe, walls and bastions of warm, honey-coloured stone still much as they must have looked in medieval times. The place lay upon its undulating plateau, marvellous, somewhere I might well have chosen for my summer's writing stint. I said as much.

'Where in fact are you headed, then?'

'Cuenca,' I said, 'in New Castile.'

'Why there?'

'I'm only going to be happy where I really know the language. Catalonia's out because I don't understand much Catalan, Galicia because I don't speak any *gallego* at all. And the Basque country – well, I'm not going *there*! Not just because I'd never learn a syllable of Basque, but because my wife would fret at home about my getting too close to terrorist bombs. Then again, I don't want to have to wrestle with local variations and dialects, so that disqualifies Asturias and Valencia. Oh, and I can do without heavy accents, so not Andalusia. At a pinch, I might have chosen Aragon or parts of Extremadura or Leon. Frankly though, there doesn't seem much point in considering anywhere outside Castile.'

'OK. But why Cuenca?'

'I'll be working at my trade – I need a town big enough to have photocopying facilities and shops that sell things like paperclips. But I don't want anywhere that's likely to be too big and anonymous. So that rules out cities like Madrid, obviously, and even Valladolid. I'm not too keen on the idea of touristy centres, either, so not Toledo or Segovia.'

'That still leaves a pretty wide choice. Why Cuenca? Why not Guadalajara, or Alcalá? Why not Soria – or Palencia, where we stopped earlier this afternoon?'

'Well, this'll sound daft, but . . .'

'Go on.'

'My brother saw bits of Cuenca in a Spanish language course on the telly. He said it looked nice. I'm taking his word for it.'

'It *is* nice. You'll like it there. But now, do tell me. Why choose Spain in the first place?'

*　　*　　*

14

Indeed – why Spain? The young man's question, as soon as I had inadequately answered it, prompted a happy daydream as the train began its long descent towards the capital. I'd made my first visit to the country in 1955. Aged twenty, with new-found aesthetic and intellectual pretensions (and, I daresay, an insufferable Oxbridge snobbery), I could have wished to travel with a party of like-minded young people: bookish linguists, clever sophisticates all. I hadn't bargained on the unlikely group my parents had gathered together to accompany us and my ten-year-old brother: Sid, a wild-eyed, rough-hewn scoutmaster; Douglas, his balding, sheepfaced friend; the widow Peacock (loud and difficult to please) and her mongol daughter, the nice little Winnie, and another widow, a certain Mrs Boon. In two cars we had progressed through France, Sid's 1934 Hillman (in which we menfolk rode) sporting kitbags on its wings like ancient cannon. At Perpignan we left the cars in lock-ups and took a morning train to the Cerbère/Portbou frontier post.

I was to enter Spain many times since then. I have arrived by sea at Santander, and by air at Barajas airport, Madrid. I have crossed the Roncesvalles pass on the classic pilgrims' route from France, and I have driven in from the abrupt slopes of Andorra. I have crossed the Bidasoa bridge on foot from Hendaye to Irún, and I have slipped through from Portugal at quiet, leafy spots east of Bragança, Portalegre and Évora. Not one of these entrances was made with anything like the same sense of excitement and incredulous wonder as when, in that quaint and raggle-taggle company, I transferred my luggage to the Spanish train on its wider gauge track.

What a train! Nothing to do with Europe, clearly: rather, a century-old Mexican monster, complete with cow-catcher, brass belly-bands and a tall chimney belching smoke not of coal but of wood; a train straight out of a cowboy film, a Wells Fargo Special with bygone carriages of nice, varnished oak – one that Hopalong Cassidy might have ridden alongside to foil a robbery while Lulubelle, simpering beneath a white parasol, waved from the window. The vast engine quietly hissed and occasionally sneezed a mild, hay-fever sneeze.

The driver and his fireman sat nearby on the platform, their backs to the wall in the shade, eating a leisurely snack. I watched them as I might have observed rare animals in the

15

wild. Real Spaniards! They tore hunks of yellowy-crust bread, sliced rounds of *chorizo* sausage, with wonderfully long, flick-bladed knives, and drank wine from squeezed leather *botas* at arm's length – the glittering parabola of liquid bridging lips and fingertips exactly as described in an ancient picaresque novel I'd been reading. Beyond in the sun, a dusty pair of *guardias* sat on a bale of cork, their rifles between their knees. My father was shocked when they rolled and lit cigarettes and in a bored fashion spat – such behaviour falling far short of the *umpity-poo* he expected from uniformed officials.

I stood in the corridor the entire journey down to Barcelona, avid not to miss one clod or pebble of the landscape. Many hours it took through the broiling July afternoon to cover the ground. Sometimes we might have gone as fast as twenty-five mph through the fields of tall maize. Straw-hatted peasants returned my waves as, gently, we swayed past. Mrs Peacock brewed up on a Primus stove in her compartment, and I was embarrassed and ashamed: not because she boiled water on a train – which was a particularly Spanish thing to do – but because she would insist on having her English *tea*, which I thought disqualified her (and by implication her companions) from the title of true traveller. It did nothing of the sort, of course: quite the reverse, in fact.

After the richness of the countryside, Gerona came as a shock. Crumbly cliffs of slum apartments, strings of raggety washing, crying babies and starving dogs were my first, sharp intimation of the poverty of Spain. High up in one peeling building I saw a white-haired man with an eye-patch lean over a perilous balcony as though about to plunge down and end it all. We waited a long while in Gerona station. Along the platform came a one-armed *venta ambulante* with a tray of bottled beer and *bocadillos* consisting of entire loaves slit lengthwise and filled with stiff rounds of *salchichón*. I bought a beer, wanting to practise my Spanish; and I suffered the pang of realizing that what I had been warned about was true: we were visiting a region of Spain where Castilian Spanish was not the vernacular. Our transaction was conducted amicably enough; but though he understood me, the Catalan hawker was obviously not inclined to accommodate me by departing from his native tongue. I was not in the Spain I had been

16

preparing for through six years of studying her language and literature. I wondered, the rest of the journey, whether I could persuade my parents and the others that we should change our plans and go on to Madrid.

But there was no reasonable hope of this; and besides, when eventually we reached Barcelona, I (as ex officio guide) had other, more urgent, anxieties. No sooner had we stepped off the train in the large, cool hall of the Estación de Francia, than we were surrounded and shouted at by a dozen hotel touts. Some wore peaked caps bearing the names of their establishments, some ran only to button-tags: all were strident, down-at-heel and in need of a shave. To my dismay, they were the standard Spaniards of crude, Anglo-Saxon prejudice. Through a thicket of waving arms, I lip-read what Mrs Peacock was opining: *typical, innit?* I hadn't bargained on my first experience in the great second city of Spain being a farcical discomfiture. I was rattled – as many people are when first arriving in this unremitting country – and I tried very hard to bring about calm. Quietly I uttered a series of courteous requests, necessitating impeccable subjunctives in the minor clauses, that the hotel representatives kindly not bother us. But by now my elbows, my lapels and my collar were being gripped and tugged and I was being exhorted and beseeched in a language I resented for being beyond my understanding. A hard ball of anger rose in my throat and I lost my temper. Abandoning the pure Castilian, I bawled in my own Brighton cockney idiom: 'Bugger off, you gits, and leave us be!' The touts fell away. I led my laughing group a few blocks up the Vía Layetana and, as though confident I knew what I was about, arranged our accommodation in a seedy-looking but respectable *pensión*.

We stayed four or five nights: long enough for my father to sample delights such as having a shoeshine while simultaneously sitting at a bar and nursing a glass of *horchata de chufas* (pressed tiger-nuts) – 'Get us an ooftie-chooftie,' he'd say; long enough for me to see my first bullfight; to take part in the evening *paseo* up and down the Ramblas – in short, to acquire a taste and a longing for more. I didn't mind, as Mrs Peacock kept on volubly minding, that the washbasins got fuller when you pulled out the plug, nor did I mind the old cabbage-water smell of cracked drains, or the shops being

17

shut all afternoon, or the filthiness of the paper money, or the tram conductors complaining if you had nothing smaller than a peseta note. It didn't matter to me if meals were served at eccentric hours, or if they contained the claws and tentacles of nameless sea-creatures, or if a cockroach occasionally scuttled at the speed of light across your bedroom floor.

Being an (as yet) unsullied and unsold-out Socialist, naturally I had grave political reservations about the country. It was then the hey-day of Franco's dictatorship, and the visitor to Spain was forcibly struck by visible symptoms of an oppressive Church and State: cohorts of overweeningly smug and superior cigarette-smoking priests ensconced at café terraces promptly at the fashionable hour; a loaded machine-gun at each street corner (no fewer than three on the steps of the *Correos*). But while the head was busy deploring, the heart was being won over. Spain belonged to a different era from that of the rest of Europe. Being there was to be translated back to Edwardian times – even in go-ahead, busy Barcelona – and I found this captivating. It was worth stealing out of bed late at night, dressing again, stepping outside for a breath of fresh air, if only to indulge once again in the ritual of summoning the *sereno* to let you back in. You would clap your hands peremptorily at your door, wait for the answering clack of his stick on the wall or pavement; and then he'd appear amid much jangling of dozens of bunches of keys, touch his peaked cap, open up for you, graciously but not obsequiously accept the few céntimos you tipped him; and finally bow you over the threshold.

Our short visit over, I realized how little time I'd spent getting the hang of the place – also how long I'd been obliged to spend in souvenir shops while members of our party got me to ask the price of *mantillas* and toy tambourines with pictures of bullfighters on them. I had scarcely explored beyond the *barrio gótico*. I'd not been able to wander about, eavesdropping on the fragments of conversations, peeping into yards, letting adventure come to me (as it always does come in Spain) simply by keeping still somewhere and waiting for things to happen. My best half-hour had been on the Sunday morning when, alone for once, I had ambled about in the Plaza Real, marvelling at the elegant palms and listening to the haggling, in their impromptu booths, of stamp dealers

18

and their customers. Brittle, vibrant syllables had ricocheted off walls like handfuls of flung pebbles. As I travelled one final time down to the ground floor in the *pension*'s engaging, superannuated, brass-and-wrought-iron lift, I vowed to come back to Spain one day unhampered by the likes of the widow Peacock.

And return I did – again to Barcelona – a few years later, at Easter: this time as a semi-professional courier with an educational travel agency.

The moment we arrived (my party was of Manchester youngsters with a know-it-all master in charge) I sensed something was amiss with our lodgings: something which, in the glaring sunlight of mid-afternoon, I couldn't quite put my finger on. After dark though, I realized precisely what was wrong. Our hotel, in the heart of the red-light *barrio chino*, was clearly, on some of its lower floors, a brothel.

'This place is most unsatisfactory,' complained the master. 'Obviously it specializes in accommodating theatricals.' At first, I took this to be a genteel Didsbury euphemism; but then I saw there was no ambiguity in the man's eyes. 'I've seen the theatre, just round the corner on that big avenue,' he said. 'You won't convince me otherwise.'

It seemed prudent and pragmatic not to disabuse him. For the rest of the week, I decided, we'd go on assuming that the unending parade of garish ladies and their consorts whom we met on the staircase landings were dancers and their stage-door Johnnies. (At the time, one of the great international ballet companies was appearing at the *Liceo*, the nearest theatre on the *Ramblas* to our hotel.)

As it happened, that very first night we saw some of the best theatre Spain has to offer: the spectacle of an Easter procession through the late-night streets. Well after eleven o'clock we took up our positions in the Plaza de Cataluña, as near the kerb as the packed crowd allowed us. There was the ceaseless hum and thrum of expectancy in the air – as of a flock of vaguely menacing birds about to roost – and then, when distant watchers first glimpsed the approach of the procession, the noise of anticipation changed. Now voices were plangent and far-carrying, like trumpets or bells, creating excitement not only by being loud but also by being rhythmically rat-tat-tatting, by bouncing metallically off cackling laughter one moment

19

and clashing with happy or sad or passionate song the next. Amidst this clamour we craned our necks and wondered what it could be we were waiting for. I smelt the reek of smoke and paraffin even before I saw the first of the torches – at the very moment when the already dense crowd began to surge and pack even tighter and press inexorably forward.

Then fell an awesome silence (as of shock, or the ghastly realization of a tragedy about to occur) as the first of the floats, the *pasos*, came into view, followed by another and another and another. Some were on carts, other borne high and swaying from side to side on the shoulders of strong, tall men. By flickering light and cackling chatter, gaudy statues of the Virgin progressed. Sometimes they seemed startlingly to move as the bearers lurched this way or that, effigies made literal with stage make-up, actual hair and children's-size, well-cut clothes: perhaps *too* real, too bedecked and bejewelled for a Protestant to be able to admire. In truth, they resembled the women going constantly in and out of our hotel; and this was unnerving – remembering what the profession had been of the other Mary, the Magdalene. Something they possessed, those trumpery Madonnas with their extravagant cosmetics and trinket vulgarity, something ordinary people seemed to know about and which had nothing at all to do with gentility or the bourgeois notion of good taste. The disturbing female figurines passed, followed by some nailed and bloodied Christs. Then began a different experience: for now came the ineffably slow, profoundly moving and spellbinding column of penitents.

At first, all seemed an elaborate artifact in motion: hundreds of men, bare to the waist and barefoot, in loincloths or tattered trousers, were re-enacting the agony of Christ's climb to Calvary. Most of them were inflicting pain upon themselves to imitate or atone for that agony. It might have been a crowd of well-directed Hollywood extras in a Sam Goldwyn Biblical extravaganza (how well the Make-up Department had done their job: so convincing the sweat, the scars, the running sores!). But then you realized that none of this was pretence; that the strange sheen on the men's scourged backs and torsos was due not to some subtly contrived lighting effect but to the steady shine of streetlamps and the licking flames of torches. The chains and manacles the men wore were real chains and manacles, just as heavy as they looked; the great wooden crosses some of them were half-carrying, half-dragging, must have weighed hundredweights; some, hauling hand-forged links behind them as they walked on their knees, had worn their very kneecaps to the bone. 'Have they come from far like that?' I asked an old woman. 'All the way down from the mountain – several kilometres,' she said, her face white with vehemence. There was still some way for them to go, too, for the procession was to take a circuitous route to the cathedral. One man collapsed under the burden of his cross not far from where we stood. I heard his gasp and grunt, the rasp of his cross in the gutter. No one went to help him; I believe he wished for no help or refreshment. More men shuffled past, some of them very old, and some of whom were on all fours; some were walking backwards and some tugging chains so long and ponderous that many of those behind couldn't help but tread on them excruciatingly again and again; and so it went on until night became *la madrugada*, that before-dawn hour for which English has no single word.

We went to our beds, paradoxically both cowed and exultant. Spain had got to us. As the days went by, I took the school party on coach-trips to Tarragona and Monserrat. We went, in Blackpool mood, up the pleasure-park mountains of Montjuich and Tibidabo. But however temporarily diverting these excursions, it was that midnight, religious ecstasy we kept remembering and muttering about. It was disturbing, shocking – even obscene, some of the youngsters thought – and, whatever our secret opinion, the memory of it was never going to go away.

Twenty years later (which is to say the day before I was to sit on the Madrid train opposite the bearded young man from the British Council), I recalled that Easter procession. I was standing at the taffrail of the ferry, about to leave Plymouth for Santander. By now I was middle-aged, my family had grown up and my life had become a muddled drawer that needed tidying. The previous year, the Society of Authors had awarded me their Travel Bursary. I had intended, then, to walk from the Bay of Biscay to the Mediterranean; but my wife had fallen ill, had had a major operation and I had spent that summer nursing her. By the time another year had passed, the romantic idea of wandering on foot from coast to coast had gone sour on me. I decided instead to stay in one place and try and write some kind of prose book. I had no precise idea yet what kind of book it should be, but I did feel quite optimistic. The bursary money was enough to live on, frugally, for three months. In the harbour there was a Spanish ship called the *Elocuencia*, which I took to be a good portent. What I needed now was something of the inspired, self-lacerating single-mindedness and staying power of those Barcelona penitents I'd seen when a young man: if anything was to get written, I mean.

It hadn't crossed my mind to use the cash to go anywhere other than Spain. This was the opportunity I'd always been waiting for. Nearly all my life – both before and after those long-ago visits to Barcelona – fragments of the country had kept coming my way. Slowly and imperceptibly (as one might fall in love with a far-flung pen friend), my interest in the country had turned first into affection, then into passion.

The sight of the tramp steamer *Elocuencia* also prompted the thought that my involvement with Spain had probably begun on a certain end of summer day in 1938, when I was rising four. That morning, my mother wheeled me to Shoreham in my pushchair to do our meagre shopping. She got a tin loaf and a bit of scrag-end at the Co-op, and there couldn't have been much left in her purse by the time we reached Brown's, the greengrocer's. Here, normally she'd have asked for just a few penn'orth of carrots, onions and potatoes to stew with the meat. Today though, unable to resist such a bargain, she also bought fifty oranges for a shilling. It seemed that a Spanish merchant ship crewed by Loyalists had berthed in Shoreham harbour and had sold off her cargo dirt-cheap to raise quick funds for the struggle against Franco. Everybody in the High Street was carrying a bag of oranges. Later, on his way home from work, even my father – who never so much as entered a shop if he could help it – was seduced into buying a bob's worth, stuffing the fruit into his lunchbag and all the pockets of his carpenter's overalls. Our tiny, dark and cluttered living-room was transformed by the glow and an incomparable aroma somehow betokening fair weather, good health, abundance and optimism.

That day's extravagance was not to be forgotten by any of us. In my mother's recurrent fantasy of happiness and prosperity, she strolls at sunrise in her own grove of citrus trees, selecting and plucking the biggest and most luscious, full-ripened fruit for her breakfast. My father, by contrast, recalls hard times: uncertain employment, the dole, the Means Test, and the bitter irony, once, of having blued all his raked-together, precious small change on, *goddammit*, a tragic, a *duplicated* luxury! Often I recall those oranges with a various (and frankly sentimental) relish. Any that weren't eaten fresh got turned into marmalade; the tissue paper wrappings with their glamorous designs were used as scented handkerchieves. And I like to suppose that, by eating my share of the fruit, I did my bit for the Republicans in the Spanish Civil War.

I now know that Spain was much talked about in our house during my early years. In 1937 my father's younger brother, then aged seventeen, raised almost enough courage to defy my fearsome grandmother and go out and join the International Brigade. I can just remember my Uncle George, a podgy apprentice plasterer forever sketching racing cars, motorbikes and (that newfangled Spanish invention) the autogyro. Eventually he did fight against fascism, losing his life during the North Africa campaign. He was *a real left bloke*, my father has said of him. 'He had this friend, name of Con Ainsworth, who was a wireless engineer and a bit of an amateur archaeologist. They used to go to political meetings at the Literary Institute in Worthing. I went with them myself a few times when the Civil War really got started. Of course, our kid never had any money. But I remember him putting fourpence – all he had – into the collection. I stumped up a bit too, and your Ma gave him the one and nine out of her savings tin. Year or two later, we saw the refugees from Bilbao and Guernica. In Steyne Gardens that was, only a step from the Literary Institute. Ten-year-old kids, orphans, poor little buggers. Our collection money hadn't done *them* a lot of good, had it?'

Below me on the ferry the car-ramp clanged shut and preparations for casting-off began. I was a foot passenger, one of only a few. Most of the motorists were English, pretty well-heeled by the look and sound of them. I overheard one group exchanging anecdotes and pointing at places in guidebooks. 'Only too bloody *typically* Spanish, of course,' one blue-rinse woman was saying to a matron with alternate crimson and purple fingernails. Her inflection suggested a long-practised disapprobation. 'Everywhere you go, roads likely to be full of potholes,' said one of the husbands, a military type. 'Nowhere near as good as they look on maps. Whatever you do, don't believe maps!'

I thought of the battered old atlas which, as a child, I'd been allowed to thumb through as soon as I could read. Its exclusively political maps of the countries of the world used five different colours to display the division of counties, regions and provinces. I'd grown up believing that Galicia was the sad mauve of woodsmoke caught on misty mornings in the crowns of trees, that Aragon was the beige of scorched rock. Was New Castile, where I was bound, really the golden yellow of wheat and sunflowers? If ever I reached the Guadal-quivir, would I pause in a green shade beside an olive-green river and nod my head with a smile, acknowledging that Andalusia had indeed been green in my fancy ever since I could recall? I knew bits of Catalonia were the rose-red of its peculiar mountains, for I had seen them for myself when taking those Manchester children on their excursions. First impressions such as those derived from the colours of an old atlas were ingrained, ineradicable, the stuff of preconception and prejudice. I listened to more snatches of conversation on deck as, fore and aft, lines were being loosened and let fall in the water. Scarcely a single complimentary remark was being uttered, except in a patronizing way, about the Spanish people and their culture.

I, too, had been brought up to believe in the inherent superiority of the British over the Spaniards – indeed over all other Europeans. My generation, whose primary education coincided exactly with the duration of the Second World War, ingested a steady diet of nationalism made temporarily respectable under the guise of a necessary sense of patriotism. We learned to hate Germans and Italians – though with a kind of glacial respect, the due of powerful enemies. We were taught to accept that nations such as France and Belgium were our friends and allies in the struggle (though, being defeated, they commanded not respect so much as a kind of tolerance and good-natured scorn). But what contempt our teachers heaped upon those countries which had remained neutral! Of these, Spain was by far the most frequent object of disparage-

24

ment and sneering disdain. At the start of each school year, moving up to a new classroom with a new mistress to mould our minds, yet again we would hear the story of the rout of the Spanish Armada. Here I was, in my forties now, sailing past Plymouth Hoe for the first time in my life, yet with the feeling that I'd been here before. In my imagination I had been. Four times before the age of ten I had been enjoined to paint a picture of Sir Francis Drake finishing his game of bowls; and four times I had had the hectoring moral rammed down my throat: that a phlegmatic, amiable, games-playing English-man was worth any number of over-excitable, passionately eloquent, intensely professional foreigners. As Blue-rinse was now putting it to Fingernails, 'Not got the first idea how to do a damn thing properly. Just you ask my husband if you want to know about the frightful Spanish. He ought to know. He served in Gib.'

My father, a Corporal despatch-rider in the Home Guard during the war, had been in the Drake tradition of British soldiery. True, he hadn't played bowls; but, while guarding our stretch of the English Channel coast, he and his chums had engaged in what had appeared to me like an elaborate game. Their 'manoeuvres' of a Sunday had seemed to me like little more than a grown-up version of the tag we boys played in the schoolyard. The Home Guard HQ was a requisitioned bankrupt private school. Among the improving books my father looted for my benefit was a much-abridged edition of *Don Quixote* which I read several times. Sometimes I was allowed to accompany my father on his adventure. His khaki motorbike was our Rosinante. Boldly we set forth, knight and squire, up to the Downs – where there were windmills, flocks of sheep and wheatfields, just as in La Mancha. A little fat Sancho, I delighted in the fun and the fantasy that what we did had anything at all to do with the overthrow of Evil; but my father, with his thin and doleful countenance – a deluded military romantic if ever there was one – believed utterly in the worth of the Home Guard's efforts and self-evident nonsense. How earnestly he carried pointless (and pointlessly coded) messages hither and yon between farm and farm! Arriving at whatever remote and bucolic destination, with what commitment he helped blow up kennels and cow byres, accepting that they had been transmogrified into the Hun's ammunition dumps or communications centres! But no doubt he would have been offended to have his antics compared with those of the Don's: because the Don was a Spaniard, and a Spaniard was a *dago*, and a *dago* couldn't have been expected to have more common-sense than to fight a windmill with a lance, thinking it was a giant. Conscientiously he cleaned his gleaming rifle (for which he had nary a bullet) as though it would stop an entire division of Hitler's stormtroopers. Never for one moment did he indulge in qualms of faith.

After the war and up to the age of fourteen, I learned about Spain haphazardly, spasmodically, yet persistently – as though knowledge acquired by the serendipity of books, stamp-collecting, films and such was becoming somehow purposeful. Myths and fictions (as well as a few vivid and true insights) clung to my memory like burrs. My fellow-countrymen – like those strolling the decks of the ferry, delivering themselves of loud and patently ill-informed opinions – were unanimous about certain national character-istics of Spaniards. They were all 'a lazy lot' who were 'swarthy' and who ate 'nothing but filthy, greasy food reeking of garlic'. They were 'cruel, slovenly, untrustworthy, forever gabbling nineteen to the dozen'. Seldom was a good word spoken for a country that had once been, according to my reading, one of the greatest and most powerful cultures the world had ever known. It wasn't until I began my School Certificate year that I began a process which was to give me the key to the truth about Spain and to help me to leave behind, once and for all, years of crass, dire, chauvinistic ignorance: I took up Spanish.

Learning the Castilian language determined the course of my life, for the acquisition of a second modern language (I was already good at French) turned me into a linguist; and being a linguist was – and still is – a necessary part of one's training as writer, teacher and traveller. Spanish struck me straightaway as a more intensely *foreign* language than French. It contained a noun like *duende* – which encapsulated the notion of an inspirational magic possessing an artist when favoured by the muse – which doesn't even exist in English; and it presented me with a verb like *embarbascar*, with its two wildly disparate meanings (to throw hellebore into the river to make the fish bite or to catch one's ploughshare in a root).

A language containing such wayward vocabulary seemed to hint at formerly unsuspected dimensions not only of semantics but also of life itself: dimensions capricious and bizarre. Spain became for me, partly also because of the strange phonemes of her language, an even more fascinating and exotic land than I'd thought. The more I learned by reading her novelists and poets in the original (and the more I shrugged off the ignorant opinions I'd had foisted upon me), the more odd and individual the country became: perhaps ultimately unknowable by even one such as I, a constant lover.

It's not unknown for a young artist to go through a phase of fancying that some foreign country is his other, spiritual, home. At thirteen I had written to the Dalai Lama, a boy almost exactly my age, telling him of my love for Tibet. I'd devoured every book about the place I could lay my hands on. In my imagination I had warmed myself by fires of yak dung, made statues of rancid butter, chanted my mantras and turned my prayer-wheel on long pilgrimages from monastery to mountain-top monastery. After three terms of Spanish I was inclined to exchange my saffron robe for a suit of lights. My first piece of written work in the sixth form was a French essay with the title: *Chacun a deux pays, le sien et la France.* In it I claimed that my other country was Spain. I had never been there, and I knew no Spaniards; not unjustly, my teacher accused me of gross pretentiousness. Like many another adolescent dreamer, I responded by dreaming even harder. Trusting my hunch, I maintained that a half-truth wasn't necessarily a half-lie.

I'd been on a school cycling party to the north of France; with the Boy Scouts I'd gone to Switzerland, a country I despised. I wanted, desperately, to get down to Spain; but I thought I had as much chance of doing so as of strolling the streets of Lhasa. The period of post-war austerity was not yet over; the era of cheap air fares and package deals had not yet begun. Spain was still a distant country for a young fellow whose sole source of income was the weekly five half-crowns from his paper round.

The summer before my seventeenth birthday, hitch-hiking on my own in France, I did chance to arrive tantalizingly close to the Spanish border. The couple in whose luxurious Humber I had been riding for several days invited me to continue with them – after Lugano, Como, Genoa and Monte Carlo – as far as the coast of Levante, there to stay with them on their friends' orange farm. I would be warmly welcomed, they said. But maddeningly, I had no visa; and besides, my money was running out: so at the Pyrenees I had to say goodbye and watch the big black car as it purred southwards without me. Four more years were to elapse before that first, ludicrous, journey to Barcelona. Since then, there had been times when I'd thought I'd never get any further into the country than Catalonia.

'I stayed up on deck long after the ferry cast off at Plymouth yesterday,' I told the bearded man from the British Council. 'Had to make quite sure the last bit of Cornwall slipped safely out of sight. I still couldn't quite believe my luck, you see. At long last I was actually on my way, alone, to the heart of Spain. And here I am! In Madrid!' I couldn't stop stupidly grinning with delight. Soon the train came to a halt amid the lofty, fascist architecture of the terminus and we said goodbye. Not many minutes before, from the refreshment car, I had glimpsed the Escorial palace in all its bleak, grey, granite grandiosity; and my inward eye was still full of the endless expanse of the *Meseta*. In Spain you needed time to adjust to the sheer scale of the works of Nature and Man. I took a taxi to the vicinity of Atocha station, found a cheap room, lay down for a few minutes (as I thought) on the sagging springs; then it was morning.

CHAPTER TWO

The tap yielded only a gasp of red air. I cleaned my teeth in
wine and ate an orange, listening to the swifts screaming at
the cliff-face of the new apartment block opposite.

At eleven o'clock I took the Valencia-bound TALGO. A
superb train: spotlessly clean, fast, air-conditioned, comfortable, with courteous staff to handle your luggage, serve you
excellent coffee, inspect your ticket and wish you a pleasant
journey. Before long we reached Aranjuez, whose name
brought to mind Rodrigo's guitar concerto, and where the best
strawberries in Spain were ripening; and then the earth
became coppery, and there were more and more olive groves,
and dead on (Spanish) lunchtime we were in Cuenca. My case
of traps and my typewriter were taken out of the guard's van
and set upon the platform for me as ceremoniously as if I had
been a Colonial Governor in a cockaded hat rather than a
down-at-heel, inky-fingered poet in a denim coat.

A few weeks before, I'd written to book myself a room in
a modest hotel a few hundred yards from the station. The
receptionist was a small, balding, middle-aged man with bad
teeth and a French-mustard coloured suit, threadbare but
beautifully pressed. His name was Señor Arias; I was to get
to know and like him well. He was standing at the threshold,
brandishing my letter and broadly grinning.

I went up to my room and made myself at home: unpacked,
bathed, shaved, changed, arranged my desk, took my typewriter from its case and placed beside it a mint ream of paper.
I had ninety days at my disposal, a room to myself where
nobody would come to knock at the door and no one was likely
to telephone. I had a comfortable bed and a balcony looking
on to the street, where I could sit of an evening and hang out
my washing. What more could a writer want? Ah . . . I tried
to persuade myself that the nausea I felt was due to travel

fatigue and one too many midday beers on the train. Maybe some of it was: no need to worry too much yet. Before the day was out though, I wanted at least some inkling of what I should spend my summer writing: next morning, at nine o'clock, I was determined to make a start. Feeling queasy, I decided to do without lunch. Then it was almost the siesta hour. I lowered the rattan slats of the blind, closed my eyes and went to sleep in my clothes, to the sweet sound of canaries singing.

A sense of panic (for that's what it was) still lay on my stomach when I woke. Never mind, I thought: I'll go and find a welcoming bar, a glass of something, a bit of cheerful company; let inspiration come when it will. Downstairs in the lobby, Señor Arias, having just handed over to the night porter, begged me to let him have the stamps off any letters I might receive. His request was a chill intimation of inevitable loneliness: but the street looked warm and propitious, thronged with people of all ages for the evening *paseo*.

It felt marvellous, strolling among so many total strangers and wondering which of them might become acquaintances, which ones even friends. There were dozens of bars and bar/restaurants to choose from. I picked one called El Sotanillo (The Little Cellar) pretty well at random. It offered a set dinner for a reasonable price and was evidently popular. The proprietor, Alejandro, bore such a marked resemblance to the American actor Phil Silvers that, ever afterwards, I thought of him as Sergeant Bilko. I asked for a glass of red wine and was given a *tapa* of a black olive, the size of a pullet's egg, on a square inch of red pepper, to go with it.

Standing at the counter next to me was a short, elderly man with sharp features and merry eyes. We struck up a conversation: first about politics, then history, then poetry. It was a great joy for me to get my Spanish out of its cobwebby cupboard, to dust it off, to retrieve words long neglected and more than half-forgotten, reassembling them with rusty grammar and blunted syntax, giving them a honing and a buff and a polish and sending them lively as a swarm of excited insects into the air. Alejandro, setting up another round, introduced us. Pedro was the old man's name: don Pedro, the Master Blacksmith of Cuenca.

'And you, don Eduardo, what do you do for a living, and what are you doing in Cuenca?'

30

I told them. Pedro grew more animated.

'We had an English writer here once before, years ago –
didn't we, Alejandro? You know! Always held his glass like
this.' He clutched his fists tight to this chest. 'Ha! I remember
him as clear as if it was only yesterday. Used to spend hours
and hours in here, singing and joking. We were all very fond
of him. What a chap – really *desgarbado*, he was!'

I couldn't remember what the word meant. I asked him to
demonstrate.

'You know what *desgarbado* is. Like this.'

He pulled his jacket awry and screwed up his tie and shirt
collar. Later, I looked up the word in my dictionary and was
delighted to find that I'd accurately guessed Pedro's charade:
'*slovenly*'.

'That's right,' said Alejandro. 'He sat in that corner over
there. Of course, in those days this place really *was* a cellar.
There were a few steps down from the street. I've made a lot
of improvements since then, one way and another. Oh yes,
I've done pretty well for myself over the years. For example—'

'Get on with the story,' said Pedro.

'The Englishman – yes. He was teaching himself to play
the guitar. Whatever I had on the radio, he'd join in. Pontifical
High Mass from Toledo cathedral or the latest popular song
– he didn't care! He'd be strumming away, whatever it was.
And wasn't he a lad with the girls!'

'He certainly was that,' said Pedro. 'Say there was a case
of live crabs delivered, all packed in ice. The Englishman
would get one in each hand and chase the women around.
They'd run up the steps and out into the street, screaming
their heads off!'

'But they all loved him.'

'Oh, yes. They all loved him.'

We had another drink on the strength of shared laughter.

'What was his name, this Englishman?' I asked.

'Lorenzo,' said Alejandro. 'Yes, that was it, Lorenzo.'

'Not Lorenzo Lee?' I said.

'Correct! Lorenzo Lee. Fancy you having heard of him!'

'Of course I've heard of him. He's very famous in my
country. Very famous indeed. World famous.'

'No, no! Not a man like that! *Vaya!* A man so *desgarbado*!'

'I assure you both, I am telling the truth. I know him slightly.

31

Tell you what: tonight I'll write and tell him about this! After dinner. Can I eat now, Alejandro?'

Doubtfully, he looked at his watch. It was nine-fifteen: earlyish, still, for dinner-time in Spain.

'The thing is,' I said, 'I'm not used to Spanish hours yet. I missed lunch, I only had an orange for breakfast and last night I fell asleep and didn't get dinner. I'm famished.'

Alejandro served me himself. For roughly the price, in an English sandwich-bar, of a couple of rounds of sandwiches and a mug of alluvial tea I had: a large plate of mixed salad; a whopping bowl of *potaje castellano* – beans with lumps of *chorizo* and black pudding; two sizeable roundels of hake in batter; *flan* (caramel custard, ubiquitous in Spain); half a bottle of red wine; a hefty bread roll the shape of an annulus; black coffee; and a quadruple shot of the local liqueur, *resolí*. When I paid my bill, Alejandro gave me a message, written on his business card, to enclose with my letter to Laurie Lee: 'Dear Lorenzo, I'm remembering those good times. When are you coming back to Cuenca? I embrace you warmly.'

At midnight I staggered out of El Sotanillo. I had made two friends, was no longer tired and hungry, and the feeling of dread and nausea (in truth, the fear of failure) was dispelled. I knew, now, what I should spend the summer writing. When I dropped a line to Laurie Lee, enclosing Alejandro's message, I'd tell him I was about to embark upon a reminiscence of childhood – my version, so to speak, of *Cider With Rosie*. The night was frosty and full of stars. Rosy with *resolí*, when I got back to my room I wrote the first sentence of *The High Path*, my autobiography of childhood.

Cuenca was effectively two distinct communities: the original, ancient, naturally fortified site high up and the more recent development below. I decided to remain in the modern part of the city – *abajo*. Most of the shops, the market, the banks and businesses were here, in workaday streets where ordinary *Conquenses* lived and went on their daily rounds. Next door to my hotel was a joinery; when I came or went, I'd stand a few seconds at the door and listen to the slap-slap-slap of the lathe-belt and the moan of band-saws biting home, sniff the new shavings and saw-dust: nice.

The upper quarter – *arriba* – was the pretty part: quiet with abrupt, twisting alleyways not wide enough for traffic; picturesque frontages many of them containing bohemian denizens, the painters and potters of the artists' colony; the bit the tourists wanted, with cathedral, souvenirs and postcards. In short the *Cuidad antigua*, with its two stars in Michelin, with its spectacular houses overhanging a precipice, its celebrated modern art museum – and precious few of the kind of shop where they sell plain things like shoelaces, or a bag of carrots.

My first morning, early, I climbed the cobbles to the very top – up beyond the Plaza Mayor, on past the castle remains and the upper gate in the fortress walls. Once there, you could better understand why Cuenca had been built where it was: impregnable, on sheer, loftiest cliffs at the confluence of the rivers Júcar and Huécar. The setting was literally breathtaking: still panting from the stiff ascent you couldn't help but gasp at the sight of the giddy drop if you stepped perhaps a yard too close to the lip and saw all of the huge and awesome yawn of the *hoz*. At seven o'clock the sun had felt warm in the lower town; this high, a full hour later, the breeze was chilling.

The vast hollow of the ravine was strident with swifts and swallows wheeling aloft; while from far below rose the heartrending song of too many nightingales to count. There was the sound, too, of a game of *pelota* in the grounds of a seminary on the opposite side of the chasm: dry, hard, percussive smacks of the ball echoing three times among the rocks. Warm air rising from the wooded riverside carried up lime petals and their scent; and all around in the grass were profuse wild flowers. A narrow road followed the upper edge of the gorge. There were a few houses more beyond those above the castle gate: one a *mesón* not yet open for business, its door and windows surrounded by pelargoniums and lobelia. A little way beyond this was a whitewashed cottage with a tethered goat in front, and a pile of dung for its half-dozen chickens to scratch at. A woman stepped outside, flung a fistful of corn, stood a few moments to look towards the further cliff, and went back indoors.

Idyllic, it was, *arriba*: but at the end of my first day's stint, I came across a more disturbing scene *abajo*. At the *aperitivo* hour I witnessed a political demonstration by the extreme right-wing *Fuerza Nueva* party. All over town, on every bit of vacant wall, the rally was advertised with fly-posters. Earlier in the day, while I was at work, it had been announced by a concentration-shattering loudspeaker van. And hundreds of light-green leaflets had been scattered in the streets, strewn by the wind like autumn leaves into every corner: floors of bars, flowerbeds in the public gardens, entrances to banks and shop doorways. Their message read:

THE NATIONAL FLAG belongs to all Spaniards who honour and respect it both in public and in private. Come to the demonstration in aid of the DAY OF THE SPANISH FATHERLAND at 8.30 pm. A motorcade will leave the railway station and pass through all the main streets of Cuenca. Afterwards, outside the former Head-quarters of the Movement, there will be a mass meeting addressed by RICHARD ALBA.

In the station forecourt I counted more than a hundred vehicles being lined up: saloon cars, mostly, and several Land Rovers, all of them crammed tight with well dressed men and women of all ages. The front four cars in the procession were bedecked with the red and yellow horizontal strips of the national standard and the banners of *Fuerza Nueva*. Behind these came the loudspeaker van blaring a martial *paso doble*.

They moved off, slowly enough for me to follow for a while on foot, first through an area of brand-new, high-density apartment buildings at the raw edge of town. The streets were lined with adults and children, many of them waving minia-ture flags. There were cries of encouragement and support as the leaders passed by. The drivers kept their horns blaring incessantly, their passengers meanwhile leaning out of the windows and bawling slogans in support of Spanish unity. Soon the motorcade picked up speed and one by one the cars left me behind. Most of the numberplates were local, from the province of Cuenca, but I saw plates, too, from Toledo and Madrid, Albacete, Valencia, Badajoz, Ciudad Real, even one from the Canary Islands.

Half an hour later, after criss-crossing the busy streets at the heart of town, the cars were parked and their occupants made their way to the little square in front of the Casa de la Cultura, or Arts Centre, where a sizeable crowd had gathered

34

to await and greet them. There were no placards on view: but there were hundreds more national flags and the banners not only of *Fuerza Nueva* but also of *Falange Española* and the *Comunión Tradicionalista*. I was startled by a stage-managed 'spontaneous' eruption of fervour when prominent party members began to take their places on a wooden dais. Chanting began. The battle-cries were 'One Spain, not Fifty-one', 'One Flag and a United Spain', 'A United Spain will never be Defeated', and 'Blas Piñar for Caudillo'.

The crowd divided. The larger group gathered around the recently paint-daubed statue of General Moscardó; the rest, though in support, stood slightly apart. In the first group there were many young men in para-military uniform vaguely reminiscent of that of the Hitler Youth Movement. Indeed the proceedings had an altogether sinister, Thirties feel to them – particularly when the assembly sang the patriotic anthem, *Cara al sol*, which I couldn't help but associate with grainy, black and white newsreels and Falangist propaganda films.

It now became apparent why the meeting was taking place by the statue of General Moscardó. (He had been the hero of Franco's army during the siege of the fortress of Toledo; the officer who, when given the ultimatum that his son would be killed by his Republican captors unless the stronghold was surrendered, calmly advised the boy by telephone to commend his soul to God, shout *Viva España*, and die like a hero.) The first item on the agenda, said the local leader of *Fuerza Nueva*, was to pay homage to the memory of General Moscardó and to make an act of reparation to the famous soldier, following the 'infamous desecration' of his statue. The crowd made appropriate noises; and then, a real *coup de théâtre*, the General's daughter, the Countess del Alcázar de Toledo, was produced from amidst the platform party. She was cheered and clapped, an infinitely sad-faced lady giving the impression that this was the kind of thing she was often called upon to do.

Then Cuenca's national *Fuerza Nueva* delegate gave a short address. He referred to an accident that had occurred the day before, in which two workmen on a construction site had been killed under a fall of rock. The sympathetic murmurings were scarcely over when the same speaker recited the Lord's Prayer: for the immortal souls of the dead men, he assured us. Yet one felt irresistibly that the prayer had been said to remind

35

us that God was still against democracy (as Franco always said He had been during the 'holy crusade' of the Civil War). And then, the centrepiece of the evening's demonstration, no less a celebrity than the National Secretary himself was called upon to make his speech, a repetitive harangue whose message was two-fold: that the 'traditional values' of Spain had to hold the country together against the violent will of the Basque separatists; and that the forces of the left, which were trying to undermine the authority of central government, had to be confronted and overcome. Three quarters of an hour after it began, the meeting ended with the singing, once again, of *Cara al sol*. The crowd dispersed quietly. There were no scuffles, no fights, no loud arguments; but there was an undeniable smell of incipient violence in the air, like the stink of decay.

I went to El Sotanillo, feeling angry. I wanted to talk to don Pedro, the Master Blacksmith. He, I knew from our talk the night before, had fought for the Republic.

'What on earth's the matter, Eduardo?' he said. 'Come on, have a glass of wine.'

I gave him an account of the meeting, wanting him to be angry, too. Wasn't democracy still a tender plant in Spain, one needing room to grow after so many years of smothering dictatorship? Wasn't it terrible, so soon after the death of Franco, for a party like *Fuerza Nueva* to emerge and attract so much attention and evident support?

'*Tranquilo*, Englishman. *Fuerza Nueva* is only another political party. They'll make a lot of noise and scrawl a lot of slogans, yes, but they'll not get far. It's the moderates who'll keep power in the *Cortes* – the centre parties, and those just to the left and just to the right of centre. Democracy still has to find its feet, remember. In Spain it's a new concept to everybody except those of us old enough to remember the Thirties. There's a good many – young and old – who mistrust it. They see what's going on in the Basque country – and what the separatists are doing outside the Basque country – and they say to themselves, "What an abomination, *qué barbaridad*, in the old days things couldn't have got out of hand like this." Did you see what happened the other day in Seville? Three high-ranking army officers and their driver killed. Almost every day innocent citizens get blown up in the street, and in cafés and bars like this one. You mustn't be

36

surprised if a few people want a tough police force again.'

'A few! There must have been thirteen hundred people outside the Casa de Cultura tonight, out of a population of – how many?'

'About thirty-seven thousand. So what? It doesn't bother me. People enjoy a parade! I just wish the left wasn't in disarray, as usual, while the right are united. That's bad.'

A youth in *Fuerza Nueva* uniform came in. His shirt was navy-blue – the colour chosen (because it was the colour of workmen's overalls) by Primo de Rivera for the shirts of the original *Falange*. Over his breast pocket was a Spanish flag, about six inches by three; above his left cuff, the party's emblem done in bronze – a sheaf of spears. He got himself a beer and joined his cronies. 'They know nothing,' said don Pedro quietly. '*Nada de nada.*' But despite his reassurances, on my way back to my room I couldn't help but feel sickened by the swastikas I saw chalked on the trunks of the plane trees outside the Town Hall.

Each morning I went out for breakfast on the dot of eight, the mellow chimes of the Mangana tower, *arriba*, playing a tune tantalizingly reminiscent of *Oranges and Lemons* before striking the hour. The traffic policeman, having parked his moped, would be pulling on his white gauntlets ready for confronting the rush-hour from his island (about the size of a tea-tray) at the junction of three roads. Metal shutters would be clatteringly opened; the usual importuning gipsy in his stubble and anorak would be lounging at the same street corner; familiar office workers would be picking up their paper at the *quiosco* where I got mine.

Having a routine confers a kind of honorary citizenship on the traveller who chooses to put down temporary roots. You know you belong somewhere as soon as you've remained long enough to have a haircut and buy a new cake of soap. You surprise yourself by being able to give simple directions to strangers; you acquire a pot plant for your balcony; you know where to get the best value in a sandwich and a glass of wine. There was a blind lottery ticket seller whose station was the doorway of a shoe shop. He knew me by my footfall, greeting me '*Hola, el Inglés,*' from twenty yards away. I was recognized by the clerks who cashed my traveller's cheques at the Banco

37

de Bilbao, and by waiters setting out chairs and tables on the pavement. I liked that.

Breakfast for me of a weekday was simple and quick: usually a cup of white coffee (*café con leche*) and a couple of little plain cakes, *madalenas*. Now and again I'd have some other item of *bollería* instead: a *suizo* (rather dry, not very interesting) or an *ocho*, a figure-of-eight flaky pastry. Sometimes I might have a *tostada*: not toast quite as we know it in England, but a square, thick slice of bread lavished with margarine both sides, fried on a hot-plate and eaten with a knife and fork. The *mermelada* served with it wasn't necessarily orange marmalade: more often than not it was peach, apricot or strawberry jam. At the counter in the *cafetería* I liked to watch the *churros* being prepared. Fluted strips of dough round as a finger and long as a hand would be extruded from a glass container into a vat of boiling oil beneath; when they were done, they were drained and piled and sprinkled with sugar. Wonderfully delicious and quite indigestible, crisp, hot and golden they looked. But *churros* were a Sunday treat, not for working days.

It was good, then, to walk in the park for twenty minutes before going back to my room. The Parque San Julián (named after the patron saint of Cuenca) was from the start a favourite place of mine: cool, leafy and delectable. In the middle of town, it was rectangular in shape, with plenty of benches beside each wide path of sandy gravel. In this part of Spain the climate, winter and summer, is too fierce for close-cropped lawns; instead there were formal rose-beds surrounded by dwarf box hedges, and avenues of tall, graceful trees – planes and acacias – whose crowns intermingled overhead. There was a pretty little bandstand at the centre, and drinking fountains, and at one end a children's play area with climbing frames and swings and such. Soon after eight o'clock every morning a municipal worker was at work with a fireman's brass-nozzled hose, sending a powerful jet of water a good forty yards among the beds and along the paths, damping down the dust and giving the whole park a delightfully fresh, after-rain scent.

It was the hour when mothers took tots and toddlers to play school, nursery school, primary school. Is there any country in the world where children are so well cared for, so well dressed and groomed? They would be brought to the park for an early-morning session on the swings and slides, beautiful confections for some Impressionist picture when glimpsed momentarily half and half between shadow and dappled sunlight.

There was no school uniform as such (though uniforms still are commonly found elsewhere in Spain, in private schools), and each student I saw made the most of his or her individuality; but in their choice of clothes they conformed to some unwritten code of what was apt. This sense of appropriateness remained with them after school hours. Teenagers you saw early in the day walking in twos and threes through the park with file and textbook under their arms were indeed the same ones you saw during the evening *paseo*: but by then the girls had changed into well-tailored and modish skirts or trousers (seldom jeans) and light woollen sweaters, the boys into zipper jackets, fashionable casual shirts or summer-weight suits. However, something else – something in addition to their clothes – transformed young people of an evening. They would sit along a wall, chattering and ceaselessly nibbling sunflower seeds like a row of parrots, or foregather in groups of a dozen or so in the squares or in the *cafetería*: and it was not simply the gaiety of release that took over from the serious business of being in the classroom. Underlying the talk and laughter one detected a sense that the social evening hours were a conscious rehearsal for the adult world. The girls, most of them, wore a little discreet jewellery; they stood, sat, held a glass, with elegance and style; and the boys seemed quite without the usual gaucherie of adolescent lads. They didn't jostle you on the street; they were courteous and charming to each other and to their families and to strangers. Often you'd see a girl suddenly break away from her circle of friends and run to greet her parents walking towards her; without self-consciousness or embarrassment she would hug and kiss them and exchange a few words before catching up with her friends and linking arms with them again.

If, by comparison with their British and American counterparts, young Spaniards sometimes seemed too good to be true, I felt that this was partly accounted for by the attitude Spanish parents adopt towards sons and daughters from infancy. Children are treated not as a race apart but as small people entitled from the very beginning of their lives to the same respect and consideration required from them. In Spain it's rare to see a father or mother cuffing a child or otherwise humiliating it. On the other hand, it is commonplace to see an entire family – babies in arms to great-grandparents – sitting together in bars. Each member of the family receives equal treatment when it comes to the ordering of drinks. The little ones – the *peques* – are not fobbed off with something they don't want, or sent off to play outside while the adults get on with their chat. If the six-year-old boy feels like it, he will make his way to the bar and ask for – and get – what he fancies. The baby's milk bottle, prepared at home, will stand to warm in a jug of hot water beside the coffee machine.

Language has a big part to play, too, in the Spanish child's early and easy assumption of dignity and good manners. When he learns to talk, he discovers that he must use the formal *usted* to his elders and betters outside the family; while *tú* and *vosotros* betoken affection and familiarity. When he has to be reprimanded, the loving *tú* is temporarily withdrawn from him, to be replaced by the frigid and distant *usted*. Early mornings in the park, I would observe how this was instilled into their tiny siblings during play by even the very youngest nursery school pupils.

Spaniards are among the best turned-out people in Europe: not only during leisure hours but also at work. The man hosing down the park wore a neatly pressed suit; building workers, clerks – even road menders and refuse collectors – dressed smartly. I, who had long inclined towards the Laurie Lee look, found within a few days of my arrival in Cuenca that I was shamed by young and old alike into taking more care with my appearance. I checked often that my toe-caps were polished, that my collar and cuffs were clean. When I'd finished my stroll in the park and it was time to go to work, I stepped it out straighter and brisker to my desk. Living in Spain made you conscious of your deportment; also it reminded you of what good manners were really about: on a busy pavement, you stood aside not only for the old lady with her basket of vegetables but also for the three-foot high *hidalgo* leading his sister to school.

I was often – and not always unwillingly – distracted from the typewriter by sounds from the street. Two or three times

40

a week, about mid-morning, I would hear the pipes of Pan being played exquisitely. Their piercing, poignant notes mingled with the trills and warblings of caged canaries singing fit to bust from the moment the sun was up. I wondered who it was who had this charming hobby; but each time I heard the pipes I was just too late at my balcony to see the player performing. The only person I saw was an old fellow in a beret and a brown suit pushing a power-assisted bicycle. It was a haunting sound, ancient and pagan, from a time before Homer, performed in my imagination by some cloven-hoof satyr cantering up the Calle Ramón y Cajal, invisible to the human eye. But one morning, stuck in mid-sentence, I happened to be staring down from the balcony as the old man came pushing his bike along. I saw him lift one hand from the handlebars and seem to wipe his nose with the back of his hand. Of course! The pure notes rang out, and the mystery was solved. I went down to take a closer look at him. He was a knife-grinder, his saddle supporting the grindstone. The pipes of Pan, I learned later, were the customary street-call of his trade all over Spain. He set the bike on its stand, and for fifteen minutes kept up his playing. Nobody brought him so much as a penknife to hone; but from the benign look on his face one might have concluded that he wouldn't have minded if the entire world had gone over to plastic cutlery.

Other noises from below were less welcome. One delivery van in particular, obstructing the free passage of traffic at eleven o'clock every day without fail, could occasion such a cacophony of car horns and hooters that I would have to stop and frustratedly watch until its driver emerged in his own good time from some premises up the street. He'd indulge in one or two baroque altercations on his way back to his vehicle, then delight in taking his minutes to rev and manoeuvre, stall and start, blare his horn and belch black smoke until – having judged the moment nicely – he could crawl forward, confident that everyone behind him was on the brink of apoplexy. I never heard anyone complain about the noise. Any amount of racket – whatever time of day or night – was tolerated, provided it came from outside and not indoors. My neighbour once grumbled (quite reasonably, in my opinion) when I had my typewriter on the go during his siesta – yet he was impervious to the ceaseless *fortissimo* air-brakes of timber trucks

41

at the traffic lights nearby. On sixteen wheels the vast lorries would judder under a load of perhaps two dozen entire pine trees on the Teruel Road; the brakes would gasp and whine and the engine would rage; and on the green light the raw, resin-bleeding trunks would have the springs bucking and straining and the low gears crashing as the driver made tracks for the saw-mills. You could have heard those timber trucks from a mile away: but perhaps I alone in our street was aware of them.

The morning stint over, I'd go down to collect my post; if there was none, Señor Arias would raise his right index finger and do an imitation of a slow-moving windscreen-wiper.

It was time, then, to do my forty-five minutes' shopping for lunch. Now, three quarters of an hour may seem like a very long while to pick up one or two items for a modest midday snack; but it must be remembered that in Spain a visit to a food store is no mere matter of entering, choosing, paying and exiting as quickly as possible. No: it is a ritual, an event of the daily social round which cannot be hurried; and this holds true for the modern *supermercado* almost as much as for the traditional grocer's shop. There's something distinctly oriental about the animated, parish-pump exchange of news and views which takes place in every *alimentación*; a throwback, maybe, to many centuries of Moorish occupation. *Tienda* means both 'shop' and 'tent' in Spanish; when you pass through the tinkling bead curtain it's not difficult to fancy yourself under canvas in some long ago souk rather than at the reinforced concrete centre of a twentieth-century town.

The other name for a grocer's is *ultramarinos*, a word I like for being so crammed with hints of the exotic. In my local *ultramarinos* I often witnessed an unwitting comic playlet for all the world like an extemporized vignette demonstrating some small aspect of the human condition. To be a minor member of the cast could be stimulating as well as entertaining.

For example, I went in one day, just before closing-time, to find the shop unusually quiet: only the shopkeeper, his wife, their daughter, and one customer – a small boy – apart from myself. The proprietor's face was glowering, for the small boy had just brought in a can of sardines, its lid jaggedly open, which his mother reckoned was off. 'Impossible,' said the boss; and he took a large carving-knife, prodded up a bit of fish, tasted it, chewed it, swallowed and grimaced. 'I told you not to sell that tin,' he bawled at his wife. 'Didn't I say it was blown?' At this he looked up and saw me, and his face lit up with pleasure because he hadn't been expecting to make any more sales. 'I just want a litre of *tinto*,' I said. 'Nothing special. Table wine, *corriente*.' He told his daughter to go and get a bottle from the crate outside on the pavement and his wife to get rid of the stinking fish. As soon as they had gone out of the shop, he reached up for an unblown tin of sardines. While his back was turned the boy snaffled a handful of sunflower seeds from an open sack. From where I stood, I could see the daughter of the house trying to get at the wine. She had just lifted a full crate of Mahou beer from the stack by the door and a litre of Tinto Especial from the crate beneath, when the small by, not waiting to find out whether I would betray him, ran out with his stolen seeds and his good tin of sardines. This startled the girl, causing her to drop the wine. Wicked, spiky shards of glass glistened on the pavement. Her father shouted at her for being clumsy. 'What do you expect of a woman only eight years old?' yelled her mother, giving me a look that demanded concurrence. 'Oh dear,' I said, 'what a shame.' The girl brought in another bottle, holding it tightly in both hands; and straightaway she went back outside to clear up the mess. Her father wrapped up my purchase in a page of *El País* and took my money, sighing. When I left, I saw that the girl was in tears; and without her father seeing, I gave her five *duros* to cheer her up. So: the shopkeeper had won the chance to say 'I told you so' to his wife and an extra customer before closing-time, but had lost the profit on a litre of wine; his wife had been able to enlist the moral support of a customer (and a foreigner at that) but had had to suffer discomfiture over selling the blown tin; his daughter had gained twenty-five pesetas but had had to endure a harsh reprimand; the boy had profited by a ten-minutes' nibbling of sunflower seeds but had in future to keep a wary eye open for a sharp-eyed witness who might report him; and I had something to smile about for the price of a couple of glasses of wine.

The Júcar never felt a warm river. It carried snow waters down to Cuenca from the *serranía*, and their descent was swift, and the spring sun scarcely had time to take the chill

43

off them before they reached my favourite stretch. It was one of those rivers a swimmer finds irresistible: fast; sometimes noisy; often deeper than you'd think; a lethal river whose cold you hadn't time to think about because your concentration, from the moment you immersed yourself, was all on dealing with its pull.

I would change and leave my things at a particular spot on the bank where I put my wine to cool in some rushes; then I'd walk about five hundred yards upriver. There was a willow tree with a handy branch from which to launch. Before I let go I would have to steel myself: not against the gasping iciness I'd got used to but against the terrible, wide-sliding power of treacherous water. It was the washed-out colour of cocktail olives. I knew I should never trust it. It throbbed through the willow branch, a branch as big round as a man. I'd let go; and at once my tree could no longer help me. For a few seconds I'd be like a dropped leaf spinning out of control, trying my best to turn and face forward with the current before the bend where the first rocks were. Then it was the purest of all exhilarations: to be borne along not quite helpless now but able to steer through gaps between boulders; hearing and feeling white water passages with abrading pebbles, and very soon being out of my depth once again and needing every bit of strength and skill to get beached where I wanted to be, not where the river would have me.

For lunch I'd have a *barrita* of bread, slices of *chorizo*, a tin of anchovies, a big misshapen but succulent tomato, a hunk of *Manchego* cheese, and then some fruit: new season's cherries or strawberries or medlars or a honeydew melon, or those curious *paraguayos* from the province of Madrid – small peaches flattened out top and bottom. The wine was dark and strong. Two or three glasses were enough, with the early afternoon sun strengthening and now standing tall above the chasm, to bring on a delicious drowsiness. I'd have a glass more, then go and paddle a few minutes in the shallows by the rushes, among hundreds of dragonflies. I'd wonder where it was my neighbour set his nets to catch crayfish, *cangrejos del río*; often I saw the nets, complicated contraptions of wire and sticks, drying on the balcony next to mine.

The river was restful to watch, though never itself at rest. Now and again a swallow would glint, or a trout might rise

44

to sip at a fly. Maybe a trail of hay and poppies and yellow-petalled flowers would come drifting past, and I'd imagine the cart from the new-mown field, far upstream, bumping over an ancient bridge and shedding those hard-won armfuls of its load. It was a skin of water too lovely to look away from: but eventually the wine would take hold and I'd wash away the orange stains of *chorizo* from my mouth and fingertips, cup some water to splash over my head and cool my nape. Then I'd carry my things to the lacy shade of an acacia, stretch out and let sleep come as it would.

In Spain, every day is two days. Twice you get up, twice wash and dress to begin life anew in the cool. If you're used to eight hours' sleep, you learn to take them in two unequal periods: five and a half at night and two and a half in the afternoon. If I took my siesta in my room instead of by the river, I darkened it first with shutters and blinds, making no bones about stretching out until the sun stopped raging. Four months of the year, the sun is the enemy in Spain. Indoors, you're grateful for small windows; outdoors, for high walls so there's always shade on the side of the street where you walk. The sun dictates. When it's strongest, you get out of its way; you give it best, the way longshore people give the sea best. It won't let you work or play effectively, so you have no option but to snooze the heat through.

People from northern countries find it hard to get used to this most practical ritual, feeling perhaps a puritanical (or maybe superstitious) guilt about losing some daylight time for ever from their lives. 'Eschew meridional sleep,' wrote sententious Francis Bacon several centuries ago. The English in particular have conserved, since the days of the Raj, their deep-rooted suspicion and contempt for the siesta. Noel Coward's song precisely sums them up. They think it a shame and a waste; and so the mad dogs really do mooch about gloomily, sweltering in near-deserted Spanish town centres throughout the afternoon and grumbling because the shops and the public monuments are shut. At night they go to bed at a 'sensible' time like eleven o'clock, thus missing some of the best things Spain has to offer. Once back home, they congratulate themselves on their own country's efficient and common-sensical routines, talk piously about Spanish children being kept up late and even maintain, with the wonderful logic

45

of the saloon bar, that it's small wonder Spaniards have to take a nap in the afternoon, given that they're up till all hours at night.

Under my acacia, with a towel and a blanket to protect against the horse-flies, I slept within earshot of the ceaseless rushings and turnings of the Júcar. On the opposite bank was a stand of black poplars, *chopos*, favourite shade and plantation trees hereabouts. If there was the slightest breeze I would hear their lacquered leaves rustling deliciously when I awoke. Once, I was awakened by the tonk-tonk-tonking of goat-bells when a flock browsed slowly past, lingering among the dabbled rocks before splashing on towards the upriver water-meadows. Their herdsman, eating an onion the way you'd eat an apple, didn't see me as he passed by. I think he had been having his siesta too because he yawned wide and made a crucifixion of himself before quickening his pace and whistling up his dog.

CHAPTER THREE

Julio's Bar, El Bodegón, was in a yard up a sloping alley. From the start I liked it and its proprietor so well that I all but deserted Alejandro and El Sotanillo. Not that I found the décor all that attractive: rustic pine furniture with the bark removed, all knobbly and self-consciously folksy under layers of glutinous, dark-toffee varnish, has never been my notion of style or comfort. No – it wasn't Julio's tables and chairs that drew me sauntering up to the Cerillo San Roque most evenings so much as Julio himself, his family, his clientele, his wine and his food.

During the early part of the evening, before the rush of pre-dinner *aperitivos* and snacks began, Julio liked to practise his small and excruciating collection of English words and phrases on me. He'd learned them some years before, during a long and unhappy period away from his family, in Torremolinos. There he'd worked non-stop in order to raise the capital to buy the bar, his own place, in Cuenca. He was proud, understandably so, of his achievement. However, about the third or fourth time we talked together (I helping him out with his patchy vocabulary), he lit up a Fortuna, poured himself a glass of alcohol-free beer called Sin and smiled ambiguously. It had been won, this empire of his, at a cost of more than mere millions of pesetas. The slog of Torremolinos had done his health no good; he needed a pancreas operation, he wished he could cut down on his intake of cigarettes, he knew he ought to relax more. He acknowledged that he was a workaholic: but what could he do, with a family to support, other than soldier on? They all had to keep hard at it to keep the business thriving in case anything happened to him or *la señora*. She wasn't in the best of health. And it didn't help matters that his eldest boy was away doing his *mili*. His daughter, about twenty, more or less engaged to the barman, José, had to help her mother all the time in the kitchen. Even

47

the youngest lad, Pico – who was still only twelve and who wouldn't be leaving school for years yet – had to do his share of fetching and carrying, too.

Between nine o'clock and ten thirty El Bodegón was always thronged. Behind the bar, in the kitchen, nobody stopped. Young José, who worked a seventy-eight hour week, would be holding two *cañas* at the beer tap with one hand, while pouring wine from the bottle into two *chatos* with the other: this, while taking yet another customer's order and keeping an eye on the microwave, or the barbecue, or both.

With each alcoholic drink a *tapa* was served as a matter of course. In Julio's, as in any bar in Cuenca, it was free, and *tapas* were no longer free – or even available – in many other parts of Spain. Sadly, the old custom was dying out, due to modern pressures, foreign influences and plain, economic exigency. *Tapas* survive in Cuenca, Julio told me, because there the customer still dictated the terms. There are very many bars competing in the city centre, and not one could survive without the attraction of *tapas* with every drink, both midday and evening.

El Bodegón was celebrated for the variety and generosity of its *tapas*. Even ordinary items were special here: potato crisps the size of small poppadoms, peanuts in salt-frosted shucks, too many not to tumble from the saucer. A group of friends would have a communal dish with a good spoonful each of Russian salad to share, an Agape, while solitary drinkers were cheered and enlivened with fiery-spiced pickled carrots. I never knew what to expect with my *tinto*: maybe ham or *tortilla* or stewed pimento; maybe cubes of pork in a sweet sauce. On my way up to Julio's I used to salivate in anticipation of what special dishes might have been prepared and set out along the bar like the subject of a still-life. Had *voladores* been available in the fish market that morning I'd wonder – those delicious tentacles of baby squid? Tonight, would it be my turn to have a taste of *morteruelo*, the local speciality, a sort of meat porage? The problem was the unwritten etiquette of things: you didn't choose what you'd have, and so your solid *aperitivo* was a lottery. It was nice to have a little fish or egg *mahonesa* to begin with, followed by somthing more solidly meaty. And what I liked with my third glass, to cleanse the palate, was a small helping of mixed salad – crisp, red-veined lettuce such as I'd seen growing beside the Huécar, with moist, mild onion, and green tomato, and strips of red pepper and black olive, all anointed with good oil and vinegar.

What I didn't ever acquire a taste for was a house speciality all too often offered to me after I became a favoured regular: pig's ear, *oreja*. Conscious of the honour that Julio was doing me, I would chew and chew with apparent pleasure (while actually feeling more and more nauseous), until, when nobody was watching, I was able to remove myself for a few moments to dispose of the unthinkable quid concealed in my cheek. On one redolent occasion the *tapa* was three spring onions (which proved to be fresh young garlic) with a necessary piece of bread; on another, it was a handful of broad beans to shell and dab in the salt jar after dropping the pods on the floor.

From the ceiling, in rows, dangled dozens of *serrano* hams and other cured meats or sausages, *embutidos*; gnarled-looking *chorizos* large and small; the salami-like *salchichón*; piquant black pudding, *morcilla*. In a stainless steel clamp at one end of the bar, its shiny black trotter daintily cocked, there was always a *serrano* ham on the go. This is quite unlike the pink, moist, rather blandly sweet York ham we know (though *jamón de York* is universally available in Spain), being strongly flavoured, cured a long age and inclined to be a stringy treat, if taken in too thick a chunk. Julio would deftly carve paper-thin slices, either to be arranged on a platter for a *ración* or slipped inside a stout roll for a *bocadillo* the size of a boxing glove.

A *ración* (portion) was a considerably larger helping than a *pincho* (skewerful), which in turn was bigger than a *tapa*. A *ración* could constitute almost a meal in itself, depending on what it was: a couple of quails; cod in tomato sauce; little lamb chops; veal tongue; smoked salmon or trout; a big bowl of *gazpacho andaluz*; mountain hare or venison; cuttlefish, squid or octopus. There was a speciality *ración*, the *zarajo*, which I have never seen since except in the province of Cuenca. At first sight a tray of *zarajos* will look for all the world like a tray of little game-birds like snipe or woodcock; however, those are not twig-like legs protruding from the body of meat, but actual wooden twigs round which have been wound, like an armature, long strips of powerful-tasting lamb's belly. They are eaten hot, sliced through and sprinkled with lemon juice. If I didn't have a *zarajo* at the bar when the crowds were beginning to thin out, it was because I'd decided on a barbecued *morcilla* instead – spicier and more moist than British black pudding – or a plate of a wonderfully strong, smelly, blue-veined goat's cheese which was kept under oil, as volatile potassium is, and which I swear moved about round the rim of the plate even as I watched.

Gratuities were neither solicited nor expected at Julio's. If you wanted to leave your small change for José or Pico, that was fine; the coins would fly from their saucer into the collective *bote*, and collective gratitude would then be expressed by the ringing of a carillon of little cow-bells. It was then that Julio had time for a grateful smoke and another chat. He'd pour me a glass of wine on the house, and a bottle of Sin for himself. Before long his wife would appear at the hatch between bar and kitchen. She was a plump, comfortable woman who wore tinted spectacles and, clearly outlined beneath her white cotton blouse, a brassière of heavy-duty material. After greeting me with formal courtesy, she'd josh her husband about his favourite football team and then smile invitingly for him to go and give her a kiss. Seeing this, I'd say how much I was missing my wife. It was a ritual we invented.

'Julio used to be away for six months at a stretch in Torremolinos,' she'd say, words to prompt Julio's frown.

'Yes, those are the worst times, the first few weeks away, no doubt about that. It gets a little easier as time goes on. But we never value our wives so much as when we can't be with them.'

At this, *la señora* would blush and look at the floor. She had a way of putting a hand to her throat through an embarrassing moment. She did not look a completely well woman; Julio hinted as much. Two years later I went back for a visit, taking my wife with me; I wanted to introduce her to all of them in El Bodegón, where I had spent so many happy hours. The moment we went in, after the handshakes and the pouring of drinks, I could tell from Julio's eyes and by the way he scurried a little less frantically behind his bar that things had changed. He told me his news. He had had his pancreas operation; it had been pretty much of a success, though he'd had to slow down a bit. His older son, now back from the army, was an immense help; the younger boy was due to leave school; his daughter and José, the barman, were to be married soon. The children would be well provided for. Before long, the place could be running itself without his help.

I explained all this to my wife, who couldn't understand enough of the Spanish to get the gist.

'And *la señora?*' I said next. *'Qué tal la señora?'*

'She died, Eduardo. A little while ago. I shall never get over it.'

He clutched my elbows, gripped them hard and shook them. I knew he must weep if I let there be silence between us.

'What was it, Julio?'

'What she had when you were here before. Cancer, of course, *claro.* Now, *hombre,* what will you and your wife have to eat?'

On the first day of June there was going to be a bullfight: not a full-blown *corrida de toros* but – very nearly as good – a *novillada con picadores,* with three matadors to kill two bulls apiece. Leaflets littered the streets; *carteles* were slapped up on walls. During the final days of May, the Diario de Cuenca carried articles and advertisements about an event which posed an interesting case for students of feminism. On one side of the equation, there was a lady bullfighter, Maribel Atienzar of Albacete, on the bill; on the other, the organizers offered free seats 'to any married or single lady accompanied by a paying gentleman, in order to honour the *torera* and to pay homage to the women of Cuenca'.

Well in advance I bought my *sol-y-sombra* ticket (the booking-office was a tailor's shop in the Calle Mayor) and hungrily waited for the days to pass by: hungrily, because the ticket cost the price of two dinners and I'd have to tighten my belt if I was to balance my books for the week. Several mornings I took my pre-breakfast walk along the Ciudad Real road as far as the *plaza de toros,* rehearsing my excitement. The way led under feathery-leafed acacias and past gardens full of marigolds and peonies, hollyhocks already waist-high. The day before the fight I squinnied through one of the gaps in the bullring wall, hoping to see preparations going on. Small boys on their way to school were doing the same. There was nothing yet to see. In such circumstances, with the sense of anticipation becoming unbearable, there's one thing aficionados can do: brag about great bullfights they've seen long ago and try to convince each other – and therefore themselves – that the imminent spectacle will be the best ever. The small boys shouted exultantly, using their jackets as *muletas* and kicking up dust. Passing labourers stopped to join in the debate; so did a dozen housewives and delivery men. I spoke my two-penn'orth about *corridas* I had seen at the Plaza Monumental in Barcelona and was gratified to be listened to politely and gravely by my assorted audience. We had grouped under the statue of Chicuelo II, on a patch of grass by the bullring entrance. Like any memory of past *toreros* he was aptly in pigtail and suit of lights and about twice life-size, his silent presence seeming to add authority to all opinions stated within his hearing.

That night I was making my way home from Julio's earlier than usual. The streets were quiet and the air felt strangely cold: so cold indeed that I thought I'd have a *coñac* somewhere before turning in. An occasional car crossed the intersection. A couple of Alsatian dogs were nosing a pile of rubbish. Behind balconies french windows were being slammed tight shut, slatted blinds were being lowered. There was a sense almost of siege, as in streets of boarded-up shop windows near British football grounds hours before the fans arrive. Something bad was on the way.

But the drab and unwontedly lifeless quarter was suddenly made gorgeous and exuberant as, bursting from a dark alleyway, sixteen young men in traditional Castilian dress appeared. Most carried string instruments. They were the *Tuna San Julián* (a *tuna* being a group of minstrels, usually students). Several times I had enjoyed listening to them, the hours each side of midnight. But I'd not seen them: only heard them, a street or two away; and assuming they were in ordinary, twentieth-century dress, I'd not bothered to go down in search.

They formed a ring between two lines of parked cars. There was a short discussion; the music began. Six mandolins in unison announced the melody, which eight guitars then developed in harmony. At the centre of the ring, the tallest member of the *tuna* supplied the beat on a tambourine; outside

52

the ring, the youngest member twirled a flag and danced. After sixteen bars of instrumental introduction, all began to sing. The song was a traditional May carol. A crowd gathered, as though out of thin air. Shutters rattled up. Entire families in the apartment blocks came out on to their balconies to listen and watch.

The musicians' costume was even more sumptuous than their playing: shoes with silver buckles; black hose and knee breeches; black and emerald striped doublets with frilly white collars; and black velvet cloaks festooned with brightly-coloured ribbons – lilac, crimson, apple-green, sapphire, white – hanging from ruched rosettes at the shoulder. The tambourinist wore white gloves. The flag, attached to a shining brass standard, was of royal velvet edged with gold. After the third refrain the song became louder and more boisterous. The tambourine player began leaping high in the air, still keeping perfect time, beating not only against his free hand but also against wrist, elbow, shoulder, thigh and knee. During one enormous leap he managed to strike both heels behind him. The carol shifted to a minor key. The flag-twirler joined the ring and sang a verse solo in an uncertain, immature tenor; a mandolin took over for a short, slow, bridging passage; there was the briefest pause; then, with all voices and instruments in unison, the final, surging chorus rang out.

Each side of the street was seven storeys high. Applause erupted, sounding like thousands of pigeons suddenly released and taking flight. There were repeated cries of *Bravo, señores*. The singers looked up, beaming; if they saw a pretty girl they waved and shouted compliments. After half a minute of this, as the clapping died down and a car edged past, they debated what to sing next. I heard the same song, like a long-delayed echo, eerily carrying from a block or two away.

It was another *tuna*: but of predominantly old and middle-aged men in everyday black berets and corduroys. They had piano-accordions as well as strings, they didn't go in for flag-twirling or leaping about with tambourines, they sported no colourful ribbons and their voices were far stronger and more assured than those of the *Tuna San Julián*. These players stood in a horseshoe. Behind them a second, impromptu, choir of men formed itself. They came sauntering up from adjacent bars to join in. The soloist was the one young man in the group. About twenty he'd have been, with the air of a Sixties rock musician: Elvis Presley haircut, leather jacket, open-neck shirt, an insolent sneer about the eyes and mouth. But there the comparison ended. When he sang, a yard or two in front of the others, his hands were kept at his sides, his feet remained stolidly together and the whole of his body was still. With the pagan emotion of the May carol, sometimes his eyes would close and he would permit himself the briefest shudder of the jowls as he hit a top note. He finished; hand-clapping and cheering broke out. A white-bearded, bohemian old fellow – perhaps from the artists' colony *arriba* – stepped forward to touch the singer's elbow in gratitude.

The bands moved off to serenade other streets. I followed a little way, then, at a crossroads, hearing new strains reverberate through a honeycomb of passageways, I tracked down several more *tunas*: groups exclusively of men, of all ages, some in traditional costume but most not, singing and playing for the sheer delight of celebrating the month of May, the last minutes of which were ticking by. No collection was taken up. If you offered a drink to express thanks for the pleasure they'd given you, it was politely declined.

All evening, thunder had been distantly rumbling. Just before I reached the door of my hotel, a few heavy spots fell on the pavement and spread, big as plums.

I took the lift to the second floor. In the short space of time this took, the rain had become a Niagara of unbroken, vertical water. From my window I couldn't see as far as the opposite side of the street. It wasn't just heavy rain, or torrential rain. 'Downpour' would not have described it adequately; 'cloud-burst' would have been downright feeble. No: it was joke rain, unnatural rain, a special-effect rain produced by expert technicians working on an Old Testament film epic. It was a liquid wall to be laughed at for its improbability.

I stopped laughing when the thunderstorm started. The lamps went out. There was the briefest, disorienting darkness. Then, indoors and outdoors, all was made bright as day by ceaseless lightning. For a long while it was like being at the epicentre of a remorseless bombing raid lit with inextinguishable flares. The thunderclaps were terrifying in their unleashing. I stuffed my ears. The entire building shuddered. My tooth mug slid into the sink. The white metal bed-head rattled. Floorboards shook. I was properly frightened, trembling, breathing fast and riveted by wonder to stare out of the window, like a little boy alone in the house who dares to continue reading a horror story.

So mesmerized was I by such quantities of hurled, spectacular weather (the like of which I'd never seen anywhere), I hadn't thought to shut my outer door. Rods of rain came slanting in to my blacony, bouncing a good foot high and each one making a couple of dozen normal-sized drops to carry to my bedroom floor. Already a fair-sized puddle was forming. What I had to do was lower the rolled-up blind outside before closing the french window: which I'd have done there and then had it not been for the beginning hailstones.

The first ones were only twice as big as any I'd ever seen, about the size of Mint Imperials. When I tried to get at the blind cord they gave me such a buffeting that I had to retreat. And immediately – tho thunder and lightning continuing unbroken – the hail was bigger than mothballs, than gobstoppers, than golf balls. The balcony above afforded no shelter. Mine was very soon several inches under a drift of hailstones most of which had ricocheted from walls and gutters and sills and flower-pots and railings and any number more of those various protuberances which adorn Spanish buildings. Cleats and metal washing-lines went zing, window-boxes dully percussed, somebody's tin bath kept pinging like a spittoon in a slapstick film. I was in awe of that hail. It hammered at my windows and made tom-toms of parked cars in the street below. Women screamed. Men with scared-sounding voices shouted advice to each other about how best to protect property. Transfixed at my window, I saw a geranium leaf drift down, a carmine petal stuck to it. This was followed by a sharp bit of tile, swift as a flung knife. If you'd stood outside under the onslaught of that hail you'd have learned what stoning to death is like. Not before it had held off for a good ten minutes did I dare look over my balcony to see, by the unflagging lightning, vehicles wheel-deep in a rushing torrent, most of them with windscreens smashed. Cowed, I went to bed and fell asleep at once. Then at three o'clock I was awakened by what I thought was the storm coming back. But the glare I blinked at was merely that of my room lights, the power having been restored. And the thunder was only that of a drum!

For up the street, shin-deep in flood water, came marching in double time a scratch band of two trumpets, two trombones and the drum, a big bass drum. The group splashed along belting out a *paso doble*, pursued by a short procession of roisterers doing their best to keep pace. The musicians pounded and blew with all their might as though defying the weather – even God Himself – to fling down anything worse. Gradually their noise faded into the distance, grew weaker and weaker, finally stopped. A light rain began, soothing to listen to; but beneath it was a shocked quiet that had descended upon Cuenca like a thick rug. I could sense how many in the city lay awake, waiting for daylight to come so that the damage could be seen and the cost counted.

By eight o'clock the sun was bright and strong. The streets were steaming. There were pools of deepish water all over town. Between these, householders and shopkeepers were hard at work sweeping up broken tiles and the rubble of stucco hacked by hail from older buildings. Yards of high wall had collapsed, chimney stacks had toppled. Some nice old outhouses and store sheds had been seen off. In the middle of the *calle mayor* were uprooted wild plants borne there by the Huécar, which had broken its banks for a short spell during the night. An emergency edition of the *Diario de Cuenca* (its presses having been affected by the electricity cut) thankfully reported no serious human casualties. Farm animals, however, had been killed in the open countryside near the city and arable crops had suffered throughout the entire province. Cereals had been flattened. The garlic fields of Las Pedroñeras had been particularly badly battered: the fresh, pungent smell of the bruised young bulbs could be smelt upon the air several kilometres away. The paper carried photographs of familiar streets which, for about an hour, had become Arctic runnels. Piles of hail had formed miniature icebergs to be dislodged and carried away by the torrents. Not even the old folk could remember a storm so severe. The first of June, everyone was saying, was like the first of December, a mini-winter.

More an autumn, I thought: a green autumn. I all but wept at the piteous sight of my favourite trees in the Parque San Julián, so suddenly stripped so bare. Everywhere there was fallen foliage and thick, sappy twigs, floatings of leafage like water-lily mats spread over every broad puddle and pool. I scuffed through thicknesses of big, wet, floppy horse-chestnut and plane leaves along paths made strange by the phenomenal weather: paths normally at this hour walked by young mothers and schoolchildren and old chaps with their dogs, but deserted now save for me and a few startled pieces of statuary. I saw the man whose job it was, every other summer's morning, to damp down the dust. Today, he told me, he'd be helping the firemen to drain basements and cellars.

It was the day when the festivities in honour of the Virgen de la Luz had been scheduled to begin. 'I suppose it'll all be called off now,' I said to him, 'the bullfight and everything.'

'Not everything,' he said. 'The novillada will have to be cancelled – no doubt about that. You can't fight bulls in a flooded plaza. But otherwise things will go on as planned. The cycle race, the travelling theatre, the funfair. As soon as everybody's got cleaned up after the storm, they'll be in the mood for having a good time. You'll see! Not that this is a big fiesta, you understand. The best thing you can do is to get your money back on your bullfight ticket and use it to get a good seat at the theatre.'

That's what I did. The Teatro Lido's marquee was almost the length and half the breadth of a football pitch. It was a wonder that such an expanse of canvas had remained undamaged by the storm. Its advertising was gaudy and cheerful, with illustrations suggesting a revue programme of comedy, song and dance, bawdy and unbuttoned without being too offensive. The line of chorus girls as depicted – scantily clad, with plumed headdresses towering to ten feet – recalled the innocent naughtiness of English music-hall on its last (high-kicking) legs in the Fifties. Franco was not long dead – but he was dead. Spain was by now cautiously testing the delights of public permissiveness; also she was becoming more and more vulnerable to foreign influences.

British things – in particular Scotch whisky, sold in an establishment with a fanciful nonce title such as a güisquería – were considered smart. The English language was, so to speak, dernier cri, even though, more often than not, ever so slightly misused: the Lido Theatre's Ballet Inglés was also dubbed las Lido Star's Girl's. (Spanish show-biz adores the apostrophe. In Galicia I was to see posters for a rock band known endearingly as Los Belter's.)

What had not changed – had not changed for centuries – was the custom of countryfolk from remote villages invading the provincial capital in droves for the *fiesta*. They arrived by bus and coach (and even taxi) for this annual treat. Through the spiky grass of the *terreno ferial* they paraded themselves in their best clothes for the benefit of the townies. Gawky boys off tractors dribbled and laughed too loud when they saw someone was watching. Demure and waxy-faced virgins, in frocks modish two years before, carried posies and licked large lollipops, lubricious. But it was the older peasants that most took the eye: wicked-eyed field-workers, each wrinkled face and dewlap brown as a walnut. The men were shrunken under broad, flat berets, wielding hefty walking sticks like medieval implements of war. They were swathed in suits of gold corduroy several sizes too big, so that trousers overlapped huge leather belts with a piecrust effect at the waist. Their ladies dwarfed them, cackling like pantomime dames and smelling of hot oil and liniment as they passed. Some were in dresses of subfusc you could have covered several sofas with; others were lovely in the way that healthy, buxom women always are, in cotton prints the colours of late-summer flowers. One was carrying a cactus in a pot as though it were a bridal bouquet; another had a live bantam cock by the legs and was swinging it provocatively, the way a tart will swing a shiny handbag.

The show comprised twenty scenes, most of them (literally) thinly-veiled excuses for revealing the female form. There were four leading ladies, *vedettes*. Stunningly beautiful they were too: no amount of tawdry make-up or tatty threads could have made them otherwise. What was more, they were thoroughly professional about doing their best with poor material. Not a hint of boredom did they display throughout the show, with bump and grind routines they had probably performed, to the same cliché-ridden neo-music, a thousand times from La Coruña to Cartagena, from Cádiz to Cabo Cerbère. With good heart and evident goodwill to give value for money – and not to patronize their bristling comb-and-water customers, eagerly gurgling in the front seats – they gave it all they'd got from the first bar of the opening production number to the final curtain. They took it in turns to let down their hair and bare all after fronting the chorus line in some dance number of minimal choreography and in ludicrous costume surreally suggestive of a theme: soldiers' red caps and boots for a battle; silver goldfish bowls and boots for a space odyssey. Interspersed with these travesties were comic sketches of (as it seemed at first) such dire archness that I felt like cringing, sliding off my seat to the grassy floor and crawling out for pure shame.

And I would have left, but for a couple of accomplished singing acts. A trio of Nicaraguan Indians (bead headbands; also, less authentic, frilly orange georgette shirts and electric-blue, lurex trousers) sang some Latin-American songs with intricate rhythms, accompanying themselves on guitars and maracas; and the company's *polifacético*, or versatile all-rounder, came on in a suit the colour of sour cream to perform, with more than a hint of wobbly *cante hondo*, a slow-syrup sentimental ballad and a modern, patriotic rabble-rouser called *My Spain Or Our Spain?* which, between them, brought down the canvas house.

I'm glad I stayed: because when Ruben García, the stand-up comic, came on stage dressed as a peasant farmer in town for the *fiesta*, there was an enraptured welcome for him, suggesting he had more audience attraction than any number of mammary glands. For a full two minutes, before he was able to utter a syllable, the marquee was loud with laughter redoubling at his merest twitch of eyebrow or lip. His beret was as broad and flat as a manhole cover; his walking stick was seven feet tall and as big round as a goal post; he could have got both legs into one leg of his cords and his jacket would have saddled a camel. When, finally, he spoke, it was in a high-pitched whine which proved to be the last straw for one helpless matron in the expensive seats: a row of buttons down her bombazine back ripped, popping off. She had to be supported by her friends until she got control of herself. As soon as she'd done so, García squeaked. She keeled backwards. A man in the row behind, bearing all the vast bulk of her, bellowed for water.

Precisely what García said in his ensuing monologue, I can no longer remember. It wasn't a matter of jokes or wisecracks. What made his adoring listeners crease was his knack of reminding them, tactfully and with dignity, of who they were and why, that day and night, they were in Cuenca. Sex was but a funny memory, riches a daft dream, high fashion and glamour a fad of folks no better than they ought to be: but it was all right, once or twice a year, to catch a passing glimpse of things that had never been theirs at all, or had seldom been theirs for long or ever theirs to keep. Laughter was a more congenial purge than tears. Those good people didn't mind being burlesqued because they had long since learned how to laugh at themselves. All that Ruben García had to do was to be a catalyst. Before their very eyes, his art was imitating their nature; and, as soon as everyone was outside in the fresh air again, nature would repay the compliment.

I saw an old couple from the audience standing by the glare of arc lights next to the bumper-cars. Each, rather sadly, was sniffing a spray of lavender brought from the fields of home. They were watching a group of ten little girls with hula-hoops so closely twirling that the hoops overlapped, making a single work of mobile art of them all.

'Raro,' mumbled the old lady. 'Husband, tell me if there ever was a thing as graceful as that.'

'Never, woman. There never was, I'm telling you,' he said. And he spat on the toe of his dusty boot and led her away and bought her a bag of coconut chunks.

In the blue marquee I had laughed life-enhancing laughter until it hurt. Now, outside again, the meretricious frivolity of the funfair was pernicious, engendering loneliness. I went to a plush and characterless hotel near the fairground for a smart drink. I'd been there before; its 'English' bar was the only place in Cuenca where I'd ever been short-changed; the only *tapa* on offer was a saucer of salted almonds: but it did me good, once in a while, to enjoy the comfort of a padded stool at a padded bar and to talk to someone (usually American) in my own language.

I got a gin-and-Italian; I swizzled, nibbled and sipped. The short-changing barman (I'd caught him out the time before) mooched moodily off as soon as he'd served me. There was nobody else in the bar apart from some glum Portuguese tourists. I thought I'd drink up and leave.

But then there entered (and such an occurrence, every bit as much as ten overlapping hula-hoopers, must be less than usual in this remote part of New Castile) five Chinamen. Four were in shirt sleeves and the fifth, who proved to be their interpreter, was in a formal suit befitting his office. With them were five Spaniards, journalists evidently. They all sat down at an adjacent table, convenient for me to eavesdrop.

The Chinamen were officials of the People's Republic team of Wushu, one of several martial arts highly popular in Spain. They were touring the country, had just arrived from Madrid and were to perform their acrobatic skills next day in the Cuenca Sportsdrome. On the pretext of being a newspaperman too, I got myself invited to join the party.

The interpreter had been speaking perfect Spanish. Now he spoke in perfect English. He told me they had been in Manchester recently, oh yes. He introduced me to the team manager, a man as programmed as a word processor.

'Where are the gymnasts now?' I asked.

'In their rooms, resting.'

'All of them?'

'All of them.'

'It would be good to speak to some of the team.'

'What do you want to speak to them about?'

'Their sport. What they do.'

'My colleagues and I can tell you all you want to know. The athletes demonstrate the following disciplines.'

He began to turn the pages of a brochure. On each page there were photographs of Chinamen several feet off the ground and parallel with it, swishing at the air with all kinds of stick, sword, club, bayonet and dagger. There was also an illustration of a sport known as *solitary boxing*.

'I should like very much,' I said, reverting to Spanish, 'to speak to a solitary boxer.'

'What about, sir?'

'Why, solitary boxing, *claro*.'

'My colleagues and I can tell you all you want to know.'

'Yes, *caballero*, but it would be most interesting to hear what an actual practitioner has to say.'

The team manager frowned. The interpreter turned to the Spanish journalists and said, 'Who is this man?'

'An English *periodista*. That's all we know.'

There was a lengthy exchange in Chinese. Then, 'The team manager offers you a cigarette and a drink in the name of world peace,' the interpreter said to me.

By the time I'd finished smoking and drinking in the

interests of world peace, the sun had set like a smashed blood-orange and now it was eleven o'clock. The great storm had long since spent itself. Walls and streets in the city were dry; the cracks between paving-slabs were already filling anew with spat husks of sunflower seeds; stone seats in the park had warmed through and it was a bitter-sweet pleasure to sit in the dark, looking up through stripped trees at the night sky. The air was cool as watercress. A dwarf widow-woman hobbled past me. Moonlight made talc of the gravel path as she stubbed it up. She stopped by a litter-bin, rummaged, found a hunk of bread and put it in her apron pocket; then she lay down to sleep on a bench, still as a dead *Infanta* on a catafalque.

CHAPTER FOUR

Cuenca was a slow starter of a Sunday morning. The bars were desolate at eight o'clock. '*Ya no funciona la máquina,*' you were told when, desperate for coffee, you stepped inside through the litter of prawn shells, cigarette ends, toothpicks and olive stones – evidence of the roisterous night before. The proprietor would tiredly wave at the coffee machine, rub a stubbled chin with the back of a hand, yawn, ponderously begin to set out one hundred saucers, on which to place one hundred spoons, one hundred packets of sugar and one hundred cups, before even beginning to think about turning on *la máquina*. 'Not that it doesn't work, you understand,' he'd say, 'so much as that I haven't switched it on yet. No, there's nothing to eat. Not yet, *señor*.' It wasn't that he was disobliging, one understood, so much as that *he* wasn't switched on yet, either.

Therefore you went instead to one of the *cafeterías* in the middle of town, noting on the way the absence of the blind lottery ticket seller but the presence of the bootblack who, this one day of the week, set up his pitch in the portico of the España cinema.

Or, much nicer, you'd go to the *churrería*.

This was in one of the short streets connecting the *calle mayor* with the park: not a wooden stall or a barrow, as many *churrerías* are in Spain, but a loveable, tall-roomed, quaintly old-fashioned establishment, whose tables were of wrought-iron, with round, white marble tops; whose waiter had a slicked black kiss curl and wore a starched white apron covering him from neck to ankles. You could fancy that perhaps the owners and the staff (and – who knows – maybe some of the customers, too) had not ventured out into the street for several decades, that they never saw a newspaper, or listened to the radio, or had even heard of television.

Chocolate con churros are as much associated with Sunday in Spain as roast beef and Yorkshire pudding are in England. Sunday is the one day when you can thoroughly enjoy them, for you need time to walk them off afterwards and avoid an otherwise certain bout of indigestion.

Spanish drinking chocolate is made sweet and viscid: if you tilt your cup, it will scarcely pour or spill. You spoon it up; or, if you carry the cup (or bowl) to your mouth, you ean have chocolate whiskers. Once that happens (and you have noticed it happening to your fellow customers too) then you can surrender utterly to your pleasure. Oh, you look after your adult dignity as best you can, with deft use of several paper napkins; but there's nothing for it but to give in completely to behaving like a child. Soon you find yourself dipping your hot, sugar-sprinkled *churro* deep down, maybe with a stirring motion, lifting it carefully, craning forward to avoid spilling ineradicable brown spots on your best Sunday shirt, and then, with a sort of pecking motion, ah, bliss! biting into the *churro's* crispness, sucking at the chocolate's softness, not giving a damn about anything except the next mouthful.

Sundays might continue in the plaza outside San Esteban's church, where I enjoyed the passing parade of best clothes. More often than not there's the charming spectacle of two or three little girls dressed all in white like child brides, first communicants; also, endearing tearful scenes created by their parents, weighed down with emotion and cameras, for whom the occasion was clearly more overwhelming than for their daughters. By now the mid-morning warmth would be falling like bran on my cheeks. I would spend half an hour inside cool, modern Saint Stephen's, fascinated by its brutal stained glass, by the constant coming and going (like that of bus station crowds) of the congregation and by the fussy, high-camp self-importance of the priests, for some of whom the congregation seemed all but irrelevant.

Then, my face by now tanned brown as a cigar, I'd go *arriba* in my field worker's demins, sit on the steps of the cathedral like a peasant and gawp at the tourists. Often I posed for coach parties in my *sombrero campesino*, affecting to be incapable of the least understanding of English, accepting kindly-meant tips in the spirit in which they were given. Sometimes I sat with a beer at a terrace table, at the edge of my benefactors' conversations, grinning like the idiot fellow who (a friend had told me) used to throw bits of wooden box at visitors the moment they stepped from coach or car.

There was a way down to the banks of the *Júcar* from the top of town, known as the Bajada de las Angustias. It was the prettiest path imaginable: steps of cobbles and flagstones gently descending first between ancient houses, then past their hanging gardens; with dramatic vistas of a rock-gorge to stop and admire through many a gap between shrubs and trees; with a carving of a lion's head, or a fountain here and there; and delicate climbing and scented plants and weeping green fronds to have lingering across your shoulder as you passed. Halfway down – as it were a landing to the stairs – the *bajada* widened for the Plaza de los Descalzos, a cool, grassy, leafy area in front of a delicious little Franciscan hermitage or monastery. This is where (certainly if you were making the journey uphill) you'd pause for a while in the shade, drinking from your knuckles at the spring or trying to edge your way past and crush into the shrine for a glimpse of the Virgin in Auguish. And then you'd continue, beginning to hear laughter and voices not far below, beside the river; but you'd want to prolong your walk just a little longer because you could see grapes growing wild, or a small knot of rock-cress clutching at a sunny ledge, or you'd just want to stand and feel the gathering warmth accumulated in a balustrade.

Weekdays I went above the bridge for a swim, lunch and siesta. Sundays, though, I went below the bridge – as did very many *Conquenses* and tired, day-tripping *Madrileños* – to the *merendero*.

A rough, loosely-woven roof of osiers supported by iron poles; an area of sandy gravel with a wooden bar counter; a barbeque pit, wine and beer crates, a few dozen tin tables and chairs surrounded by a stone wall: that's all the *merendero* was, unless you also count, immediately beyond the wall, mature trees rustling above the well-worn patches of green and dirt, and the wide dappled slab of the river.

The first time I went there (finding it by accident, drawn by the smells of woodsmoke and roasting meat and the sound of families playing), I knew straightaway it was a congenial oasis to make a beeline for at the end of each week. Accordingly, I chose my table with great care and, when I got an *aperitivo* of a bottle of beer, I tipped the owner's ten-year-old son to keep the table for me. I recognized his dad: I often saw him about in Cuenca, Mondays to Saturdays, obviously on various paid errands for other people. Sundays he was his own man, lording it over his family and the patrons of the *merendero*, blithe. He came himself to take my order for lunch: a salad, and then a mixed grill comprising *lomo* (a slice of good loin of pork) and lamb chops, *chorizo*, *morcilla*, stewed peppers, kidneys, half a loaf and a jug of red wine.

'You wish me to put ice in your wine, *señor*?'

'I'll not come here again if you do.'

'Some people like ice in their wine.'

'Not I.'

'Nor I.'

From where I sat I could see the river, matte olive in the shade. A certain sparrow was forever flying in. It would cling to a reed, be gently lowered to the surface and delicately sip before being lifted clear of the water again. Here was a place of refreshment such as you seldom encounter. Fatigue fell away. Wherever your eyes rested, there was calm: not silence, not quiet even, but an absence of stress and anxiety.

In Spain, wherever there are people there is certain to be sound. From somewhere in the trees, beyond where I could see, came girls' voices that at once grew louder. They were beginning to sing, to the rhythm of hand-clapping, a quick paso doble. I thought it might be a coach party from a Madrid secondary school, probably with a trio of nuns in charge: on the low wall nearby were draped duffle-bags, satchels and cardigans; and on a patch of clean grass near the river there was an old wicker hamper as yellow as sunlight.

A massive acacia trailed a weeping-willow-like curtain of leaves which suddenly parted as the girls burst through singing, dancing and clapping; thirty fourteen-year-olds and as many others, aunts and younger sisters, all of them in cool summer frocks. As soon as they emerged into the open, they finished the lively song. They joined hands in a ring and began singing a song not requiring them to clap. It was hauntingly sad, with many verses and refrains, making the passers-by on the opposite bank stop in their tracks. Then dancing began again; a fast dance following a slow, a slow one following a fast; for an hour without stop, with ever more intricate steps.

Weaving round the trees as though in a trance, they went one final time to a measure more serious: the girls with the air of the women they would become; the women recalling the girls thay had once been. I wondered where all the brothers, husbands, uncles and fathers were. Out hunting rabbit in the high sierra? Gone to the match in a blinding stadium? Mending bikes in a trellised yard? None had seen the afternoon dance, heard the singing or joined in the happy chatter and out-of-breath laughter.

The time had come for the spreading of white cloths for their picnic. I'd finished my meal. I had wine and water to see me through the afternoon. Most of the tables under the canopy were once again free. I thought that, lunchtime over, the *merendero* would gradually empty except for the laughers at the bar. Replete and somnolent, we would all stretch out in a bit of dapple of our choosing. The smoky air from the barbeque was closing more eyelids than mine.

I'd not reckoned on a game of bowls beginning.

Bolas can in no way be compared with *pétanque*, let alone English lawn bowls. It's a game requiring a good eye for accuracy: but that would have been of little use without a chinful of Sunday stubble and the strength of lumberjacks.

The bowls themselves were large, rough-hewn near-spheres of South American hardwood, partly hollowed out and with a couple of holes for the fingers. They'd have weighed two and a half, perhaps even three, kilos. They were not rolled, lobbed or pitched but out-and-out hurled. The rink was an oblong of flattened dirt not far from the *merendero*, about twenty-five metres by fifteen. The referee was a tiny, bald man dressed entirely in black. He had nine willow wands, slender as a baby's little finger, which he set up equidistant from each other in three rows of three. To get them standing upright in the hard-baked ground, he poured water into each hole, puddled it about to make mud, then worked the wand gradually in. Spectators sat on tree trunks at the side of the rink or (the intrepid ones) at a slightly higher lever at each end.

The game was played as singles; or between sides of two, or three. The object was to send as many wands as possible flying out of their holes, the complication being that when you'd flung your *bola* from one end to another (how satisfyingly it clattered against the boundary trunk!) you had to take your return shot from wherever it came to rest. So long as you kept one foot on the spot where you picked it up, you were allowed to stretch on the other leg as far as you could to line up the wands remaining; the more you stretched, though, the less you could keep your balance, and the less accurate you'd be.

Players braced to take their shots were furious-faced, intent, grunting like malcontent gorillas. Team-mates and opponents alike would observe them, swig beer from the bottle, spit flecks of tobacco. The tiny referee would scuttle this way and that, adjusting and replacing wands – a black widow spider holding them in thrall. When the *bola* was flung – fast, chunky, knee-high and rising – everyone gasped involuntarily as though in shocked anticipation of what damage could be done. A wand would be hit, leap out of its socket like a snake from a fissure and, with a whiplash crack, go spinning high in the air while the bowl fell to earth and slithered and skidded and thudded and bounced at an unpredictable angle back into the rink.

As the afternoon wore on and even in the shade the heat intensified, the bigger, beefier, most hairy-armed players cried that they'd had enough. Taking a last brown bottle from the fountain trough, they slumped to the base of a tree, took a suck of beer, pulled caps over eyebrows, yawned, fell asleep, thus leaving the rink to the wiry young lads with more ambition and stamina than they.

With the first light breath of cooler air, a long raft of cars assembled on the Madrid road. By nine o'clock, Cuenca belonged to herself again: an old-fashioned town in an old-fashioned country. Though Madrid was only a hundred-odd miles away to the west, its twentieth-century sophistication was as remote as that of capitals in far-flung continents. The fashionable place to go to in Cuenca of a Sunday evening was not some smart cocktail bar but the ice-cream parlour.

Returning from the *merendero*, I bought a cornet to take to the park. There was a nice elderly couple sitting on my favourite bench. She was crocheting, with very fine thread, a lacy white tablecloth to a pattern of remarkable complexity; he was biting a toothpick – a common habit of Spanish men – and contentedly patting an ample stomach. The temperature was still in the nineties but he hadn't taken off his jacket.

'Señores, do you mind if I sit next to you and eat my ice-cream?'

'Of course not, señor, please sit down,' the old chap said.

We fell into conversation. I said how much I enjoyed living in their city. Conquenses loved being told they lived in the most beautiful place in Spain – therefore the most beautiful place in the whole world.

'You have come from far away, perhaps?' the old lady asked. 'A Frenchman, no doubt?'

'No, señora, I'm from England.'

'We, too, came from far away to live here, my man and I.'

'May I ask from where?'

'From Sacedón. When we were newly-weds.'

Sacedón was all of eighty miles away, in the Alcarria. I'd seen it on route maps in the bus station. Not long since, a new bridge had been opened over the Júcar; now you could drive straight to Guadalajara on a fine black road, by way of Sacedón, in an hour and a half. I did a quick calculation then said, 'How far is it – a hundred and thirty, a hundred and forty kilometres?'

'We did it in less than a week – didn't we, woman?'

'With all we possessed. On an ox-cart.'

'Got out. Just left, like Alfonso the Thirteenth!'

'That's right. Ha!'

A Sunday might be out of the ordinary, with a romería to make it special. A romería was anything from an afternoon picnic outing to a full-blown, long-lasting pilgrimage lasting several days. However big or small, it involved a journey to some sacred place: a shrine, perhaps; a cave once inhabited by a holy man; the site of a miraculous vision of the Virgin Mary. There'd be feasting and jollity, dancing and singing. The pilgrims would be members of the same community or congregation.

Being invited to take part in a romería by don Pedro, the Master Blacksmith, I regarded as an honour and a privilege: a touching gesture of friendship and loyalty I hadn't earned and didn't deserve, given that lately I hadn't taken the trouble to go and see him and Alejandro in El Sotanillo.

The invitation came about like this: skulking and ashamed of my neglectful ways, I went into the bar one evening with a letter I'd just had from Laurie Lee.

'I've heard from Lorenzo,' I said. 'Guess what?'

'*Hombre*, we thought we'd never see you again,' said Alejandro.

'I've had people come here to meet you,' said Pedro. 'You were never here. Now they don't come.'

Reproach hung on the air like stale smoke. I felt awful and serve me right.

'I'm very sorry, *señores*,' I said. 'Can you forgive me?'

'You've been busy with your work. For an artist, work comes first. I am an artist, so I understand. It's nothing, *nada*. Don't apologize. You still drink *tinto*?'

'Yes, please.'

I took out the letter from its envelope. It was on four sheets three and a half inches wide. Pedro hissed through his teeth, marvelling. '*Qué raro! Lorenzo, el Desgarbado!*' he said as I began translating into Spanish:

Dear Ted,

Your wondrous letter came; and too brief & too late I'm answering it – but the letter I'll keep by me. Cuenca I loved & next to Cuenca Alejandro de El Sotanillo whose photograph I had for years drinking out of a wine skin at a bullfight – though I don't know where it is now. How glad I am you met him & that our paths crossed that much. Ask him if you get this what he did with the 10 shilling note I signed & gave him & which he nailed to the tavern wall.

I always meant to return & get it back. What a shame I couldn't be there with you. I went there by train from Madrid through fields of caves (inhabited then). Let's go back together some time and give Alejandro a proper scare.

I'm v. glad to hear about your book and I'm sure the signs, the place & the man are right . . . I admired your Spanish poem more than I can say, & shall keep it by me. Let me know when you get back & we'll meet & talk about it. Meanwhile please give Alejandro & his mates my salutations & warnings that I will be back.

Yours
Laurie

The poem was one I'd had in the *Diario de Cuenca*, full of my mawkish homesickness. The letter passed from Pedro to Alejandro.

70

'Follow me,' said Alejandro.

Pedro and I trooped behind through the ornamental wrought-iron gate that led downstairs to the dining-room.

'Nailed,' said Alejandro, witheringly, 'to the wall of the *taberna*! Don Eduardo, this establishment no longer is a *taberna* but a *mesón*, a smart restaurant. Nobody knocks nails into my walls these days. *Mire!* I have come far. But the past is not forgotten. Once a friendship, always a friendship. Here's the banknote of *don Lorenzo, el Desgarbado*.'

On the wall there was one of those glass-fronted frames, such as you see in bars and cafés all over the world, containing small denomination notes of many different currencies. Plumb in the middle was Laurie Lee's ten-bob note, signed by him with an expression of warmest good wishes. The ink was rather faded.

'Once a friendship, always a friendship – yes!' said don Pedro when we were once again upstairs in the bar. 'Will you come on Sunday with a party of *vecinos* on a *romería* to the Sanctuary of San Julián el Tranquilo?'

Vecino is a nice word. It means 'neighbour' but also 'inhabitant' or 'citizen'. My *vecino* in the hotel was the young Cordovan schoolmaster in the room next door who dried his crayfish nets on his balcony; I was his. He being an *Andaluz*, I being English, we could neither of us ever be true *Conquenses*. But were temporary *vecinos* of Cuenca and of each other.

On the Sunday morning early I went as arranged to a small, nondescript bar near the bridge on the Madrid road. Outside, perhaps fifteen or twenty small Seats were parked. They had all manner of shapeless brown-paper bundles in the back seats and on the roof-racks. I went inside the bar and found it full to bursting with mainly working-class people both young and old in Sunday best: scrubbed, glowing, full of high spirits and looking forward to an enjoyable day. At first, I couldn't see Pedro. I felt embarrassed and out of place among so many who were well known to each other but strangers to me. But soon he arrived; and we had a *café-coñac* which he wouldn't let me pay for, despite my protests.

'Everybody's brought something for the *romería*,' I said, indicating the loaded cars outside and bags on the floor in the bar. 'Let me at least pay for these.'

71

'We'll have another round,' said Pedro. I thought he meant the round would be mine. But when we'd downed our *copas* and coffees he wouldn't let me pay for those, either. There was no time to argue because everybody was moving outside.

There were many large ladies, which meant that much good-natured teasing went on as the men tried to work out who should travel with whom and in which cars. I was wedged in a back seat between a soft matron smelling of lavender and a sharp bundle smelling of tar. Pedro, in the front passenger seat, kept offering cachous to the driver, the matron's son, during the short drive along the gorge of the Júcar.

We parked on a strip of roadside grass. The spot was not remarkable. I was baffled. Anywhere but hereabouts, I could have understood why it had been chosen for a picnic: the river was no distance away, the rocky chasm through which it flowed was leafy and picturesque with great boulders. Lovely enough: but in the environs of Cuenca you could have picked a thousand more beautiful and convenient sites. No doubt about it, though. Cars as they arrived were placed in shady corners. Their boots and interiors were emptied, their roof-racks unloaded. There looked to be enough in the way of provisions for a tidy expedition.

An expedition was precisely what we were embarking upon. A few of the younger and more vigorous couples had already shouldered their loads and were beginning, like sherpas, to climb the hill path. Their children scampered on ahead.

'What shall I carry?' I asked Pedro.

'Why – nothing at all,' he said. 'You are our guest.'

'*Vaya*,' I said, 'you've got to let me do my bit.' I grabbed the brown-paper package I'd had next to me in the car and set off up the track with it. I had a peep inside. It was kindling wood, bits of chopped-up chestnut paling.

The procession continued through mixed woodland; up and on, the women singing to themselves and the men offering hearty words of encouragement whenever the way became steeper or more difficult underfoot. Somehow old Pedro got ahead and was waiting for me when I reached our destination.

'Here you are,' he said. 'The Sanctuary of San Julián el Tranquilo. Don't you think it's the most peaceful, most beautiful place in the world? *Venga*, let's have that firewood.'

I gave him the bundle. After he'd walked off with it I was

able to see where we were. The path had levelled and widened considerably, forming a long, broad patio of freckled sunlight and full shadow. Green iron railings protected the drop one side, a stone retaining wall the weight of the hill the other. A fountain spring and then the sanctuary chapel itself continued the line of this wall: a disarming, endearing, plain white box roofed with bright orange terracotta pantiles, with a round window above its two-pillar porch and an aperture above this for a bell. Beyond, a single-storey, four-arch colonnade, then the path led on and away.

It was enchanting. Farther off, one could see the scrub-covered shoulder of the mountain, its outcroppings russet in the strengthening warmth of the sun. It was going to be hot up there: but where we were should remain cool, with deciduous leaves rustling delectably and the mingling scents of rosemary and pine and woodsmoke filling the air. Pedro had got his fire going; as more and more people arrived, so the benches and tables and parapets were covered with white cloths that flapped until they were laden with loaves, bowls of salad, bottles of wine and beer. Everyone talked at once. You couldn't hear the bees humming any more; the river below was only its remembered roar. Cackling old ladies sat chipping cucumbers, being kissed by sons and daughters, grandchildren and great-grandchildren. A lovely young, heavily pregnant woman in a billowing frock arrived, supported on each arm by husband and brother. Puffed out, she subsided on to a frail tin chair, looked in her hand-mirror, dabbed powder on to a cheek fuzzed by the sun like an apricot. Hardwood logs were being fed to the fire now and a clatter of cooking pots and ladles began as a burly man in a red-spotted shirt strode up with a knobbly sackful: tins of corned beef with which to make *morteruelo*.

I was introduced to thirty or forty people. Then I had to fend for myself: Pedro had quite enough to think about, making a fire fiercely hot but flameless to cook with. You could see by the way he raked the embers that he knew a blacksmith's thing or two. Somebody gave me a bottle of beer. From that moment I was an honorary *vecino*. I opened tins of corned beef, peeled onions, talked to babies under their pram parasols, tested the lads on mental arithmetic and the history of Spain. I felt at home.

73

I was thinking all that was needed now was a little suitable music. Almost at once, over by the fountain, I saw a trumpet glint and heard a snare drum being tested. And there were black instrument cases stowed among the boxes of apples and bananas; and suddenly (where they had sprung from, I couldn't tell) the bandsmen were all sitting together and playing a morning hymn. Next they struck up a military march, and when the final chord of this crashed home, one of the cooks took the bandmaster by the elbow, whispered in his ear, eased the baton gently away from him and put a glass of wine in his hand.

It was still not yet eleven o'clock: but the smell from savoury pots and the stiff uphill climb into fresh mountain air had made us ravenous. We were each served a hunk of bread, two ladles of stew, some *longaniza* sausage, fruit and a glass of whatever we fancied from where it was cooling in the fountain basin. I was just swallowing my last sliver of apple when the chatter subsided and everyone turned to face the path by which we had come.

The guest of honour was arriving: the little girl whose first communion we were there to witness and celebrate. Head to toe in white satin, white ribbons in her hair, carrying a white missal, she smiled when we applauded. Walking in front of her parents, she approached with that firm-striding gait Spanish girls acquire as infants: not shy, not abashed by the occasion, confident, self-possessed, quietly happy about being the centre of attraction. Father and mother, older brother and two grandparents accompanied her into the chapel. Only a few others followed them in. Mass was to take place outside after private family prayers.

I found a level spot above the patio from which to view the service. This lasted no longer than it took to smoke a small cigar. While I watched, I fed a length of *longaniza* to a three-legged dog which had attached itself to the *romería*. The priest was tiny and aged, so frail I wondered how he'd managed to toil up to the sanctuary. His voice all but dispersed in the air like smoke from the dying fire before it reached me. I could hear the bees again, and the amens of the congregation were like sudden short rushes of white water.

Immediately after the blessing, the band began to play. The priest scarcely had time to take off his vestments before he was roped in to do a jolly hands-joined-in-a-circle children's dance to the march that had been nipped in the bud earlier. Old Pedro must have missed me. He strode about the perimeter and talked briefly to a knot of boys, one of whom pointed up to the trees where I sat. I scrambled down.

'Come and meet the girl and her parents,' he said. 'I told them I'd be bringing you.'

We stood in the waiting line. When it was my turn to be presented I did a formal bow from the waist, as I thought they might expect a Frenchman from England to do. I kissed the little girl's hand and the mother's, and I shook hands with the father.

'Enchanted,' I said to him.

'Enchanted.'

'You must be very proud of your daughter.'

'Very proud, *claro*. She speaks English, *señor*, as well as your Queen Isabel. Say something to the *caballero*, Pilar.'

'I no go to Londres,' said Pilar.

'You see?' said her father.

'Enchanting,' I said.

Now the band started to play a *jota* (an Aragonese dance: Aragón begins not far from Cuenca), and I was whisked off by the prancing lady who had been in charge of the *morteruelo* ladle.

'I don't know the steps of the *jota*,' I said.

'There aren't any steps. All you do is dance.'

She worked my left arm like the handle of a village pump and the dust rose all around us. After this dance I was passed on to her sad-faced friend, another widow. We did an uncomfortably fast paso doble during which we made many circuits of the courtyard and knocked over a pile of cardboard boxes. Then I got a different partner, and after her, another different one.

The hotter it got, the faster the band played and the shorter became the interval between dances. Each time I thought I'd have a quiet bottle of beer in the colonnade, I would be sought out by one or other of the ladies and manhandled back to the dance. In the middle of one marching tune the trumpeter, a wag, inserted a two-bar quotation from *Rule Britannia* into the music and winked as I was bundled past. When old Pedro said he was going, soon, to walk back to town along the high ridge path of the gorge, I said I'd join him – tired as I was.

It was only a couple or three miles, but the journey took us a good two hours. Pedro, who loved to talk, was one of that generation of Spaniards who find it impossible to do so without looking the listener in the eye. Every few steps he would stop in the middle of the path, lightly squeeze my elbow, have us turn to face each other foursquare, then look up into my face and say something like, 'You know, of course, who it was your John of Gaunt married?' At which, whether or not I knew the answer to his question, I would say. 'No, don Pedro, I've forgotten, please remind me.' This, so that I could enjoy his expression of triumph upon proving, yet again, his theory that even educated Englishmen have scant knowledge of things he thought really mattered in history.

Close to the edge of the city, it was I who stopped us. I thanked him for having invited me to go on the *romería*.

'You enjoyed it?'

'I can't tell you how much.'

'The sanctuary is named for the patron saint of Cuenca. Did you know that, don Eduardo?'

'Yes, don Pedro. San Julián.'

'The second bishop of Cuenca.'

'I knew that, too.'

He pointed towards the vast stone statue atop the hill on the opposite side of the gorge.

'That's him over there.'

'I know.'

'You see the glory round the saint's head? The weight of it is something you'd know too, perhaps?'

'Of course not! Pretty heavy, I'd guess.'

'Seventeen kilos. Wrought-iron. I made it. *Venga*, one of these evenings you must come to my workshop. *Hombre*, I'll show you some real blacksmithing!'

For *romerías*, communities sally forth; for *verbenas*, they stay put. Traditionally , the *verbena* occurs only upon the eve of a saint's day; an open-air jollification confined to the parish of the church named after the saint. In practice nowadays it's found convenient to hold your *verbena* on a Sunday; and though it remains strongly parochial, anyone from outside is welcome to attend.

I came across one in progress one Sunday evening, on a circuitous way back from my usual afternoon at the *merendero*.

Where the little river Huécar met a complicated conjunction of steep streets and alleyways below the craggy bluff the ancient city was built upon *arriba*, something unusual was going on. Bars were no more than usually full of noisy chatter: but one had glimpses of yards and lanes of sweet stalls being trundled, of orange and red national flags being draped from balconies. There was an occasional fizz of fireworks. Laughter echoing off walls wasn't the laughter normally heard of a Sunday.

To the side of this street there was a district of Cuenca – and a considerable one – which, until now, I hadn't realized was there. Curious, I followed a stepped, cobbled alley upwards through a slow S-bend. This gradually and tantalizingly opened into a small, irregular plaza. Here the way divided: to the left it passed through a gateway beyond which it culminated, after a few small houses, with the small church of Cristo del Amparo; to the right, it continued its sinuous climb between the poor dwellings of the quarter, or *barrio*, of Los Tiradores.

Closely parallel with this alley was another, sunken, one: maybe ten feet lower and fifteen feet across between its walls, quite dangerous. The hollow this formed was packed with children playing round a vast pyramid of fish crates, fruit boxes and other combustible material: the bonfire to be lit after dark.

A man in a baseball cap came down the hill. Over his shoulder he had a framework cross entirely adorned with fireworks and fuses. I sat on the parapet dividing the upper and lower alleys to watch the preparations: a perch I shared with some older folk who, so immersed in their chatter, scarcely flinched when a boy unintentionally flung a cracker-jack too close to them. There were perhaps two hundred people gathered in the little square now; subdued, mildly expectant. More and more sweet stalls arrived. On the level above, a couple of makeshift bars were swiftly erected, spread with resplendent white cloths and loaded with bottles along three of the four sides of their squares. Couples, young families, widows, old men with sticks, kept coming and going through the gate leading to the church. The waiting folk

77

became noisier. There was more animated movement. Some urchins found a fish-box full of slush to pelt each other with. Then, startling us all, the church bells began to peal, a triple whose hard, metallic echoing between wall and wall made a repeated refrain that sounded like *bacalao de Bilbao*.

The church was tiny, crammed with people of all ages sitting, lolling, standing, walking about, smiling. Some were even quietly laughing: not without reverence but yet with the air of persons feeling comfortable in an accustomed public place: a market, say. I was content for a while to observe from the doorway. A woman in a pew at the back broke off a conversation with her neighbour and abruptly went down on her knees, crossed herself and prayed. Her companion, patient, smoothed the creases in her skirt, evidently prepared in a minute or two to take up her sentence where she had left off. So natural and unself-conscious were the two women that you had to remind yourself that the kneeling one was not, say, looking for a contact lens. The altar looked for all the world like an exhibit at an English flower show – a tumultuous bank of roses, carnations and gladioli, the gilt and silver crucifix a kind of epergne at the centre. Indeed, the entire atmosphere was that of a Sussex marquee in summertime: an impression made even more intense by a much-garlanded float, two long supports bearing its weight across several rows of pews on the right-hand side of the nave.

Moving forward for a closer look, I became aware of the overpowering scent of the blooms. Thickly it overlaid clinging accretions of incense steeped in the stone like smoke in a pipe-smoker's tweed. There was another aroma, too: deeper, darker, more subtle, arising wherever I trod. Underfoot was not rush matting but strewn sprigs and bunches of herbs: lavender, rosemary and thyme brought down from the nearby bee-encrusted mountains. I picked up a woody stem of thyme to wear in my buttonhole – all the men had one – and as I stopped I noticed that there were rose-petals, too, like a generous confetti, on the church floor.

The float contained a figure of the Virgin Mary. In the side-aisle, by the light of a row of candles, were two other figures; I couldn't get close enough to see what they contained for the bells had ceased pealing and, now that the congregation was about to begin the next stage of its

78

devotions, it seemed the tactful thing to go outside again.

Everybody was free to come and go at will; but on occasions such as these it's hard for a stranger not to feel an interloper. Just outside the doorway, this feeling was confirmed: *vecinos* constantly trickling in and out of Cristo del Amparo, greeting each other with a hug or a kiss or a smile or a wave of a sprig of fragrant herb: so that it was like being present at a family party to which even the most distant cousins have been invited. (Many of them may well be related. I learned later that this *barrio* was settled in the Twenties by extended country families from humble villages within a couple of days' march with mule or donkey. The old couple I had spoken to in the park were a typical example of this. They set up small industries – they were carpenters and joiners, mainly – and within a generation had become the close-knit community they were to remain.)

At the gateway to the plaza, the man in the baseball cap had lashed the timber cross, with its yards of fuse and dangling fireworks, to a tall pole. During the next half-hour I kept catching sight of him erecting such set-pieces, including some in an open-sided alley which I hadn't noticed before, opposite the churchyard gate and at right-angles to the main street. And at ten-yard intervals he fixed strings of fireworks across the sunken street. They looked like empty washing-lines with the clothes pegs left on them.

It was growing dark. The crowd had swollen to about five hundred, and was beginning to seethe.

Something dramatic erupted at one of the bars: a violently angry argument between a black-cassocked priest and a group of half a dozen working men in their Sunday best. All were shouting and gesticulating wildly. The priest spilt his wine. The quarrel was about the route the procession was to take, and the timing of it.

The men, bitterly anti-clerical, suffered the *cura* to give them a talking-to. But something he said was too much for one of them, the shortest, who had a harvest-moon face and rose-bud buttonhole. Protesting, constantly ignored, he put his hand on the priest's arm, trying to get a word in edgeways. The priest brusquely pushed the hand away, without looking to see whose hand it was; and the little florid man struck him a savage blow in the chest.

There was a momentary shocked silence. In even the most rabidly anarchic eye there was, I fancied, a sudden, residual, maybe superstitious gleam of fear. Everybody seemed to be waiting for the little man to be struck dead in a blinding blue flash from heaven. If a stray firework had exploded close to us at that moment, we should all have been down on our knees in terror. But before anything else could happen, apologies were exchanged. There were handshakes, a short coda of argument, then the dispute abated, the tension eased and the group dispersed.

At once the bar began doing a brisker trade. All manner of wines, soft drinks and spirits were available. The favourite local tipple for a warm summer evening's *verbena* was *zurra*, taken by the jugful from a huge earthenware crock. Zurra is an old word for 'drudgery' or 'hard grind', as well as for this cooling beverage. Concocted from white wine, brandy, vermouth and sugar, diluted with water, chinking with ice-cubes and garnished with quarters of oranges and lemons, it's closely akin to sangría.

It was already dusk down in the square. Higher up, a brilliant shaft of final sunlight was lighting outcrops of rock from which grew the simple houses of Los Tiradores. Briefly it slanted on scars of peeling plaster, the irregular muddle of pantiles on flattish roofs, the spindly harvest of television aerials; then it was extinguished and we were in the night. You saw the flames of matches and lighters. Windows lit up. And then, in the street, strings of coloured lights came on between stalls you hadn't noticed arriving.

Within minutes the crowd doubled itself. Old single men, bachelors and widowers, appeared at their doorways. Some, dandyish, wore black berets and jackets of op art black and white herringbone; one sported a dashing white cheese-cutter cap and a white scarf. Also in white, several first-communion girls were in evidence; as were their male counterparts, attired in light-coloured suits and – round their shoulders like a mayoral chain of office – a golden rope, elegantly tasselled at the back, bearing a gold and silver crucifix big enough to cover a man's palm. And soon, threading through this ever-thickening, shoulder-to-shoulder press, there came a single file of seven grown-up girls in white, sporting red and yellow sashes and carrying aloft great bunches of gladioli: the Fiesta

Queen and her entourage, passing through the gateway towards the church.

The little square looked entrancing. By daylight it had been picturesque but drab; now, with illuminated candy stalls and lamps at lace-curtained windows, it had the glamour of a fairground a hundred times its size.

Over a *copa* of Soberano brandy, sleepily contemplating the few fierce blue stars that had come out, I was scared rigid by three almighty detonations that reverberated in the sunken street. They echoed and re-echoed between the constricting walls, making the ground shake, the dogs bark and the people cheer and clap. Nobody looked at the source of the explosions: all eyes had turned towards the gateway, where the first float had appeared with its attendants.

Borne on the shoulders of ten young men, it began its slow progress up the main street. In the half-dark the crown subsided like a treacly liquid to allow it through. In it was a doll-sized figure of the infant Jesus, crowned and garlanded. Behind this came two similar floats; one for the Miraculous Virgin and, in pride of place, one for the Cristo del Amparo.

Amparo means shelter, refuge, protection. The Christ of this name is the one for whom the little church was named and for whom this celebration was held every year. In the faces of the oldest men and women – those who originally came to this *barrio* with only one small bundle containing their poverty – there was genuine adoration. By contrast, at the bar three of the men who had argued with the priest raised their glasses of *zurra*, drank them down and then, clasping each other in mock helplessness, barked with mocking laughter.

The procession continued up the hill. As it passed out of sight, the firework display began: Catherine wheels, rockets, Roman candles, strings of deafening crackers. The timing (perhaps more accidental than contrived) was exquisite. When the procession reappeared, having made the entire circuit of the *barrio*, the bonfire in the sunken street was sending flames twenty feet high. The timber cross at the gateway, too, was aflame, a torrent of sparks and spangles to welcome the images home for another year. I stayed a little while longer to watch the bonfire die and collapse upon itself. Nobody went home. Youngsters poured in from other parts of town, filling what space was left. On a ledge of raw crag a band of rock musicians

81

with the usual paraphernalia of microphones and amplifiers took the usual long time to get ready. Four hours later, when I came back after dinner, dancing was still going on: rock, but also Latin American rhythms for the large-rumped wives to sway to over a second jug of zurra. On a beer-crate, between the bar and the flaking wall, a five-year-old boy, his *verbena* over, sleepily sucked a lollipop shaped like a hammer.

CHAPTER FIVE

It was Thursday: but being the *fiesta* of Corpus Christi, it had
a Sunday feel to it. I went for morning coffee to a brand-new
bar in a newly completed steel and concrete block at the edge
of town. It smelt of wet plaster and cardboard packing-cases.
The *dueña* was a fading widow with a teenage daughter. I
supposed she'd invested in the place on the proceeds of her
husband's life insurance.

On the wall was a map of the environs of Cuenca. I studied
it while the milk for my coffee was being heated. The daughter,
still in her pink dressing-gown, went outside to strum a guitar,
not very well.

'I see there's a village called Palomera not far from here,'
I said. 'What's it like, *señora*? I could do with a walk.'

'Palomera? Why would anyone want to go there?'

'I like the sound of the name. And I see on the way there's
a place called Molinos de Papel. That's even nicer-sounding.'

Molino means 'mill' and papel means 'paper'. I visualized
a kind of Flanders field not of poppies but of those toy
windmills on sticks which, as a child, I used to hold high and
run with towards the wind.

'I must go there,' I said. 'I'm taking the rest of the day off.'

'Nothing there, *señor*. Nothing at all. It's not worth going
to see.'

The sky was overcast, the air on the chilly side: ideal walking
weather. I bought a copy of the *Diario de Cuenca* to shove in
my jacket pocket. Ten minutes later, I was at a different edge
of the city, on the Palomera road.

The river Huécar, unlike the Júcar which it flowed into just
below Cuenca, was only a few feet across. If you'd broad-
jumped it, you'd only have got the back half-inch of your heels
wet. But the gorge it had cut through the sierra was colossal,
of stunning grandeur; perhaps three-quarters of a mile from

cliff-top to cliff-top, sometimes narrowing at two fairly close spots to form natural amphitheatres. In its valley bed at the outskirts of the city were *huertas*, plots of cultivated ground whose rich soil was ridged into exact geometrical patterns for irrigation. Whatever grew looked as if it had been earthed-up like potatoes. Indeed potatoes did grow there as well as French beans and a species of tall, crisp, delicious, dark-green Cos lettuce, red-veined and red at the leaf-edge. On the far side of the river the ground was terraced. Grape vines grew across pergolas. Every so often there was a white-walled, orange-tiled cottage built against the lower rocks of the gorge. Above – high above – the houses of Cuenca *arriba* (and not only the most celebrated *casas colgadas*) seemed upward projections of the cliff: cream-coloured, higgledy-piggledy, perilous slabs with windows opening above a drop of several hundred feet. It gave me vertigo simply to imagine what it must be like living up there, a permanent aviator above the trees I was now walking past: acacias, poplars, aspens, almonds, figs, osiers and willows, their thick summer leaves hiding many nightingales.

The road rose and twisted gently through the valley. Before long the city was left behind, out of sight. I caught up with and overtook an elderly lady returning from church. I got a fair way ahead of her; but then I began to stop every so often to look at the view, or to pick a wild flower for pressing in my notebook. She would catch up. Each time, we'd exchange a few words.

'You're not from around here, *caballero?*'

'No, señora, I'm a long way from home.'

'It's hard to be away from home, a *día de fiesta.*'

'Yes.'

'The countryside evidently pleases you.'

'Very much, *señora.*'

'Go with God.'

I passed a kilometre post, then another. She was no longer there when, at a bend, I looked back before the previous bend disappeared. She must have lived in the last cottage I'd passed on the left; one with a *parral*, a shady trellis of vines which began above the front door and extended over the patio and halfway down the path to the gate. There had been a young laughing couple, one of them possibly her grandchild, sitting in the shade of her walnut tree. They were doing a crossword.

By now the gorge was less tamed, with fewer cottages. Across the river browsed a herd of goats, most of them chestnut-brown but some spectacularly pure white; a carillon of goats, perhaps I should say, for I heard their bells before I saw them. Another bend, another; and now the rocks at the cliff edge demanded to be looked at.

These *torcas* had taken on extraordinary configurations. Their basic shape was that of a blunt anvil: but they'd been eroded into camel's heads, sphinxes, dinosaurs, monstrous mushrooms, reclining figures by Henry Moore, wooden quayside bollards with waists worn away by strangling ropes. Beneath them the slab face had been as though corbelled. Every fifty feet or so along was an unclimbable overhang. Their colours were endlessly varied: predominantly salmon-pink; but also rose, chalk-white, ochre, cream with stains as from rusty nails; and all gradations of grey to almost black. While I was trying to understand the geology, my eye caught a pair of eagles soaring within the jaws of a minor ravine. At once, such now was my unassuageable greed for beautiful, natural things, I began to see all manner of other birds of prey marauding along the cliffs. The rest of the day I was to see kites and buzzards and solitary smaller hawks – merlins, maybe they were.

I was still stopping to pick wild flowers, wanting an entire anthology to send home. There were so many, so varied; I lusted for one of each. Soon I had all my pockets full. One flower I bent to pick for its remarkable intensity of blue sprang up at me, becoming a butterfly. There was so much lavender, rosemary, thyme, fennel and Old Man growing at the roadside, I could scarcely see any grass. You'd have said the entire verge to Palomera was a linear herb garden. I took a good sprig of each woody one to take back to my room and hang in a bunch at my balcony.

The skies had cleared. It was getting hot. In a field arable between scattered olives, men in bright yellow straw hats straightened their backs and leaned on their hoes as I passed. One wiped his brow and went for the water-bottle dangling from a branch. Nearby a woman was cooking their meal over an open fire whose smoke of olive-wood smelt sweet. The crickets were noisy and so were the jackdaws. The sun fell like shovel blows on plots of barley and beans.

I reached Molinos de Papel, whose name of course did not mean 'paper windmills' but, more prosaically, 'paper mills'. The widow in the bar had been right to say there wasn't much to see. Only up to a point, though. True, the place contained little enough beyond some long, thin, shed-like buildings – the former mills; but when I looked carefully at the village's huddlement of flower-bedecked dwellings around an endearing courtyard, I felt grateful for the woman's notion of 'nothing'. White roses spilled like foam from the windowsills; a few petals fell; an old couple dozed in rocking chairs.

I left the place behind. It was getting on for three o'clock. Suppose in Palomera there was nothing to eat or drink? I was not bothered. Every few hundred yards there was pure water gushing into troughs through piped channels in the bank. And in that heat I wasn't likely to feel desperately hungry.

By now the valley was rising closer to the cliff-tops, becoming more pastoral, less dramatic. There was a cottage or two smothered in climbing plants. Women were washing clothes in the river on flat rocks that probably their great-great-great-grandmothers had also used. There were moss-roses gone wild by the river bank. Some ailing plum trees and apple trees at the roadside yielded, if little fruit, good shade. Huge rocks, too, gave shade. Canted over, they made caves of themselves, their ceilings covered with a thick impasto of swallows' and martins' nests. On the road were the flattened remains of a frog, big as my hand: black, stiff, the shadow of a frog, if shadows can be a millimetre thick. Lizards flicked and flickered into chinks of dry-stone wall. I saw a bird I couldn't name – like a long-tail tit but all black except for a long and slightly swallow-like russet tail. It began to feel very remote, a very long way from Cuenca.

My first glimpse of Palomera was a muddle of roofs grouped around the taller roof of its church. There were also a few cow-byres set into the hillocks above. There was no sound save that of ceaseless crickets. The place had the air of a ghost town. I came into its street, stumbled on the broken surface, passed houses terribly quiet yet – with open doors and windows releasing cooking smells – evidently containing people.

I saw a bead curtain below a Coca-Cola sign. I could hear neither voices nor laughter. I couldn't be certain it wasn't a private house. But I parted the beads anyway and went from blinding sunlight into what seemed like utter darkness. When my eyes adjusted I saw with relief that it was indeed a bar and that I was not its only customer. Relief turned to disquiet when I became aware of an interior like one in a painting, an atmosphere as of suspended animation. At one table two teenage boys had been playing cards. At another, a priest had been drinking beer from the bottle and a hundred-year-old woman had been munching a crust. At a third, three men and a gipsy-like woman had been drinking wine and cracking monkey nuts. Now no one was doing anything. And nobody spoke. All eyes, though their lids were almost closed, were upon me. I knew they knew I had been on my way to Palomera.

At the counter I asked for *tinto* and a sandwich. I could tell through my shoulder blades how my accent was being appraised, how glances were being exchanged. I sat down, feeling welcome as the Angel of Death. But the moment I spoke to the room at large, tension dispersed like smoke in a gale. 'How did you suffer here, *señores*, the night of the great storm?' I asked. 'Not at all,' they said in unison. From then on I might have been an *hijo preferido* of Palomera, a lad of the village who had made a name for himself and who had now come home to visit, loaded with renown and banknotes.

The landlord's wife brought me a *bocadillo* eighteen inches long containing two hot *chorizos* in tandem. The landlord himself poured me a good half-pint of wine. While I ate and drank we all talked about what grew in our vegetable gardens. We exchanged useful wrinkles and boasted a little, the way gardeners will. I noticed one of the men whispering something to the gipsy-like lady. She went out, returning ten minutes later with the corners of her pinafore held before her. She was carrying three dozen walnuts for me. I thanked her and said I'd keep them for later.

The man whose tree they came from, who called me *Jefe*, 'Chief', grinned and patted his jacket pocket.

'May I look at your newspaper?' he said. 'Here *en provincia* we seldom see newspapers.'

It was only a few miles from Cuenca. Had the day remained cool and overcast, my walk would not have seemed so long. But what with the heat and the ever changing, majestic scenery – and now this man talking about Palomera as though it were in unexplored, dragon country – I felt remote and dispossessed, homesick for my room and my odds and ends of belongings. I listened while he read aloud, for everyone's benefit and in beautiful Castilian, articles he made sound like a formal reading from the Constitution. The priest swigged his last inch of beer, bade me goodbye and left.

'I must go too,' I said. 'Please keep the newspaper.'

I deliberately left a litter of walnut shells over the first mile back to Cuenca. Anyone passing that way to bring cattle in or to stroll for a sprig of rosemary would see that I hadn't after all kept the nuts for later. It pleased me to think I'd be remembered a little longer in Palomera.

The day was at its hottest: but a breeze laid the top of the barley over. It got into meadows of tall grass, troubling the petals of poppies growing scarlet in them. On a cottage balcony a girl threw her hair forward to bleach in the sunlight. In a patio a little further on I could see a wedding party in progress, with dancing to accordions and guitars. It was all too perfect, a dream of the Garden of Eden. But then there was a moment of comedy of a kind which often occurs in Spain. Coming towards me was an old peasant in a black beret, carrying a mighty walking stick. He wasn't twenty yards away, in full view of the dancers at the reception when, without ceremony, he dropped his corduroy trousers and squatted in the ditch and began to read a scrap of newspaper. As I passed him he gave me the time of day. I felt there ought to be a ritual phrase to utter, like the *que aproveche* you said to anyone as they ate. The old fellow strained and heaved, shrubby and fragrant lavender poking into him. Nothing in the world could have been more natural.

The postmen went on strike. It was an intolerable and lonely business, having no letters. It drove me out of Cuenca for a change of scene one morning: ironically, on the mail train.

I went a nineteen-kilometre journey to a station called Los Palancares. 'Station,' I say. It was not a town or a village or any kind of actual place. When I got off the train I was in a fix. I could see no way out. The station comprised a length of platform with one building in a deep cutting ending with a tunnel. The guard, seeing my perplexity, asked if I wanted to climb aboard again. 'Where are the houses?' I asked him. No houses, he said, only a clearing in the trees where, in mid-

July, there was an annual children's camp. It was raining gently. The next place of any size was Cañada del Hoyo, where the next station was. He pointed down the track. I could see a sandy path going into the woods. 'It's a long way round,' he warned me. 'The train goes more or less direct, through tunnels. The path takes you out of your way.' The gentle rain stopped, leaving a mushroomy smell on the air. 'I'll take my chance,' I said. The train eased forward. I watched it disappear into the black tunnel toward Valencia.

The path led down between the sides of a small ravine of rock and sandy ground. Most of the trees were pines. After a mile or so the ravine opened out into meadows of grazing land not unlike tracts under the western South Downs. Flowers here grew in even greater profusion than those along the Palomera road: poppies, spurges, knapweeds and vetch that grow (though in much smaller numbers) below Bow Hill or Harting Hill in high summer; but also strange sundews and orchids and phenomenal wild roses with blooms entirely covering bushes big as pink pavilions. There were cistus shrubs in blossom too, and a kind of lily on one long stem that arched over the path. All this was wild yet felt like a walk through an artful piece of landscaping.

The butterflies were astonishing. Chemical pesticides clearly were not used in this part of Spain. I strode through tangles of grasses and flowers, putting up cloud upon cloud of tortoiseshells, painted ladies, peacocks, fritillaries, little blue ones like the chalk hill blue I'd not seen at home for more than a generation. There were some I'd certainly never seen before in my life: black and white barred ones; some like orange-tips – but with orange more vivid against a background more deeply yellow. Some were like bluebottles – until they landed and spread little red wings. And others still – much, much bigger – seemed hardly able to fly at all, flopping from flower to flower on sagging wings like lilac-coloured silk.

At the edge of the woods grew brightly-coloured fungi such as the wicked red agaric. From darkness under the trees beyond came the drumming of a woodpecker. The path was getting more and more constricted; but suddenly it led out of the pines into open, prairie-like country with no more than one wild rose-bush and one single tree, an ilex, for cover. In the shade of the ilex were perhaps thirty cattle, most of them lying down. How like a country walk at home this was becoming, I thought. However, when I was within twenty yards and one of the lying-down ones stood up and faced me, I realized that this was not after all a group of amiable Friesians but a herd of *bos ibericus*. The vast creature now contemplating me in his territory was born and raised for the sole purpose of rushing at a man and goring him to death.

I froze to the spot, not knowing what to do. One or two more stood up, displaying a curiosity I didn't find comfortable. To turn and go back was surely not a good idea: it would be cowardly, inviting a charge. To go left would be as bad, the terrain utterly exposed as far as the eye could see. To go right would have meant cutting across swampy ground and jumping over a stream – and I didn't fancy making any sudden movement. The path itself led closer yet to the ilex and the herd; then swung half-right, past the rose-bush and, after another three or four hundred vulnerable yards, reached the cover of scrub and small trees. I'd keep to the path, I thought.

The evening before, I'd been watching a bullfight from Albacete on the hotel television. One of the matadors had been badly trampled and had received three *cornadas* in his thigh. I knew, intellectually, that a fighting bull will usually charge only when he's alone; that when he's with cows he's fairly docile. I also knew (and never mind about intellectually) that he's one of the very few animals that will attack a human being on sight. I came close enough to be at the edge of the shade of the ilex tree and to hear breathing and swishing sounds. In that briefest of moments out of the sun, a host of flies assailed me. I got one in my eye and I let it stay there. At a gentle amble I reached the scrub and sat down and lit a cigar. I got the fly from my eye and looked back. All were standing now, all facing in my direction: gorgeous, with huge shoulders and long pointed horns, massive, noble, black, heavy but not ponderous like farm bulls. I had been in no danger, I told myself; but I was trembling and exhilarated. I promised myself that one day, if only to prove I was alive, I would get inside a ring with an unaccompanied bull.

I continued through wilder and wilder country; open and rocky as it rose, swampy and oozing as it fell. Often the path was under water. There were frogs croaking with a noise like the bleat of a deep-voiced goat. A yard of snake coiled away

90

like lightning. There were meadows full of herbs: marjoram growing in clumps and cushions, drifts of two sorts of lavender all acrawl with bees and butterflies. Then I came to a few cultivated fields – sunflowers and beans growing in poor earth that was mainly sand – and caught my first glimpse of the small *pueblo* of Cañada del Hoyo.

A *cañada* is a drover's road; an *hoyo* a hole or hollow. What I saw ahead was an escarpment drawn half across the horizon. Where it abruptly finished there was a ruined castle at the very tip; far below this, a line of poplars: between trees and ruins, a conglomeration of orange roofs and creamy-brown walls. Travelling extensively by car through all the regions of Spain I was to come across such places very frequently, always with gratitude and always with the memory of Cañada del Hoyo vivid and searing as that of first love. Just once you need to come to such a village footsore, having had nothing to eat or drink for hours and having had no human company. I could hear distant goat-bells; the temperature was ninety-odd; the slow bluish shadow of an eagle moved across the rock. I had come fifteen miles through paradise. Famished, I was going to be happy with whatever was on offer.

This was a can of cod in tomato sauce in a loaf as long as my arm, also two bottles of beer at once. I accidentally broke a tooth of my denture, swallowed it and didn't care. In the bar there were genial, noisy old men playing cards. I stayed with them there in the cool until nine o'clock, when I went a mile down a lane to a station like a Spanish Adlestrop. I sat with legs dangling over the edge of the shallow platform. A hoopoe flew overhead and a hedgehog sat on a rail till I turfed him off with a stick. It was getting dark and I began to wonder whether there would be a train as, in the bar, they'd said there would be. Not before the first stars appeared did it come, its brilliant headlight towing it up the long hill. Fifteen minutes it took in and out of a series of tunnels, to get back to where I'd started.

The *Diario de Cuenca* published an interview with me. The reporter had posed the conventional questions a poet gets asked about his philosophy and work in progress. I had said ingratiating things about Cuenca, *Conquenses* and the surrounding countryside. About midday, I got a local phone call.

'Señor Walker?'

'Yes.'

'You won't know me. I'm a writer and former journalist. I've just read a piece in the *Diario* and I'd like to buy you a drink and introduce you to somebody you'd like to meet.'

We arranged to meet within the hour in a bar called 'El Trébol' which had just been opened by three brothers called Jesús, José and Ángel. I recognized the caller straight away. I'd often seen him about. He looked not unlike the poet Michael Hamburger: fiftyish, dressed in a russet-coloured sports jacket and with dark and thinning wavy hair. He said his name was Pérez. He got me a *fino*.

'*Salud*,' I said, raised my glass. 'What can I do for you?'

'Later, later,' he said. He looked at his watch. 'In thirty minutes, I'll take you to meet somebody. Somebody important. But let's talk about literature for a while.'

The half-hour passed agreeably enough. Pérez knew his stuff about nineteenth-century European poetry.

We crossed the street and walked as far as a formal-looking bespoke tailor's shop. In the window were bolts of sober cloths and some pattern books. Pérez was about to open the door.

'I can't go in there looking like this,' I said. I was in a grimy denim jacket, threadbare trousers and the only pair of shoes I owned, much scuffed and down-at-heel from all the walking I'd been doing. But Pérez was through the door and was holding it open for me.

The tailor was impeccable: in shirtsleeves, with his tape measure round his shoulders, he was drawing chalklines on a suit length. He was a very big man, in his early forties, at a guess. His hair and his temples glistened. Never once in his life, one felt, had his fingernails been dirty. His shop smelt like the interior of a new car. We were introduced. With infinite caution, he put down his chalk, shook hands with me, picked up the chalk again and resumed work.

'This is the man I was telling you about,' Pérez said to him. 'The English writer interviewed in today's paper. The man with the right ideas.'

'Get the bottle of Málaga, Pérez, and three glasses.'

'Yes, sir.'

'You must excuse my appearance,' I said. 'I had no idea I was going to be brought here.'

'No importa. You enjoy living in our city, señor?'
'Very much.'
'Enchanting, is it not?'
'Wonderful. Marvellous.'
'And the people?'
'Equally, claro.'

Pérez brought in an elaborate silver tray with three glasses of the syrupy wine. We took one each; then ritually we toasted our respective countries before sipping gravely and continuing.

'You are generous in your praise of our people. Not all of our citizens are worthy of such praise. Most of the older folk, yes. They were brought up to have correct values. It's not their fault, either, that so many of the young are growing up into immorality and wrong-headedness.'

'Foreign influences,' said Pérez. 'Books and films.'

'And pornography. The young absorb everything bad. They believe in divorce, marriage for the clergy, even worse things. They believe every single wicked thing they read, or see on television.'

'Like democracy,' said Pérez.

'Or Holocaust,' said the tailor.

The documentary series about the Nazi extermination of the Jews had recently been shown on Spanish television. I had seen it not long before leaving England. On the telephone and in the Trébol bar, Pérez had kept breaking into fluent German. He did so again now. My German isn't up to much and though I was getting the gist of what he was saying, I asked him to say it all again in Spanish.

'I don't understand,' I said. 'What do you mean?'

'There are people who actually believe that Jews were sent to gas chambers. They can't see that it's all international Zionist conspiracy financed by American millionaires.'

I remembered where I'd seen the tailor. He'd been one of the platform party at the Fuerza Nueva meeting. I put my glass down on the counter and turned to Pérez.

'I don't know why you've brought me to meet this man,' I said. 'I am a member of the British Labour Party. I believe in democracy, free speech and a free Press. There's been some kind of awful mistake and I'm going. Thanks for the drink.'

'I guessed as much, Pérez,' said the tailor. 'How could a man like this desgarbado have the right ideas?'

As I left, Pérez was blustering and taking the *Diario de Cuenca* from his side pocket. I nipped quickly across the street to the *quiosco* and bought another copy. I hadn't read the interview very carefully earlier in the day. Now I saw what had happened. The 'not' in 'I'm not in favour of dictatorships' had been left out.

Full of dismay and angry embarrassment, I made straight for the station, hoping none of my friends would see me and that no stranger would recognize me from my photograph in the paper. I bought a ticket for a place called Enguídanos, drank several brandies, slumped in a corner seat on the train and fell asleep with menacing dreams full of flick-knives.

The station called Enguídanos was a long way from the village of that name. I learned this from the plainclothes postman who took a satchel of mail from the guard, strapped it to his moped carrier and set off in a deafening cloud of purple exhaust smoke. The nearest place was Narboneta, eight kilometres in the other direction.

My gloom wasn't helped by the intense heat; or by the fact that there had recently been a fire which had reduced the pine trees to black trunks and limbs. Weirdly, crickets still creaked their song amid the charred and cindery remains of the forest. At first I thought I'd be walking all afternoon through similar, sombre terrain: but the road rose and fell and soon emerged into the valley of the little river Narboneta. I was passed by a man on a donkey carrying panniers full of carrots. I guessed how he would tell them in the village that a stranger was on his way there.

Narboneta might have contained fifty *vecinos*, whose siesta time it was when I arrived. There was but one oldish lady in the street: fat; in bright clothes so not a widow.

'Is there a bar here or a shop?' I asked.

'I am the *dueña* of the bar. You'll find it in the square, next to the church. Just knock. My husband will attend to you. I'll follow in a few minutes.'

It was as she had said. After he'd watched me drink half my beer, the old man struck up a conversation. I told him who I was and where I was from. He had lively eyes and he opened them very wide.

'There has never been an Englishman here before. Strangers

94

never come. The road ends here. Narboneta is on the way from nowhere to nowhere. What brings you, *señor?*'

I told him what had happened that morning in the tailor's shop. Then I asked him what had happened in Narboneta during the Civil War. Surely there may just have been some foreigners there then – Germans, Italians, Americans, British, French?

'No, *señor*. Nobody from outside comes here. During the Civil War not even Spaniards came here. Not Reds, not Blacks. You needn't feel badly about that newspaper article. Nobody in Spain gives a damn what anyone from outside thinks politically. Oh! You mustn't think I don't know about such things just because I live in this remote little pueblo. Yes, I was born here and I've stayed all my life here. But, *mira!* I've children and grandchildren who live elsewhere. I go and visit them. I go to the provincial capital, even. I know everything that goes on in the whole wide world, *hombre!*'

He got me another bottle of beer and one for himself.

The *dueña* came into the bar. She had put on a floral wrap-around pinafore. She opened the ice-cream cold-box and rummaged about. As she bent over you saw how her fat, fat legs touched at the knee and splayed out below. A doe-eyed child came cautiously from the passageway, accepted an orange lolly and sprang back to the dark like a gazelle.

'A granddaughter, *señora?*'

'Staying with us, yes. Forgive her. She was curious to see an Englishman.'

'Can you find me something to eat? I know I'm really too late for lunch.'

She provided me with an enormous *tortilla*, a plate of black olives, half a loaf of bread, a bottle of *tinto*, an orange and a dish of sweet yellow-pink cherries straight from her tree; also a *bocadillo* for the journey back, containing a chicken wing and two different sausages. All this, with my two beers and a packet of cigarettes, came to the price, in England, of a take-away meal of fish and chips. I couldn't offer a tip, of course, as the old couple were the proprietors; but Doe-Eyes reappearing briefly, I gave her something for her money-box.

I was overtaken again by the man with the donkey and panniers. There was nobody waiting for the train. I doubted whether many people ever got on or off the *correo* from

Valencia at Enguídanos. The down trains had to stop so that the small satchel of official mail from Madrid could be picked up; and the up trains had to stop if only because the time-table said they did.

The station house, like all the others along the line, was absurdly large: a typical piece of grandiose fascist railway architecture. Its pointlessly ample proportions housed not one porter or ticket collector – let alone the full complement of station staff it could have accommodated. Not long before the train arrived I was certain I heard rustling noises coming from it. Nervously squinnying in through the dusty window, I saw that it stabled two carthorses and their harness.

When I arrived back in Cuenca I no longer minded whether any of my chums had read the interview in the *Diario*. In fact, late as it was, I went to El Sotanillo and found old Pedro and told him about my day. At midnight we walked to the College of Technology where, in his workshop, he showed me the massive wrought-iron gates he was making: a commission for a church in a far-off town whose name I'd never heard of. The gates lay on the floor. I walked round them, kneeled down and touched them; saw under Pedro's bench the filings and off-cuts and swarf which had had to be taken away to leave the finished work. The craftmanship was exquisite. Pedro was a small man; you wondered how he could manage the weight of so much metal, even with the complicated system of chains and pulleys overhead. Before long the job would be finished. He'd have to go and supervise the hanging of the gates. If I were still in Cuenca I was to go with him. Perhaps my book would be finished, too, he said. We'd both have something to celebrate.

I'd have liked that very much. I was quickly acquiring a taste for looking further afield in a country which, during the last twelve weeks, I had just begun to know something about. But the following morning brought bad news from home. Within an hour I had packed and paid my bill and was on a bus to Madrid. There wasn't even time to go the rounds saying goodbye to friends and acquaintances. On the night train to Santander I was too full of anxiety to think much about my experiences. That would come later. But the moment I stepped on board the ferry and went to

96

the bar and saw a knot of my fellow countrymen talking cricket twaddle and standing awkwardly in trousers of a funny cut, I realized the extent to which I had been changed by Cuenca, by Castile, by Spain and her people. Before long, when the bad thing had been sorted out, I'd be back.

CHAPTER SIX

The aging couple at the next table to mine on the Santander ferry four years later seemed all too familiar. He, pot-bellied, with an officer's moustache and a wah-wah accent, had been in the Army and the Colonial Service before going into oil; she, scrawny-beaked as a gargoyle and on perpetual vodkas-and-tonic, had made a career through Camberley, Kandy and Qatar as a lush. More than anything, it was her terrifying witch's fingernails that gave me a sense of *déjà-vu*: these were painted alternately deep purple and shocking pink. She bragged about their wealth: they would simply *have* to change the Merc when they got home. He, sighing, nodded. Twice, urgently, he had to go and relieve himself, having stuffed so much the night before ('Two hundred quid a night, old boy, that Plymouth hotel: but fair do's, you could have as much as you liked to scoff'), thus leaving me to listen to his wife's opinions. 'Glad to have your company,' he murmured in my ear one time as he struggled to rise. 'Saves my monosyllables, what?'

'Got this little place in Marbella,' she said. 'Had a bit of bad luck. Bought an *absolutelysuperapartment* in a *brand-new* block in Mallorca some years ago. Thought it'd be jolly marvellous for spending the odd summer in. Quite nice old couple from Leicestershire, think it was, next door. Went back following year though and what d'you think had happened? Never guess. Not joking. Rest of that nice property been bought by Spaniards. Imagine anything more ghastly? *Spaniards*, I mean to say. Everywhere, nothing but Spaniards, Spaniards, Spaniards. Hopeless! All one wanted the place for, after all, was a little warmth and sunshine.' She was very awful indeed; unforgettable, therefore the sort to make a traveller glad he has travelled, gladder still that journeys and voyages must come to an end.

Just off Santander a fleet of little craft drifted, all painted with broad bands of white and primary colours and with small, plum-coloured mizzens. Their skippers and crew jiggled with handlines for squid. The boats were bright and cheerful in the spring sunlight; but during the hour it took to free the ramp pins on my ferry, the weather turned round. It became overcast, shivering-cold and drizzly. I had nothing more to declare to the pointlessly sunglassed official than that I felt cold and miserable, whereas I'd expected to feel exultant at being back, this time with my car.

I switched on the windscreen wipers, turned up my jacket collar and drove south out of town. This was not an auspicious start to three months in search of Spaniards. To aggravate this louring of the spirit, at the edge of Torrelavega there occurred the kind of incident that drives the visiting driver crazy: a three-kilometre jam of traffic, with a badly managed diversion for road works. Worse, my arrival coincided with a change of shifts at the chemical works. Then some misleading sign-posting at the end of the diversion led me to smaller and smaller, more and more improbable streets until, finally, I found myself in somebody's back yard. Shamefacedly I backed out, watched by a dog and a petulant baby in a pram.

Some culture shock is due to small differences of detail such as those of road signs and road-side advertising. In Spain, cows in cattle-warning signs have longer horns than those of their English sisters; falling rocks look much more threatening than ours; children, as one approaches schools, are depicted not walking but running; the conventional pedestrian, enjoin-ing one to keep to the left of the carriageway, wears a funny, old-fashioned hat. You soon get used to these, just as you get used to the enormous, hill-top, two-dimensional Osborne Brandy bulls and the ubiquitous white-painted letters on flat-faced rocks announcing ULLOA OPTICA of Madrid or Seville. You become accustomed to vast Pegaso lorries with defective exhaust systems and their violet cab visors bearing not his'n'her Christian names but CRISTO ES AMOR and SANTA MARÍA LA SIN PECADO. It's not long, even, before you stop smiling at tankers purporting to transport RAM milk.

The clouds descended lower and still lower; by now pro-longed, heavier rain had begun. The countryside was vividly, well-nigh overbearingly, green: it might have been Glamorgan-shire. Glum, I pressed on through alpine or Scandinavian (therefore for me, yawningly boring) country of dairy cows, pretty-pretty little horses and carts, miniature haycocks each with its own, quaint little hat; and came eventually to Reinosa, at the edge of Castile. Looking south from an upper room balcony in the newish, comfortable but very ugly Vejo hotel, I could see the *meseta* beginning. Hereabouts they have high hopes of becoming a tourist centre. Winter sports facilities are available at nearby Alto Campóo; you can take a chairlift to Tres Mares Peak, where tributaries of three rivers spring to flow into three different seas: that of the Híjar, which becomes the Ebro and reaches the Mediterranean; that of the Pisuerga, which flows into the Duero and makes for the Atlantic; and that of the Nansa, which takes the short route north to the Cantabrian sea. Reinosa itself I thought disappointing. A sickly chemical smell hung (and looked pink) on the air. It was going to have to be a remarkably good dinner to make adequate recompense for such a dreary first day back.

As so often happens in Spain, an unprepossessing establishment produced a superb meal. First, to warm me through, I had *cocido castellano*: gobbets of fat pork, hunks of bread, bits of *serrano* ham, cheese and tomato swimming in boiling hot broth – in which the yolk of a just-cracked egg began to harden like a watery autumn sun in a morning mist. Next, delicacy after robustness, *gambas a la plancha*, a dozen large prawns, fried. Last – always a consolation when one is down – a silver chalice of strawberries and cream. In the hotel bar afterwards I talked politics with two Basque lorry drivers and got drunk on brandy. I went to bed, assuming that the morning would bring warm, sunny weather: this was after all Old Castile.

Next day though, the weather was still Mancunian: more January than mid-May. Last year at this time, the breakfast waiter told me, they'd been suffering a bad early drought; this year they'd had thirty days of downpour on the trot. 'No use making tracks for Andalucía,' he added, as I took my bags out to the car. 'It's like this everywhere.' Passing through Aguilar de Campóo, I got an attack of nausea from a sickly-sweet smell emanating from the biscuit factory; but in Frómista, during a brief break between clouds, I was much cheered by my first sight of a stork at its nest. It laid its head back until beak touched tail, then made a loud, fast clacking – like a ratcheted

100

football rattle – with its great beak. Storks' nests were to become commonplace, looking like rough, ill-fitting toupées on the crowns of church towers.

I arrived in Palencia, a long, thin, intractable town, as the midday rush-hour began. I drove about on the look-out for somewhere to stay; but was unable to find anywhere to stop the car, let alone park it, in the mayhem of traffic and pedestrians. It wasn't until I'd decided to cross the oddly-named river Carrión and leave the town that I saw a few square yards of vacant space in front of the Hotel Rey Sanchez de Castilla. You don't have to crawl across a desert to a wadi to experience a sense of blessed refreshment. I got a room in which to hole up for a few nights. I wanted to get warm, and I had a radio script to finish.

I had a friend and former colleague, one Julián de las Cuevas, who came from Palencia. Now he was teaching in the University of Tarragona. Some years before he had lived in my village in West Sussex with his blonde, liberated, Catalan wife. Julián took Spain with him everywhere he went. He was as though cocooned in the very threads and texture of Old Castile. Entering his newish, English house was like entering a *casa señorial* in the most ancient *barrio* of the most proud and ancient city. Quiet, serious, beautifully dressed, immaculately groomed, he would be standing at the head of a long oak table to welcome you to share a decanter of wine. He was in his mid-twenties: but the gravity of expression on the features of his long Castilian face was that of a man in his nineties. His smile was wonderful – as though one of El Greco's grandees in *El Entierro del Conde de Orgaz* beamed through the very varnish at the memory of an old absurdity. He had come to be a teaching assistant, at the same time seeking to improve his spoken English. My brother was the Spanish master in the once fine but now ruined school where the three of us worked. George and I used to tease a smile from Julián; exploiting his Spaniard's inability, without the run-up of an 'e', to pronounce an 's' followed by a consonant.

'Say "Strindberg," ' we'd say.

'Estrindberg.' He'd be trying not to laugh.

'Strauss, Stravinsky, Scarlatti.'

'Estrauss, Estravinski, Escarlatti,' he'd say, his cheeks beginning to twitch.

'Now, "Smith's Crisps, specially spicy,"' we'd say, playing our ace. And Julián would get no further than Esmitesses ecrispesses, before radiating the sunshine of a July day in the *meseta* throughout our wintry campus.

Julián had used to speak with great affection about his home town. From start to finish, I had nothing but bad luck with it. There was a shortage of good bars; *tapas* were few, uninteresting and to be paid for. The pricey dinner I ate in a Michelin-recommended restaurant was a disgrace. It included a scrambled egg dish called *revuelta de cosas* containing leftovers: *cosas* (things). Municipal elections had just taken place throughout Spain. The Communists had taken Córdoba. There were strident posters everywhere. On my final evening in the town, a quiet discussion with the local publicity officer of *Alianza Popular* (the Spanish equivalent of the Tory Party as it used to be in its more benevolent days) turned into a shouting match. I had no particular quarrel with the man: he was amiable enough and had obligingly laughed when I called Reagan a *vaquero*, cowboy; but unremitting rain had got to me and I converted frustration and dank discomfort into political spleen and a generalized complaint against Palencia. The experience of travel (by which I understand being, not going, somewhere) conforms to a straightforward formula: memories of places plus the people in them are determined by one's state of mind and one's well-being while there. It's pointless taking photographs. The lens admits what the cornea refuses to record. I shook hands with the startled publicity officer and asked his forgiveness. The best thing to do about Palencia was leave it; which, the following morning, I did.

The wheatfields I passed were vast. In a couple of months all would be dusty and golden; but now the stalk was only knee-high and the land as green as the South Downs. Occasionally I passed a vineyard. There was scarcely a sign of a leaf yet, though buds were beginning to break. Antediluvian stumps, gnarled and tight-pruned, were shiny black, like small, brisk bonfires suddenly doused. There were hundreds of birds about. On the road surface larks, pigeons and starlings grazed. I wondered why, instead of being constantly harried by the traffic, they didn't take advantage of rich pickings in the quiet fields. Many had been run over. There were pathetic bundles of loose feathers every few yards: and there were flattened cadavers of cats and foxes, like stiff, neglected wash-leathers. Where there were trees and bushes there were magpies and jays. Above the road and the fields birds of prey both large and small prowled and soared and hovered and swooped. One flew about a hundred yards ahead of me, doing remarkable aerobatics. It rolled through 360 degrees and then, doing a sort of backwards dive, pounced into the thick tangle of the roadside ditch. I stopped (as I believed) at the exact spot, hoping to see the bird with whatever it had caught: but though I made a commotion through the grass and poppies and yellow cabbage flowers, all I got for my trouble was wet trouser bottoms: hawk and quarry had vanished. I gazed across the expanses of the Tierra de Campos and was rewarded by two marvellous images: that of a great flock of sheep moving like low smoke across the plain and that of a peasant broadcasting seed with a fluent, unhurried action.

I reached Medina de Rioseco, needing to do three things: get money, post my script to the BBC and buy fruit for lunch.

The function of the little town was to serve the local agricultural community. What it knew about best was John Deere tractors and grain. Its usual commerce was not with itinerant Englishmen but small farmers from the province of Valladolid. The first three banks I tried dealt almost exclusively with the small savings and borrowings of men like the one I had seen sowing. The desk clerks were loth to have anything at all to do with my Eurocheque card. They passed it from one to another, peering with incredulity and fascination, as though I claimed it to be a holy relic and they were the devil's advocates. One assistant manager, to show willing, telephoned his central branch in the provincial capital and said I could have £50 worth of pesetas if I made out the cheque in pounds. I explained that the whole point of the Eurocheque was that it was made out in the local currency. He smiled tolerantly and with a practised condescension as though I was the result of many generations of interbreeding and had come into his nice clean bank with mud on my boots and chaff in my hair. Across the street was a branch of one of the Spanish big banks, the Banco de Bilbao. I duly transacted my business there with no bother at all. With common sense I'd have gone there in the first place; but the traveller with too much common sense misses some memorable encounters.

The main street was arcaded on both sides upon stout wooden pillars. This time of year usually one would have been grateful for shelter afforded from the sun; today, the arcade was a blessing to keep you dry. Unfortunately for me, the ancient covered way didn't extend as far as the modern *Ayuntamiento*, or Town Hall, one corner of which housed the post office. The building, serving a town of five thousand-odd souls, was colossal. I bumbled my way into an office the size of a football pitch penalty area with a ceiling so high angels might have nested on the architrave. There was space enough for a hundred clerical workers. Two young minor officials were in occupation, seated a comically long way away from each other at their typewriters. They directed me to the *correos* with solemn courtesy. It took a long time for my package to be weighted and stamped. Colleagues were brought from inner offices to cast an eye upon me, a visitor as from Mars.

On the way back to my car, I entered the *frutería*. I asked for an orange and the old lady weighed me two. I asked for two bananas and she weighed me three. I asked for three tomatoes and she weighed me four. Fancying half-a-dozen apricots, I asked for five and got seven. I left the shop, feeling as though I'd taken part in a Marx Brothers sketch.

I went on to Toro. At the entrance to the town, against a long, precarious wall, was a tented encampment of gipsies: vivid washing, open fires, bits of ailing or dead cars and ribby dogs like mobile wire maquettes. At the highest point, by the former prison, I could see clearly why the huge plains are known as the Tierra del Pan and the Tierra del Vino. Below, the Duero snakes past the foot of Toro and towards Portugal. To the north, wheat as far as the eye can see; to the south, all vines. Preparing a stand-up picnic, I placed loaf and wine on their appropriate north and south sides of the roof of the car and passed the time of day with an old chap sitting nearby with his grandson.

'Would you like some?' I said, observing the ritual. The invitation would be just as ritually refused, of course; but I made a show of extending the Rioja bottle and demonstrating that I had a spare glass. I offered a banana to the child.

'You carry on,' said grandad. 'Take no notice of us.'

I poured myself a generous glass.

'You've got wine from somewhere else,' he said. 'That's criminal – not drinking the good *tinto* of Toro while you're here. *Hombre!* We make the best wine in the whole of Spain. Don't just take my word for it. Buy some before you drive away. Taste it – then you'll believe me! Forget about Rioja. Forget about Valdepeñas. Forget about Jerez. Forgive me. Eat and drink. Don't let me put you off.'

The little boy found a boulder somewhat larger than his head. Without being reproved, he sent it tumbling and crashing and bouncing out of sight down the long drop. The wonder was that he didn't (as far as I could tell) kill anybody. It was a moment from a medieval siege.

'What was it like here during the Civil War?' I asked.

'Barbarous. Families divided. Brother against brother, father against son. I fought for the Nationalists. Three years I was at the war. Lost my father and my brother, both with the Reds.'

He gave me a discourse on the languages and dialects spoken in the Iberian peninsula: this, because I had said *castellano* instead of *español* when alluding to the best known Spanish tongue. Castilian *was* Spanish, the old man insisted. I tried to head him off; but once a Spaniard decides he's going to tell you something, he goes ahead and tells you to the bitter end. He had a political, nationalist, point to make: if you didn't maintain that *castellano* was the offical language of every corner of the country, you were aiding and abetting the cause of regionalism and the disintegration of the centralists state.

A party of little boys arrived, friends of the grandson. They knelt to play marbles, all except one. He had his music case and recorder with him. While the game progressed he performed Beethoven's *Hymn to Joy* for us, beautifully. One did not have to be Sherlock Holmes to guess that in the Toro schools the topic of Spain's possible forthcoming entry to the EEC was being discussed: a subject it seemed tactful not to raise with grandad. What would he have found to say about centralized European wine lakes *vis-à-vis* the excellence of his local vintage? I did buy a bottle or two of the latter; marvellous, strong, fruity stuff it was too.

On the road, I kept my valuables in a locked document case secured to a bracket under the passenger seat with one of those cable and padlock devices for securing bicycles. Upon arriving in Tordesillas I discovered that something had gone wrong with the padlock spring. I couldn't get the case out; and there was no room under the seat to get it even half an inch open. Tordesillas stands at the busiest of crossroads: Valladolid to Salamanca and Madrid to La Coruña. I stopped at this junction, miserably wondering what to do. I opened my guidebook. Previous visitors included Joan the Mad, Peter the Cruel and a Borgia Pope. The treaty by which Spain and Portugal had carved up the South American continent between them had been signed here. In the continuing downpour, with a ceaseless, hideous cacophony of immense container lorries shuddering and belching by, wanting nothing so much as a warm room but unable to get at my passport and money, I was in no mood to think scholarly thoughts about the historial significance of the little town. I wound down the window and wished, in English, aloud, the adjectived place in hell.

'*Dígame*,' I heard a voice say. I was mortified to realize I'd been observed and overheard. I was outside a Ford garage, I now saw. A young mechanic in spotless overalls was attending me. I opened the passenger door for him. He climbed in out of the rain. I explained my dilemma. Maybe he could take a pair of chain-cutters to the cable, I suggested.

He took my keys, fiddled with the lock for at least three seconds before it sprang open. I felt very foolish.

'What do I owe you?'

'Nothing, *claro*. I did nothing, *señor*.'

'You saved my life. At least have a *copa*.'

'Very well. A *copa*.'

For half an hour he gave me a seminar on the history of Tordesillas and the architectural beauties of the Convent of Santa Clara, using a set of plug sockets on the bar counter as a visual aid. It was a staggering performance. Again and again during my travels I was to be amazed at the ordinary Spaniard's encyclopedic knowledge of his country's and his home-town's past. Later, I checked his facts against the guidebook's. He'd got everything correct. Taking his advice, I stayed at the *parador* in the pinewoods. He was right about that, too. Accommodated in splendour like an American, I sipped a gin-and-tonic in a hot bath and had fennel in cream sauce for dinner. By bedtime all the clammy rigours and irritations of the day had vanished.

* * *

The sun was shining warm in the morning. I was soon on my way to the town with, surely, the most poetical name in the whole of Spain: Madrigal de las Altas Torres in the province of Ávila. The name conserved its magical charm for me even after I'd learned that *madrigal* meant not what it seems but a briar patch; even after I discovered that it was not high towers you saw from a distance over the plains (there once had been *altas torres*, of course) but a pair of futuristic grain silos and a water tower. Every year there must be scores of touring motorists bound for Portugal or Andalucía who make a detour to indulge a taste for the romantic, the medieval; and most of them probably end up like the middle-aged couple I saw in a scruffy bar – vaguely resentful that the town looked so undelectable, irrationally disappointed not to have caught so much as a glimpse of a wimple or a cuirass. Looking nowhere except at each other, the couple drank a coffee to the whirr and clink of the fruit machine, watched by a curious bunch of dusty labourers; then beat a self-conscious retreat.

Madrigal was desolate, silent and deserted even at mid-morning; anyone less nosy and vigilant than I could have made a complete perambulation without seeing a soul. At the edge of vision a slippered foot disappeared under a bead curtain; a black beret bobbed beneath a garden fence. Many houses were built against – even into – the perfect circle of original walls, parts of which had broken away to leave an effect like that of the crumbled edges of a monstrous hunk of dry Cheshire cheese. You could see by joist marks left on the wall where there had been houses now gone. There was no evidence of new building in progress; but I did see a mason pointing the brickwork of a chunk of wall that had fallen, useless, away from the rest: a perfect metaphor *in parvo* for Spain as a whole. The liveliest human figures I came across were two statues at opposite ends of town. One was of Isabel la Católica, Queen of Castile, born here in 1451. She stood holding her sceptre, slightly cracked and unearthly as she stared from funny, bulbous eyes. The other was powerful and looming, charged with the personality of its subject, don Vasco de Quiroga, a son of Madrigal who had become a paternalistic bishop in the New World. Donated by Mexico, the statue and its inscription catch the spirit of quest, vision and *hispanidad* that began in that *annus mirabilis* of 1492, when Isabel and

Ferdinand, rulers of a newly united Spain, heard how the Genoese Cristobal Colón had made landfall in the Americas. I couldn't help but wonder what the benign 'instigator of social security' (as the inscription described him) might have thought, half a millennium on, of what had become of his native country – in which so many hundreds of thousands with no work, their period of dole entitlement expired, were reduced to sitting about like conquered Indians waiting for something to happen.

Later that day I reached another small and sadly reduced town which, like Madrigal de las Altas Torres, had seen better days – indeed better centuries. This was Alba de Tormes, where the great mystic poet Saint Teresa founded her Carmelite convent and where, in 1582, she died. She is characterized in one guidebook as an 'indefatigable woman'. (Just so: thinking of certain latter-day lady poets, one senses precisely what the writer is hinting at. Anecdotes proliferate about the holy lady's indefatigable way of hectoring God Himself.) When asked if she wanted to be taken back to her native Ávila to die, she could hardly have put her considerate interlocuter at his ease by saying, as she is reported to have done, 'Have you no place here for me?' She has no fewer than three resting-places in the convent church. Most of her is in a kind of trunk-cum-casket high above the altar, but her heart is in a glass, heart-shaped vessel supported by an amazing gold contraption. One of her arms is in a glass vessel too, this one boomerang-shaped. More startling to me even than these grisly relics was the reconstruction of her cell, which you peep at through a grille at the west end of the church. There a horribly realistic effigy of her is in bed, dressed in her habit, her cross in her left hand, for all the world as if she's taking forty post-prandial winks in a *parador*. I fled.

Opposite was a shop manned by monks, selling mainly Teresiana. I bought a book containing her poems and those of San Juan de la Cruz. She made the divine human, according to the blurb, whereas he made the human divine. I don't know whether either, or neither, of these approaches is theologically respectable; but my instinct is to regard the former with greater suspicion than the latter. On the back cover of the book was a photograph of a pair of castanets said to have been owned by Saint Teresa. They looked as if they could have made a tidy old clatter.

There was a sense of pathos about the unfinished basilica I saw: dressed blocks of stone lying about here and there; and, hard against the building, a gardener (with what struck me as a proper sense of priorities) had just filched several pieces of carved stone and statuary to mark his boundaries. Now he was bedding out pansies.

The town looked handsome from across the river. So did the new countryside I drove through. In the distance rose the Sierra de Ávila and the Sierra Candelaria, snow-tipped. The ranges looked like brazen Yale keys on edge, with teeth silvered from long use. I got to Béjar late in the afternoon, spent. Too tired to be choosy, I took a room in a run-to-seed commercial hotel where, foolishly grateful for the mere existence of a bathroom, I didn't notice until too late that there was no plug in the wash basin and that the water emerged from the tap tepid and, as near as not, the colour of blood.

Next morning, Sunday, dawned fine, propitious, with an intense golden light that suffused the countryside south of Béjar with an unearthly glow. The effect was paradisiacal: the rich inflorescence of broom shrubs was more than usually golden; the green of broad-leaf trees gleamed yellowy where low-slanted rays hit them; the meadows between were of closest-touching buttercups. And lest this magnificence should fall short of twenty-two carat perfection, fast and low through this Eden a golden oriole flew.

I came to a place called Cristobal: hardly a village; more a scattering of cottages and farm buildings, with a bar lying back a bit from the road. I stopped for a coffee.

An old, stooping man came in. He was stooping because on his back he carried a fifty-kilo bag of cement which – though he stayed talking to me for a good quarter of an hour – he would not put down. I didn't know the Spanish for golden oriole. I described the wondrous bird I'd seen and its manner of flight. The old man knew at once. I looked the word up later and found *oropéndula*; but he called it (writing the word down for me, painfully slowly, on an empty cigarette packet, the cement surely getting heavier with each thick letter fashioned as though out of Plasticine) *guirupéndula*.

The main road bypassed the centre of Miranda del Castanar;

but, wanting a quick peep at the village, I was barmy enough
to try to drive through instead of leaving my car at the edge
and walking. My barminess was occasioned less by sloth than
the fear of running the gauntlet of a multitude of dogs. Each
house had a matched pair of terriers or Alsatians outside the
door; and they looked even more hostile than the suspicious
or downright surly human inhabitants. I eased my little car
on through streets that became narrower and narrower –
cobbled, too, with great ruts and low, much-protruding corbels
– until at a blind, downward-sloping, impossibly tight corner,
I found I could go neither forward nor back. A woman in a
turquoise shawl appeared at her door and watched me sweat
as I heaved this way and that on the wheel and changed from
reverse into forward gear, forward into reverse, changing
position by the barest fraction of an inch with each hard-
slogging manoeuvre. She said nothing; but observed my every
move with absorbed interest. There was the most awful
moment of scraping metal as, finally, I made my turn. The
woman gleefully clapped, had me stop and told me I was the
first driver for years to have attempted the turn successfully
instead of reversing back to where the street was wider. By
now I was surrounded by barking village dogs and small boys
wanting to tell me my steering wheel was on the wrong side.
I cut the courtesies short and bumped away. I daresay most
British motorists bring back from Spain at least one such
incident to remember with horror and relate with glee.

Whether or not the chauffeured Sitwell family Rolls-Royce
got stuck in Miranda del Castanar is not recorded. The vehicle
is known to have been in La Alberca and the surrounding area
of Las Hurdes at a time when this part of Spain was still not
easily accessible; moreover the car nearly ran out of petrol.
Its occupants were obsessed with the vagaries of Spanish
regional dress and it was their quest for costume that brought
them to the strange locality of Las Hurdes. The more I learn
about the Sitwells, the more I fancy they looked no less
outlandish to the local inhabitants than they to them. Nowadays, though the sign-posting is still not all it might be, so
many tourists of all nations find their way here to gawp at
picturesque, medieval La Alberca and its residents (who are
occasionally to be seen in traditional dress) that perhaps the
latter, without ever setting foot far beyond their doorstep,

acquire a more comprehensive knowledge of foreigners and their quaint ways than most world travellers do.

Lamentable epithets such as 'picture-book' and *típico* are all too applicable to La Alberca. Somehow (largely on account of its isolation) the town's dark, rocky, unpaved, tightly winding streets of stone and half-timbered, overhanging upper storeys have survived intact down the centuries. Until fairly recently an unself-consciously communal way of life, knowing no alternative, went on in the arcaded Plaza Pública and the barbaric streets. But now that the place is widely publicized and easy to get at, its vibrancy is doomed. The thoroughfares have already been neatly paved and cobbled; there's an *hostal* full of sincere and deeply appreciative burghers from Hamburg and Hackensack; and when you go into a shop you don't feel like an interloper. I bought a small round loaf with a *típico* crust five millimetres thick, a peril to teeth. Back outside I watched a bearded Belgian darting about, crouching, taking (as it were) action snaps of architecture. He looked, as photographer tourists often do, through a glass darkly but not face to face. He was never to see how, above his head, a long black cat crossed the street by extending one paw very delicately from one roof to another, scarcely having to spring.

Now I headed for the heart of Las Hurdes country by way of the 4,000-foot Portillo Pass on the Las Batuecas Road. From the pass I descended perilously down seven miles of hairpin bends before reaching the valley.

I was to drive hundreds of miles of even more stunning routes in Spain, with scenery of even more overpowering grandeur: but at that time of year – late spring – with the cistus in flower, the landscape as far as the great reservoir made me want to exult with actual cheers. The cistus flowers, on their ubiquitous shrubby plants, were like billions of fried eggs, each with a dark quartet of stains around the yolk. It was as though so many ladies' handkerchieves had been draped by gipsy laundresses to dry in the sun. I stopped to pick a bloom (the white turns yellow with pressing) and found the stem unpleasantly sticky. Reaching Caminomorisco, I saw a nice old lady sweeping up geranium petals in the yard of a bar. Before I got out, I checked the word *jara* in my dictionary and was struck to see that, as well as meaning 'cistus' in Spain, in was slang in Mexico for 'the cops'. I told the old dear this; and she was much amused and fetched her husband out and had me repeat what I'd said. He looked as George Orwell might have done had he lived to seventy: same shape head, same haircut, some moustache.

'Don't suppose you get many Mexican policeman here,' I said, to make him grin.

'Fifty years ago we got hardly anybody coming here, even from Salamanca,' he said. 'We were all but cut off in this valley. Nobody knew we were here. We didn't know how we got here, either. Now people come from all over just to look at us. So we're famous, you might say!'

We sat together chatting for an hour or so. Scholars from Madrid had come to Caminomorisco to study the local people, he told me. A television company had made a film about them, too. He was proud to be an anthropological curiosity: it made him feel special. I said I was too interested in people to become an anthropologist, and that made him grin and take my hand in a strong grip and shake it. When I rose to go he wouldn't let me pay for my wine.

Two years later when I went back to see him, he'd had a stroke. He recognized me, I'm sure, but he couldn't make any words come: though his lips moved as they would have done for speech. A big tear rolled down his cheek when I gripped his hands in both of mine. His wife made encouraging noises. One of the granddaughters gathered a bunch of roses from the trellis for my wife. 'You remember the English *caballero*,' the old lady said, and I felt his hands tremble. 'He brought some *jara* down from the mountain.'

In something I'd read about Las Hurdes, stress had been laid on the interbreeding of the people; the madness, the goitre they suffered from. I saw no Derbyshire necks. There was, however, a typical local face – rather do-lally, with eyes well apart and a vacuous expression, sag-jawed, as it watched from a porch; a kind of Middle Ages, gargoyle grimace. The whole area looked and felt other, bizarre, out of real time. I saw cherries ripening; there were two orange trees with all their fruit but not a single leaf – like thrown-out Christmas trees in a January yard, which have dropped their needles but which still bear their pretty, vivid baubles. I passed a couple of dozen goatherds during the afternoon. Each had no more than about eight or nine animals of a nice, light-brown colour, which leaped nimbly up the roadside bank as I approached. Some, extraordinarily, had CB radios, which must, I suppose, help relieve the loneliness of the job; others carried neatly rolled black umbrellas such as are carried by city gents; others again wore the kind of bright blue overalls you see on petrol pump attendants.

Candelario, another *típico* mountain village, had streets with channels at the side, down which the melted snow-waters run. When the thaw begins, they must flow torrentially fast: though not perhaps quite as fast as the gabbling of the priest I heard in the parish church. His Hail Marys gushed with the speed of delivery of South African tobacco auctioneers, while the full-to-bursting congregation mouthed responses like infants doing the three-times table. Outside, the village band, in navy-blue uniforms, was gathering with its instruments.

Back in Béjar, the closed Sunday shops had laid out their wares – from ladies' dresses to babies' po's – for display on the spotless floors. I saw a cripple in a hurry who had twisted his three-quarters of a right leg round his crutch like down-twining ivy. What I wanted was a red-water bath.

CHAPTER SEVEN

There were hunks of cork on the road, fallen off lorries: I was in Extremadura all right. South of Plasencia, on the way to Trujillo, I saw the first commercial yards and depots of the stuff. Bales were piled high, like so many thousands of comfy, brown surgical collars. Soon I was to see de-barked trees: 'de-bagged', one wants to say, for the bark is taken from the trunk to as high as where the branches divide – a process that leaves a cork oak standing sheepishly on one leg, nude below the armpits.

A dark, dry, spiky, louring green characterizes much of the rolling *extremeño* countryside. As well as cork oaks, there were ilexes and strawberry trees growing close together. There was a lot of scrubby stuff between, too, such as the ubiquitous *jara*. But the contrasting and frequent open patches of viridian and flower-spangled grass and the sudden flightings of partridge and woodcock, hoopoes, bee-eaters and azure-winged magpies ensure against monotony.

There was no lack of man-made eucalyptus plantations, either: sometimes extensive, but often consisting of no more than half-a-dozen trees. I find the eucalyptus a distinctly odd – even disturbing – tree. It stands in a litter of its own shed bark which curls into strips like whopping cinnamon sticks or cedar cigar-wrappers, all the gradations from almost white and palest green through to richest rust red. Its leaves are a sickly shade of green, often (especially in a young tree) tinged with red. Its colours, its pendulous habit and general configuration give it rather a depressing air. Birds won't nest in it. Animals won't climb it. To some, the scent may be the very breath of spring; to me it's redolent of hospitals and childhood anxiety.

At Villareal de San Carlos I saw the first of tens of thousands of the woolly, free-range pigs of Extremadura; brown ones

114

these, but most are bluey-black. As I climbed towards the Tagus reservoirs and the Nature Park of Monfragüe, it was nice to have a mountain hare spring a hundred yards along the road ahead before darting off into undergrowth. Human beings were thin on the ground. Tracts of this remote region are *despoblados* and *dehesas*: deserted, weird, unsettled places or cattle ranches with occasional gateways and entrance drives but seemingly abandoned.

Not thirsty but wanting someone to talk to, I stopped for a beer in a little place called Torrejón el Rubio. I asked the bar proprietor why he thought so many *conquistadores* had been men of Extremadura. Was it, as books suggested, because the land was poor and difficult to farm?

'Don't you believe it! Nonsense! What a *tontería*! Listen, we're adventurers, pure and simple, we *Extremeños*. Curiosity – that's all it is – wanting to find out what's round the next corner. And greed, of course – well, that's natural, isn't it? Take me, for example. Granted, I've not been to Peru like the Pizarro brothers. But I travel wherever and whenever I can. Where to? Andorra, mainly. That's a fair way from here. Why Andorra? A change of scene. Yes, but also the chance to stuff the car full of cassette recorders and crates of whisky! Cortés wouldn't have had to go to Mexico for all that gold and silver if he'd been living today. He'd have had fleets of lorries going back and forth to Andorra!'

A hoarding at the approaches to Trujillo advertised a firm called EXPLOTACION PIZARRO. It stood among huge, grey, rounded rocks which, like stranded whales or lame elephants, littered the ground everywhere. Pizarro is a common name hereabouts. Somewhere in this bleak vicinity the young Francisco exercised his trade of swineherd before, from curiosity and greed (if the barman was right), he went to do such great – and such unspeakably barbaric – deeds in Peru. In the Plaza Mayor there's a fine equestrian statue of him, twin of the one in Lima; frighteningly purposeful he looks, too: plumes fly like snakes from his helmet; his elbows, beard and visor are sharp-pointed; his wicked long spurs are about to dig hard in; his sword is drawn and eager to kill.

The square was a marvellous, dramatic enclosure to walk about in: on several levels, with steps and arcades and loggias; with unexpected angles and corners; with towers and emblazoned seigneurial mansions on every side. And with Pizarro dominating all, you expected to be caught up at any moment in a fierce piece of filmic action. What actually happened was that a bombastic and self-important little car-park attendant came strutting along waving his pencil, instrument of authority, as though I were his Inca victim.

Cáceres claims to be 'the city of storks' but I would hand the title to Trujillo. On the walk up to the Moorish castle I got intimately close-up views *down* into the birds' nests, such as I was never to enjoy in the provincial capital. You could see every feather on the fledglings. When an adult, red-legged bird took off (the way a hang-glider does, standing at the very lip and dropping several feet before soaring up again), you suffered a brief attack of vertigo and took your heart into your mouth. There were human activities worth watching, too. A precarious fat man was cleaning moss from his roof with a dinner fork. Each move he made I imagined he might go to his death or at least suffer serious disablement, crashing through the much cracked pantiles and ancient rafters. His wife, out of sight from where he was, nagged him for his dilatoriness; he flicked a good mouthful of moss down at her and it hit her fair and square in the face. Neither of them was to know – any more than the storks knew – how their behaviour had been observed.

The Amazon explorer Francisco de Orellana, like the Pizarro brothers, was born a Trujillo boy. So was the fabulous strong man, Diego García de Paredes: small wonder the little town gave its name to three cities of the New World. But it was the name of a village less than a third the size of Trujillo – Guadalupe – that became even more celebrated throughout not only the Americas but the entire Catholic world. This was not on account of anything its intrepid, warlike or Herculean sons achieved. What put the place on the map was the discovery there of a small, dark-oak doll, the much venerated Virgin of Guadalupe. In her presence, papers were signed that led to the very discovery of the American continent; Columbus named a West Indian island for her; in her shrine, the first indigenous Americans brought to Europe were baptized. If you want to understand certain fundamental aspects of the Spanish Catholic turn of mind, you have to pay her a visit.

I knew there was a *parador* in Guadalupe, very grand, as

116

well as a few humbler hotels and *hostales*. I fancied staying in the monastery itself.

I arrived by way of Zorita, past the stunning scenery of the Sierra de Guadalupe. From whichever direction you come the first glimpse of the place is astonishing. (Subsequently I have arrived from the higher ground of the Navalmoral road. That approach too, is breath-taking: but I have a particular affection for the abruptness of the view that fills the windscreen after the short avenue of monstrous eucalyptus trees on the lower road.)

The monastery, of rich ochre stone, vast and impregnable as any castle, dominated its subservient cluster of brown houses with a grandiosity, a richness of tracery and a variety of architectural detail which left me wondering whether I would, after all, find courage enough to seek bed and board there. The *hospedería* was not how I imagined a religious house could be: not austere, not redolent of self-denial and self-infliced scourge. To gain admission I had to tug on a big iron bell-pull. I waited a full minute: was I being observed from the tower above? The great door was thrown open. One step inside – and I recognized all the usual trappings of a modern hotel reception desk. The front-of-house Manager wore black coat and striped trousers; though the Director, as I learned later, was a Franciscan in a brown habit.

I signed in. A young, smartly-dressed porter (was he – surely not – a novice in mufti?) went ahead with my bags. We crossed a Gothic cloister. This had been the original pharmacy of the monastery hospitals but was now one of those deliciously cool patio gardens with dozens of old roses, climbers, trailers, monsteras and red-flowering shrubs in scattered tubs and pots. Then (I've been there since, and they've installed a discreet lift) we toiled up a staircase to my cell. The door was opened. I saw at a glance that the room contained utter comfort: well-laundered linen and twentieth-century plumbing in a manner speaking of luxury albeit in the vernacular of plain wholesomeness. In I went, turned to say thank you but the young man had vanished leaving me startled and embarrassed to have fifty pesetas of change in my hot fist. I should have known better than to think of tipping; but the status of the institution and its lay staff, both in the hostelry and the sacred apartments, was at times ambiguous.

I stepped outside and looked for him in a corridor with flamboyant arches. My shoes clattered on the resonant, highly polished floor. I was rebuked by a framed notice in medieval script enjoining me to silence.

I lay for a long while in a hot bath, with a wonderfully big whisky and a Cuban cigar, wondering what kind of Franciscan I might have made.

Then I went for my guided tour of church and chapterhouse, *camarín* and sacristy.

It was an hour and a half of stupefying and indigestible richness: of copes, chasubles and altar-fronts bejewelled and embroidered with gold and silver thread; of enormous illuminated volumes – ponderous books of hours and antiphonaries, each of the dots of whose crochets was a good inch square; of gallery-sized collections of Zurbaráns and Giordanos; of pearls and emeralds, rubies and sapphires, wood carving and filigree work, gold and silver, jasper and silks; of gilt baroque stucco and marquetry; of simple but priceless treasures; and, regrettably, of vulgarly elaborate artifacts and sinister reliquaries: all of them, all, to honour and celebrate one small, crudely carved effigy.

I was in a party of ten in the roof of the *coro* when I set eyes on her. She was at the far end of the building, on the same level as we, high above the altar. Very tiny she looked, her little brown face visible above a widely-flared white dress: an affecting apparition. A young friar took over from a uniformed lay guide. He began, parrot-fashion, to chant information at us.

Shortly after, we found ourselves (I couldn't quite understand how: the building is complicated) on the first floor level immediately behind the statue, in the sumptuous room known as the *camarín*. This is where the figure is dressed and regaled for procession; it is to all intents and purposes her boudoir. Her wardrobe, we were informed, is even more extensive and costly than that of Jacqueline Kennedy Onassis or the Princess of Wales. Between us and her is a panel of superb pictorial tiles, each representing a significant event in the times of the Madonna since her discovery in the thirteenth century by the cowherd Gil Cordero. The friar spoke a few sentences about nearly every one: effectively a potted history of Spain. Then (an obviously much-rehearsed dramatic effect) he turned the panel on its concealed axis: there she was, within only feet

118

of us, holding her sceptre. We were face-to-face with her! My companions, with much gasping and many frantic crossings of themselves, fell to their knees. Three were large ladies. I alone of the group remained standing, but was not alone in being aware of the fact that one of the matrons was going to require help to get to her feet again. Several Hail Marys were said. Then, while the others accepted an invitation to kiss the Virgin's medallion, the friar regarded me steadily, as though defying me to make him laugh. Despite how it may appear from my description, I swear there was no lack of reverence on his part or mine. Though an outsider, I was deeply moved by the display of fervour I had witnessed. Genially, we all shook hands after the two husbands in the group and I lifted the lady, gasping, up.

Outside, coaches full of pilgrims were arriving from all over Spain. I went to a bar, looking forward to a glass of the powerful local wine, reputed to be seventeen-degree strength: but was disappointed to be told that there was no *tinto*, only *mosto*, must of wine, available. This was to become a fairly regular occurrence in Extremadura. At first I wondered if this might be due to traditional local abstemiousness: cloudy must, alcohol-free, the unfermented juice of the grape, being an appropriate tipple for inhabitants of holy places such as this. The hard-drinking men of Guadalupe disabused me of this belief. Soon the bar was noisy with forty to fifty card players. Few drank *mosto*.

Television news was showing the annual El Rocío *romería* in Andalucía. In a white, candlelit sanctuary, with fireworks, mounting hysteria and the singing of the *Ave Maria*, the float bearing the gold and orange, life-size effigy of the *Sin pecado* was seen in the chancel behind a semi-circular, ten-foot high railing, in readiness for her procession outside. Two men were with her behind the railings; one clearing the float of flowers and candlesticks, the other fending off anyone who, before the proper time, might try to climb in. A mob of young men pressed against the railings, grabbing them tight. The *paso*, white-canopied and as though sugar-iced, might have been the winning entry in a confectionery competition and the vehement men schoolboys avid for a handful of it. The last bunches of gladioli and carnations were thrown aside. At a signal, about a hundred men swarmed over. There was

119

mayhem, a scene reminiscent of what happens in a football stadium when one set of fans invades another's territory. Many were fighting to reach the statue; others added their weight to an unco-ordinated mêlée, like a loose ruck at rugby. A few, less vigorous but caught up helplessly in the press, could do no more than look towards the Virgin with an expression of religious fervour and with arms extended in a gesture of supplication. The float rocked unsteadily this way and that and nearly toppled over. Could it ever, without being crushed and splintered underfoot, be brought out of the sanctuary and processed among the people?

It was, of course. Card-players who had suspended their games in mid-trick in order to watch now turned their attention back to their squares of green baize. I overheard mutterings about over-excitable *Andaluces*. In general though, for a short while a dignified quiet prevailed – that of folk who don't need to prove their superior dignity. Then the tension of the cards took over once more and the noise of pagan amusement resumed.

The centre of Guadalupe was packed with souvenir shops. These contained much predictable tourist-trap kitsch; but there was some good, reasonably priced, local craftwork on offer: brass, copper and splendidly colourful, well-designed Talavera pottery ware. (I rightly suspected several items of the latter of being 'seconds', an imperfectly glazed oil jug I brought home being ever liable to leak.)

I encouraged the proprietress of one shop to gossip about the friars. There were only a handful left, she said. The young one who had been my guide earlier was clearly her pet. I had heard one of the others in the cloisters, I told her, coughing like a three-badge stoker. 'Father Juan,' she said. 'A chain-smoker. You'd think they'd set us a better example, wouldn't you?' I was to see Father Juan, Director of the *hospedería*, the following morning. While I was at breakfast, he sat at an adjacent table working on accounts, one cigarette in his mouth, another burning on the ashtray and an open Ducados packet near at hand. His ceaseless, hacking cough made the spoon in my saucer rattle.

For dinner I had *ternera a la riojana*, beef in wine sauce like *boeuf bourguignon*. I sat with a young, glum, non-smoking, non-drinking, bearded German, a member of the Green party, owner of a red Spitfire car. He told me he had driven the length of the holiday *costas* from the French frontier to Gibraltar before turning inland. He had no curiosity about Spain or (as far as I could judge) about any actual place anywhere else: only a generalized anxiety about the continuance, given the threat of nuclear war, of the world 'considered as a planet'. I couldn't help but wonder why he wanted the earth to go on turning, seeing that he took such little relish in it. He ate a bit of salad and drank a glass of mineral water. He would live to be a hundred – and serve him right. But next day, outside the *Centro Nuclear* at Valdecaballeros, I thought about him and his ceaseless worry. I saw a bed of flowers – perhaps they were mesembryanthemums – of a hue I had thought unknown in nature, glaringly vivid purple. I was depressed and distressed by them. Were there to be a holocaust, any surviving flora would take on that colour.

Entering Cáceres, like a fool I drove straight to the heart of the medieval quarter. But Spain is a country where a fool can get lucky. After ten minutes of being ironically cheered by a party of schoolkids I passed and re-passed in the constricted knot of narrow streets, I found a way not up to the modern district, but, by blessed instinct, down: to a lovely street built, at a guess, not long after the end of the Peninsular War. At once I recognized it as a *barrio* where I'd enjoy staying: a place to feel at home in, where I could wash some shirts and socks and write letters and get to know a few people.

The Calle General Margallo wasn't the kind of street that overwhelms with elegance or prettiness. It wasn't picturesque; indeed it was downright workaday, where ordinary people lived, with roofs bristling with television antennae; with balconies, if not loaded with flower-pots made from empty bonito tins, then all festooned with washing. It was, its entire length, gently winding. Its plain white or washed-pastel houses were sometimes of two and sometimes of three storeys and no two neighbouring properties had floors at the same level. With a sigh I imagined how artified it would become if the Spanish cousins of Hampstead or Clifton trendies got hold of it. I stopped the car and got out. Above me a fat lady, hanging out her clothes, let curiosity get the better of her. Leaning over to get a better view of me, she accidentally dropped a pair of tights: which I caught, deft, and lobbed back up – a comic moment, not without an element of flirtatiousness on the part of both parties.

'Where's a good place to stay, señora?'

'The hotels are not in this district.'

'But I don't want an hotel. Just a clean room, small, quiet, decent, running water.'

'You are a Frenchman, perhaps?'

'No, señora.'

'Norteamericano?'

'No.'

'Try the Fonda Salamantina, Señor.'

The Fonda Salamantina, though its front door was wide open, seemed deserted. A hundred yards farther on I came to a similar establishment advertising camas, beds. I went in the bar door, took one look at the proprietor and made up my mind to stay. It was one of those faces, much lined, not exactly grimy but (like the face, say, of an old, washed and scrubbed coal miner) showing signs of a lifetime's hard graft. His name was Miguel Guzmán.

'I'd like a room, please, if you have one.'

'I have rooms, yes. However . . .'

'Yes?'

'I should have to charge 400 pesetas.'

'May I see the room?'

'Claro.'

Two pounds a night: a doss-house price. But the room was immaculate: fragrant with lavender-bags, with brass bedstead, heavy mahogany table and chair, cotton sheets looking and smelling freshly laundered and aired in the sun with the white, hand-crotcheted bed-spread: all this and a view of the bullring. I stood at the window, enjoying intimate glimpses into people's back yards: their old bikes, their dogs, their caged birds. There was a lovely outhouse roof of golden pantiles; the tiles were irregular and in slightly uneven lines, like corn on a newly-ripened cob. A lizard skittered the length of the roof, rousing me from a day-dream of living here the rest of my days. Behind me, Guzmán was mumbling apologetically.

'It's not a room of luxury, of course. More for relatives from the country when the stock fair is on.'

No private bathroom, of course; but there was a spotless

122

communal one along the corridor. I should have to heat my shaving water in the kitchen and for sure I'd replace the thin cardboard loo paper with Kleenex.

'It's fine,' I said. We went back downstairs, into the bar, where Guzmán gave me a glass of white *mosto* and a *tapa* of baked barbel.

'You'll have to help me fill in the *ficha*,' he said. 'I'm not used to dealing with passports in foreign languages.'

I did as he asked. For our mutual dignity, it could not be admitted by either of us that he was all but illiterate. We smiled at the notion of the guest doing the host's job. When it was done, I handed the form to him. He picked up my passport and looked with yearning at the frontier stamps.

'Like yourself, *señor*, I am a much-travelled man,' he said. 'During the Sixties and Seventies, as a *Gastarbeiter*, I went to Germany several times. There were lots of us – Spaniards and Turks, mostly. Wait, I'll show you my records.' He went behind the bar. 'These facts had to be kept for the Authorities,' he said. 'You understand?' he added, with a furtive glance round the roomful of empty chairs and tables. I could picture *guardias* in Franco's time off-duty, lounging, drinking *mosto* and eating baked barbel, coming to spy for the Revenue on Miguel Guzmán. From the topshelf he took a piece of torn shoe-box. On it were scrawled, in the large characters of a childlike hand, some figures and dates and the names of three or four German towns. It was Guzmán's autobiography. He handled it with loving care, as though it were some priceless bibelot or an heirloom.

'They were good days,' he said. 'A man had money and freedom. Whereas now . . .' He waved vaguely towards the kitchen.

Next morning, in the modern end of town, I bumped into him. He was in a hurry. I had the impression that he had been on some nefarious errand.

'Don Miguel!' I cried, grasping him by the shoulder, 'why the rush?'

He was on the point of running; then recognized me. 'Come and have a coffee,' I said.

'I ought to be getting back.' He was breathing hard.

He poured a sachet of Maxwell House into a cup of hot milk to make a *descafeinado*.

'My nerves, you understand. I suffer from my nerves very much. In the old days, I never suffered from nerves like this.'

He sipped, bending his head to drink like a budgerigar.

'Thank you, sir,' he said. 'I am grateful not to be running. I'll say how I met you and how we spent a long time – maybe an hour, would you say? – chatting over a cup of coffee. And I'll say how you called me "Don Miguel". That gives me pleasure – to be called not "Mr Guzmán" but "Don Miguel". I enjoyed respect of that kind in the old days.' Then he skedaddled.

I spent the rest of the morning in the market. It was a huge one, taking up ever so many winding and hilly streets. Vendors and customers alike looked as though they'd come in from far-off country districts: fresh-faced, expectant, mildly amused at the clamour; old chaps in whipcords and carrying great sticks, their buxom or scraggy ladies in gaudy cottons and weighed down with bundles and wicker baskets. Most stalls were loaded with fruit and vegetables, bolts of cloth, confectionery or kitchen tools. But there were two others doing a brisk trade: one with day-old chicks dyed bright pink, purple or lime – novelty toys for children; the other with every conceivable medicinal herb, set out in open sacks and marked clearly 'for gout', 'for rheumatism', 'for piles' and so forth.

Old Cáceres was wonderful in the first cool of the day and by fading light. The stone blocks of which the walls were built had not been smoothened by the original masons or their recent restorers but left with a nice rough texture. Their colour was of the richest golden-brown to be found anywhere in Spain: as though drenched, steeped, saturated with all the sunlight of centuries of summers. There was nothing fancy or fussy about the architecture to detract from an immediate sense of solid worth and achievement. Noblemen constructed these houses: that was clear from the coats of arms prominent on each façade; and, being noblemen, they had no need to be showy or over-assertive. An itinerary listing the names of houses, palaces, towers and other monuments of the medieval quarter would read like a half-forgotten litany:

Past the House of Storks and the Weather-vane House,
Past the Towers of Swordsmith, Postern and Pulpit,
Through the Arches of Star and Succour I went
To the Palace of the Golfines.

Walking down from the Arch of the Star, I noticed that the sky above Cáceres was thronged not only by storks (a commonplace enough sight to me by now) but also by that marvellous little hunter, the sparrow-hawk. A beer, El Gavilán, popular in Extremadura, is named after it.

In a crowded bar off the Plaza del General Mola I sampled a bottle, found it good, so had another. I was much amused by the chance juxtaposition of a shelf of two advertisements: one for a product called Bum (cheese footballs in a packet like those used for potato crisps) and another for Bitter Sin, an alcohol-free Cinzano. Upstairs I dined very well on a small dish of *paella*, a leg of roast sucking pig and strawberries: the latter served on a stemmed silver cup shaped like the urns, colonized by storks, at each corner of a certain tower up in the ancient quarter. The restaurant had been empty when I entered. An hour later, I had finished my coffee and still there were only three other diners: a bachelor Spaniard and a middle-aged French couple. The room was subdued, nobody caring to talk except to order. I felt inclined to settle my bill and leave. But then two men came in, comically dissimilar; and the atmosphere changed at once.

The much older of the two had very pronounced horizontal lines on forehead, cheekbones and moustache, and a quick glint in the eyes; he kept a sporting, wide-brimmed trilby on his head and from under it there sprouted bushy white hair falling to the collar of his light-grey suit. He was drunk and he chain-smoked and there were all the weathers of sixty years on his face. I'd have bet he was a horse-trader up for the spring sales. His companion, with whom, it was clear, he had not long been acquainted, was a twenty-year old Portuguese lad, dark-complexioned and black-haired but yet with curious blue eyes. He was dressed in a navy-blue suit and white, open-neck shirt. He looked very frightened, not knowing how to read the Spanish of the menu, not knowing what to ask for, and acutely embarrassed by the old man's loud voice and his indifference to what anybody might think about their unambiguous relationship.

'Tomorrow we shall cross the frontier back into Portugal. There will be no difficulty about that. No, we shall cross with ease at a place I know. Waiter! Place us bread, wine and water here. You will have something to drink, boy? No? A lemonade, if nothing else? Waiter, bring good lemonade for this beautiful boy. We shall each have a cup of soup, no matter of what kind. I have been everywhere in the world. Morocco, Ceuta. I have been there and am known and liked. Your country too, boy. Every corner of it visited by me. You are lucky to have found a man like me to be your guide and protector.'

The waiter was bringing items singly so he could overhear much of this. I was writing it all down on the back of my bill.

'The bread is excellent here, but the water is terrible and the wine no better than good enough. Everywhere in Spain, I know where the good water is, and the bad.'

The boy fell upon the bread like a wolf on a chicken. It was all gone by the time his soup arrived. He slurped this from the bowl, ravenous. The waiter and his colleague from the bar downstairs stood behind the screen muttering 'maricones', and digging each other in the ribs. The old man adjusted his hat and looked around him, a spoon in one hand and a cigarette in the other.

'There are few here. What time do people eat in Cáceres? At midnight? Tonight we shall sleep in a big bed. There will be plenty of room to turn over and do anything we like. This soup looks contemptible. In my village we know how to make soup.'

Downstairs on the bar television was the bullfight from the Madrid San Isidro fiesta. One of the matadors was the ageing Antoñete: half-bald, worn, genial. Another was El Niño de la Capea, young, ostentatious, all style but little substance, his cowardice smothered with gestures like bad meat disguised with too spicy a sauce. A bull called Sincero gave up and decided to die. El Niño strutted and struck poses, trying to incite. Meanwhile (the camera getting in close on him) Antoñete, watching from behind the barrier, sighed with mild, bored exasperation. You could tell he was thinking it was a bad bull, that the only thing to do was kill it at once as professionally as possible. The sword went in at the wrong angle, into the lungs. Blood gushed from the bull's maw fast as water from a hydrant. 'Fulminante, fulminante!' screamed the commentator. As El Niño prepared to have another go, the action replay began with bits of slow motion, close-ups and inserts. After Sincero finally toppled over interviews were conducted with the matadors. The prying television eye, with its unnecessary ritual, made a monotony of the necessary ritual of the bullfight, the essence of which is unpredictability and unrepeatability within an unchangeable form. Few in the bar bothered to watch. Most of the drinkers looked as weary and exasperated as the old *torero*. Then, 'Come and see this!' hissed the waiter from the top of the stairs. And not only his colleague but half the clientele took the steps three at a time to go and witness a different kind of moment of truth.

The bullring was where I spent most of the following morning. On my way back to Guzmán's after breakfast (great *churros* that came in coils, cut with shears of a size you'd take to steel cable), I heard the approach of shrill chanting and singing. Barbers, not putting down comb and clippers, came on to the street to watch followed by their swathed customers. A troupe of marching girls appeared, younger ones (up to twelve years old) in front, older ones (up to eighteen) behind. The song they sang, the *Redoble*, was lively, catchy, making you want to swing your arms and step it out with shoulders thrown back. Every single school in Cáceres, a *vecina* told me, was converging – from snooty private schools and convents like the Josefinas at the smart end of town down to poor little primaries from local villages – for the annual festival of dance and song in celebration of *extremeño* culture.

The junction of streets near the bullring was packed with minibuses, coaches and long, fairly orderly crocodiles. '*Adelante,*' ordered a serious, bespectacled six-year-old when a policeman waved the line on. Most boys wore the colours of Extremadura: white shirts, black trousers, green neckerchieves. They carried banners and flags of the region, three equal stripes of green, white and black. Some girls (the smaller ones) wore the traditional local dress of wide, knee-length skirts in bright colours with horizontal bands, white socks and a much-embroidered shawl like a small tablecloth over a white or black lace-trimmed blouse. Their hair was worn up in a bun or as earphones. They had not been made to look cheap by their use of eye shadow and lipstick, or by long earrings and necklaces. Two or three in a hundred wore the strange hat, or *gorra*, from the district of Montehermoso. It was of straw, lined with silk, the shape of a shako or a picador's inverted stirrup, with woollen bobbles and embroidery down the front, all bedecked with pearls and little mirrors. (The

127

mirrors once had the function of proclaiming a girl's availability for marriage.)

The stands quickly filled with children and parents. There wasn't quite a capacity crowd (the bullring could hold 13,000) but the noise was terrific. It got even louder when the first group of performers, *peques* from an infants' school, began to do a square dance in the centre of the arena: louder still as they finished, bowed and curtsied and made their exits. They were followed by a team of dancers from a junior school, in South American costume. The girls wore striking, off-the-shoulder dresses in primary colours and the boys were got up like gauchos. They did a series of dances from Argentina, exciting and exuberant. One girl, half-negress, moved with stunning, sinuous grace which was noticed and remarked upon by the comfy mum next to me with her toddler boy. *Hispanidad*, the sense of community of Spanish nations in the New World and the Old – something like the so-called 'spirit of Commonwealth' which claimed to bind together former member countries of the British Empire – is strong in Extremadura, home of the *conquistadores*.

That evening, on my way up to town for dinner, I stopped for an *aperitivo* in a bar not far from the bullring. A boy of nine or ten came in to get his father's lighter filled.

'Were you there with your class this morning?' I asked him.

'No, *señor*.'

'How come? Weren't you well?'

Not answering, he took the lighter, plonked three duros on the counter and ran off.

'Paco doesn't go to school,' said the proprietor. 'Nor did his brothers and sisters.'

'How can that be? What about the law?'

'It happens.'

On the pavement I found a note that had presumably been dropped by one of the schoolchildren from the festival. *Dear Sylvia*, I read, *I am sending you this to ask which of us, Jorge or me, José Luís, you have decided to pick to be your sweetheart. Please don't tear this up or throw it away but let me know your answer. José Luís Días Romero.* Young Paco, I thought, would never be able to write a love-letter. Both now and later he'd have to do what Miguel Guzmán did.

Next morning Guzmán, with much help, made out a receipt

128

the size of a stamp for me. He signed it, laboriously, with my pen. He wore a sad face.

'I told you there was good security in this street, señor. That is no longer so. Last night, a motorcycle was stolen. I don't know what this country is coming to.'

'Such things happen everywhere, Don Miguel.'

'The *moto* was chained to a drainpipe outside the Civil Guard barracks! I hope you find more honesty in Portugal.'

'What are the Portuguese like?'

'Serious. Correct.' This is what Spaniards say about their neighbours. Seriously and correctly, Guzmán waved as I drove away.

In Valencia de Alcántara, just before the frontier, I stopped for a coffee and to look at the grandiose war memorial. A white Mini with a Portuguese registration plate drew up beside me. A youngish couple got out. They were in their late twenties maybe, but with faces prematurely ageing due to excess: of sex, possibly; of drugs and drink, probably; of sun, certainly; and (I guessed) of three decades of selfishness and total disregard for others. He was a big, silly blond bear with a permanent grin behind a copious moustache, not much practised in the use of human speech. She was thin, hawk-featured, determined, undelectable, incapable of listening to talk that didn't contain information she wanted.

'Where we ged sompn' d'eat?'

I looked at my watch. The dot of noon. I nodded towards the bar I'd just come from.

'You could get a snack in there. A tortilla or—'

'We wahnna salad. Hey! Wadda you – English or somp'n? We're from California. We gahdda have salad.'

'Not here, then. Try the centre of town.'

'We just wend there. Them guys standing around the place. Nothing. Chrisd, we *hade* Spain. We prefer Pordugal. We jusd came from there. Spaniards – they're so *unfriendly*. Why, the people in Madrid—'

'Ha! You ever been in New York City?' Even as I spoke, I knew the point would be lost on her. She'd think I was just enquiring whether, literally, she'd ever been in the Big Apple.

'Yeah. One dime.'

'Anonymous big cities. London—'

'See thad guy on the burro? I just wahnned dake a photograph. He waved his arms and wouldn't led me. Whahd these people afraid of?'

'Perhaps they think it's an invasion of privacy.'

'Jesus Chrisd!'

'Not dignified.'

'No place, huh, ged a salad?'

I thought of high-piled, freshly-washed lettuces in the eating-places of Valencia de Alcántara; tomatoes about to be sliced and glistening with droplets of water; cucumbers about to be chipped; onions and peppers which, that same morning, had been brought into town on the backs of dignified donkeys led by masters who had never heard of Disneyland. I thought of flasks of oil and of vinegar; of large-grained salt.

'In Spain,' I said, 'we don't have lunch before two o'clock at the earliest.'

'We been eadin' so lade. We been in a *pousada*. We go back, Honey, *huh*?'

Honey-bear shrugged. I heard a grunt.

I drove on. After half a mile they overtook me. Theirs was the car immediately ahead of mine at the frontier post. She got out and shouted at my windscreen.

'No place change money, *huh*?'

'There'll be banks open when you get to a town. It's still quite early.' I spotted an Exchange Office, but I thought, damn you. She saw it too though, with eyes that could have seen cash through brick walls. Before starting my engine, I watched them drive off fast with their money towards Lisbon.

It was true, what I'd often heard: first that there's nothing like a short visit to Portugal for getting Spain into sharper focus and second that people will love the one and dislike the other and vice versa. My impression was of neatness, a kind of English Home Counties gentility and propriety. Portugal seemed to have English countryside, too, lush and compact, with bus stops every few hundred yards. Marvão, the first town I came to (up on a mountain top, a view to stop you in your tracks), was in spotless whitewash, mint condition, preserved and conserved as though by the deadening hand of the National Trust: not a living soul in sight to spoil everything by dropping so much as a toffee paper. Portugal was obses-

130

sively clean, like awful Switzerland, whereas Spain was carelessly untidy. Not a dirty country, as Britain is, though: Spain got dishevelled and littered all the time but was forever getting cleaned up too. A country so exuberantly lived in was bound to get messed up and battered. A few miles further on, at Beira, I had a lunch of steak and egg (ubiquitous, I was to discover) off a green Pyrex plate (ubiquitous, too) that I'd found upside down (the custom). The red wine was excellent and the people in the restaurant were very sunny, chummy, helpful, quiet, undemonstrative and nice – not to mention serious and correct. At Portalegre I got a perfectly acceptable room at the Hotel Dom João III, and in the evening I went out for a meal (chosen from a menu I couldn't understand) of *sopa de casa* followed by another steak and egg off another green Pyrex plate I'd found upside down; and more of that good red wine. For the first time in my life I found myself in a country where I spoke no more than a word or two of the language. I assumed (correctly) that it might be insulting to the Portuguese to suppose they'd know any more Spanish than English. I was reduced to pointing, practising mime. I vowed to be more tolerant in future of non-linguists helplessly floundering and waving their arms in desperation, like drowners. In a shop where I bought stamps an obliging man taught me some useful, basic food vocabulary so that in future I could eat a more varied diet. The effect upon me of being able to recognize even a few phonemes was instantaneous. No longer was everybody seeming to say nothing but *fash quash poish* down their noses.

In the evening people were saying almost nothing at all. In a café containing upwards of fifty people sitting together at tables for four there was less of a hubbub than you'd get at a Quaker meeting. In Spain, that number of people would have been making an uproar. I drank a glass of *aguardiente* which tasted of cloves (or could it have been ipecacuanha?) and which I considered so awful that I had to have another, to ascertain that the first glass had been offered in all seriousness. Then I went into a blue and white tiled church. I was the only man among forty women parroting decades, led by a priest with his back to them until a soldier, a mere boy, came in and occupied a pew at the back on his own and prayed, keeping his beret on. Next morning, as soon as I could I gobbled up

131

the kilometres from Portalegre to Elvas: all downhill, through neat villages with red pillar boxes all but identical to those in England. Soon, 'Home, sweet home again,' I was saying to myself, with a sigh of pleasure, as I crossed the frontier back into Spain.

Beside the road from Badajoz to Mérida there were many acres of peach and apricot orchards. The trees were growing in espaliers, or cordons, like lines of male Greek dancers with their hands on each other's shoulders. At Lobón, from a vantage point known as el Balcón de Extremadura, I was able to gaze over a vast plain not made fertile until comparatively recent times with the series of reservoirs and dams constructed under the 1952 Badajoz Plan. Here I crossed to the north bank of the Guadiana and headed east for Mérida: which meant that I entered that city from the same direction as did the aqueducts built by the Romans, the region's previous great water engineers. Not a patch on the wonderful Segovia *acueducto*, these at Mérida: but elegant for all that, with brickwork and tiles among the great granite blocks: picturesque, too, with cattle grazing on waste land under the arches.

I arrived early in the afternoon and was brought to a halt by deep ruts outside a bar in a street not far from the centre. Parched, too weary to drive another yard, I went for a glass of *tinto* and to enquire about cheap accommodation. The barman said, 'Turn right outside the door, then immediately right again. Go to the end of the passageway and you'll see the *fonda* – it's called La Mezquita – straight in front of you.' Wonderful, I thought: the clearest possible directions given at once. If only I'd drunk my wine at a gulp and passed *instanter* through the bead curtain back into the street, I could have had a bath and a couple of hours's sleep; whereupon, armed with my Green *Michelin*, I could have tackled all the many ancient monuments of Roman Mérida with equanimity. As it was, I let myself get into conversation with a little man called Don Pepe. Three hours later he was still talking at me.

Is it an Irishism or a wise paradox to claim that some monotonous encounters can be fascinating? I think the Ancient Mariner was the archetype of the kind I mean: the compulsive bore, who, against your wish and in however

132

unlikely a fashion, compels your attention – not necessarily with gleaming eye and skinny claw.

Don Pepe was short, portly, thinning, with a fair, freckly complexion suggesting he may once have been a ginger small boy. He wore a greenish-brown suit and was three-quarters drunk. His speech was slurred. He pronounced '*sí*' as '*sair*,' expansively, to rhyme with the English word 'fair'.

'I am not, as you may have assumed, sir, a native of this region,' he said. 'I am Catalán, born in Barcelona in fact, but brought here to Mérida by my parents at the age of eleven. I tell you these things because I wish to be of service and a good Catholic, *sair*.'

The barman and two young customers exchanged winks and gave me a look which indicated that, sorry though they might be for me in my misfortune, I was Don Pepe's chosen victim today for ear-bending, and there was no escape.

'Englishman, you find yourself in a country which, whatever its shortcomings materially, continues to have moral superiority over the rest of the world – certainly over the rest of Europe. This too, señor, I tell you because I wish to be of service. And, of all Spain, it is in this very region of Extremadura that you will find the best of men, the greatest men, the men of most outstanding achievement and moral worth. *Sair*. As an Englishman, of course, you will not have heard of Pizarro and Balboa—'

'Oh, but I have, Don Pepe.'

'Such men went forth from here, conquered the New World, took to that New World the Light of Faith. I tell you these things only from the desire to be a good Catholic. Needless to say, there was civilization here long before your countrymen, señor, had abandoned their primitive and savage ways. *Sair*. Let us begin by considering the Celtiberiáns, the Phoenicians and the Greeks.'

I realized that he intended to give me the history – not so potted, either – of Spain, from earliest times to the present. He had taken a grip of my shirt collar and was looking up at me like a supplicant as he spoke. I nodded to the barman to fill up our glasses, determined that, after I'd heard about the Visigoths and maybe Carthage, I'd go. At once, I regretted this move: for he insisted on paying for the wine; and this gave him the opportunity for a digression on Spanish hospitality

133

and its possible derivation from the time of the Arab occupation. This, in turn, prompted him to say more about himself ('I am a very celebrated local man of business, a rich draper') and about the increasing prosperity of the working-class ('A car at every door, Englishman, *sair*').

I got to the doorway and was through the bead curtain, but he had grabbed me by the waistband: had I tried to continue walking, we should have looked like little boys playing trains.

'I shall show you the way. Wherever you want to go. Whenever you want to go. *Dondequiera, cuandoquiera*.'

'I am going to the *fonda*, Don Pepe,' I said, '*Now*.'

'I fought in the Civil War,' he said. 'I was an officer under Franco. *Sair*. I once stood closer to him than I am to you, Englishman. Like me, the *Generalísimo* was a short man. There couldn't have been more than a centimetre between us. You ask me why I was standing so close to him? You wish to know? Of course you do. Because he was pinning a medal on my chest. *Sair*. I had been wounded, fighting for Spanish traditional values, from the wrist halfway to the elbow. I suffered greatly. Look here.'

He pushed up the cuffs of his jacket and shirt and I saw that he had indeed got a long white scar.

'I tell you such things, show you such things, merely to be of service. I shall show you the way to the Fonda La Mezquita in order to be a good Catholic and a good Spaniard. First, however, I shall show you my *casino* and my *negocio*.'

We were by now standing on the steps of his club: an impressive establishment it looked, plush.

'I couldn't possibly go into a gentleman's club dressed like this, Don Pepe,' I said. 'Look at me, *desgarbado* that I am, in shirtsleeves. You go on. I'll go and get my luggage and find my own way to the *fonda*.'

I fancied I saw him smirk, so feeble had been my attempt to ditch him. It served me right that he should patronize me.

'*No haga caso*. We're very democratic here, oh *sair*.'

The club was palatial. In the bar, while Don Pepe went to relieve himself, I was given a drink and a diatribe about the moral benefits of hard work by a solemn, doltish accountant who had just won a seat in the interest of *Alianza Popular* on the Mérida Municipal Council. Don Pepe returned restored and refreshed.

I tried to be matey. To keep my end up I said, beginning to feel Pooterish, 'In my club we have a billiards room.'

Don Pepe hustled me along a corridor and opened a door to a long billiards hall. It contained several pocketless tables, not one of which was being used. He closed the door, saying nothing. Further along the corridor he opened the padded door to the Chess Room. Several games were in progress, with Staunton sets on beautiful boards of light and dark woods. The players, too absorbed to look up at us, might themselves have been ivory bishops. Don Pepe closed the padded door on them. He gave me a look. Again, nothing was said. It was more than I could stand when, still with nothing being said, I was shown a Reading Room, a Philately Room, a Concert Hall-cum-Theatre and a comfortable and commodious Conversation Room, the *Sala de Tertulias*. We sat down.

'You have everything here, Don Pepe.'

'*Sair*. I show you these things only to be of service and to be a good Catholic. In this room it is expressly forbidden, under club rules, to speak of politics or religion. You met my friend, the newly-elected Councillor?'

'Yes. Did you vote for him?'

'No. I voted for the PSOE.'

I was staggered. Surely a man like Don Pepe, one of Franco's officers, would not have voted for the Spanish Labour Party?

'You surprise me, Don Pepe. I would have imagined you as a member of the *Alianza Popular*.'

'It's the man you vote for, not the party. Gonzáles has done more in five months than anybody else could in five years. The time before, I voted for Suárez, *sair*.'

Don Pepe began to tell me about the growth of Spanish political parties, left, right and centre, since the restoration of the monarchy and the coming of democracy. I was drowsing off. I could have wished to snooze in my armchair. Had I been a resident of Mérida, I thought, I'd have become a member of that *casino* even if it meant having to outwit Don Pepe each time I went there. The annual subscription was about £35.

'Now it's time to go and see my premises,' he said.

On the way, he boasted about how much he was worth. I worked it out at £350,000. He owned property apart from his draper's shop, he said. 'The stones for the aqueducts came

135

from what is now my *finca*. They made their mortar with sand and gravel from the bed of the Guadiana. *Sair*. Sand, gravel and salt from the river.'

What had seemed from the street like a small shop turned out to be cavernous inside. Many hundreds of bolts of fine material were piled high along the extensive shelves.

'I stock everything: from the best silks and velvets, down to the humblest calico like this,' he said. He took down a bolt of plain white cotton cloth, unrolled a metre or so and draped it in front of himself. 'Stones from my *finca*, and mortar from the Guadiana, *Sair*. Tomorrow, Englishman, my daughter will drive us on a tour of the Roman monuments of this, the capital of Lusitania. We shall see the bridge, the theatre, the arena, the patrician villa with its wonderful mosaics, the archaeological museum containing statuary . . .'

'No, no! I won't hear of it, Don Pepe! I've taken up far too much of your time already. Really I have! I wouldn't dream of inconveniencing you or your daughter tomorrow.'

'No inconvenience. It is all arranged with my daughter already. I telephoned from the *casino* while you were in the bar with the new Councillor. Tomorrow is Sunday. I'll be able to give you the whole of my day. There will be no hurry at all. We shall call for you at the *fonda* in the morning at ten o'clock on the dot. *Sair*.'

That evening I met a nice American couple from Washington State, Ruben and Lois López. In Spain to track down the graves of Ruben's forebears, they were on their way to a village north of León. I had salad, trout, woodcock, bread, wine, fruit: a meal a man might have had in Mérida twenty centuries before. They had spaghetti, which they'd been yearning for ever since leaving home. I told them about Don Pepe. Sympathizing, they told me about the truly marvellous Roman monuments they'd felt, well, kind of obliged to visit. Later, after a *copa* in a bar full of bullfighting memorabilia, I traipsed miserably about for a bit. I saw the temple of Diana and the Trajan Arch. I found the Alcazaba shut and felt too tired to walk further than halfway across the bridge. I turned and gazed at Mérida, Emerita Augusta, in the last of the daylight. It looked marvellous. I sensed how the Roman town would for ever be remembered by me as it was in that one second: containing Don Pepe, the poor man's Cicero, draped in a makeshift toga of calico, boring them all rigid at the baths.

136

CHAPTER EIGHT

Nine o'clock next morning I was speeding south on the Seville road. Coffee-time found me in Zafra, an airy place of white-washed walls that boasted an ancient castle with pointed merlons like cogs, now a *parador* named for Hernán Cortés. Before the end of late-morning Mass I was entering Jérez de los Caballeros, home town of yet another *conquistador*, Vasco Núñez de Balboa. Arriving here, you see a statue of him shielding his eyes as he stares into the distance. Having discovered the Pacific, one assumes, now he is looking toward Eldorado – and is soon to have his head chopped off for his trouble. Perhaps he is simply admiring the five highly ornate towers that command the skyline of his birthplace.

Somebody had renamed the Plaza de España in bold chalk letters for a latter-day hero: John Lennon. In the middle of this square, outside the church, old men were walking gravely up and down at a slow, measured tread, arm-in-arm, exactly between imaginary parallel lines. They were waiting for the womenfolk to emerge from the west door. At each end of the parvis they would stop, unlink arms, turn, link arms again and solemnly retrace their steps through invisible slots. They had an air of nobility about them. The Knights Templar, whose town this had been after taking it from the Moors in the thirteenth century, would still feel at home here.

The churches emptied. In the company of strolling family parties I climbed up the castle. This was the best vantage point from which to see those marvellous belfries, much encrusted with strange and glorious decorations of glass mosaic, blue tiles and colourful plasterwork, that dominate the streets of simple white houses. In the castle grounds there were beds of vivid orange flowers not unlike petunias. I asked several people what they were called, but nobody knew. (Spaniards seldom know many names of flowers, wild or cultivated.

137

Unless obviously a rose (*rosa*) or a carnation (*clavel*) any bloom will be dubbed *margarita*, be it a red-hot poker or a lady's-slipper orchid.)

On the way to Oliva de la Frontera I passed a few herds of pigs, nice brown. Dusty brown too were the backs of birds of prey – kites, buzzards and harriers – circling sometimes quite low over the road. In this corner of Extremadura, at the edge of Spain, lush meadows under the cork oaks were being grazed by long-horn cattle, donkeys, goats, horses and sheep. Spotting a hoopoe and some magenta rock roses, I stopped at a place where a spring of purest water oozed from a fissure of rock. A Portuguese station was quietly playing Bach organ music on my car radio. I could have wished for nothing – unless for just one human being with whom to share the scene and the exquisite moment: so much beauty, otherwise, seemed pointless. Grass vistas were sprinkled or strewn, spangled or swathed with remarkable wild flowers: lakes, sometimes rivers, of white, gold, red, purple, as drifts merged or mostly did not.

Coming to the top of a rise, I experienced another of the sudden heart-stopping first glimpses of a human settlement: Alconchel, which comprised two Mount Fuji-shaped knolls, one with a square fort and the other with a more solid bastion and tower. After another twenty kilometres, I came to Olivenza. A Portuguese-looking town, this, spotlessly white and with a lovely avenue of palms. I thought I might stay the night; but there being no chance of getting into my room until the dueño returned some hours later (I was told this by the breathless woman sweeping the bar), reluctantly I continued to Badajoz. There too my heart missed a beat: for I recognized from clips of newsreel film the very spot near the old bullring where Republican soldiers had been gunned down, executed in a spirit of merciless reprisal by Franco's troops.

Badajoz is one of those maddening cities where it's all but impossible to find somewhere handy to park while looking for somewhere central to stay. I settled for a room in a flash new hotel on the wrong side of the Guadiana. The plumbing was eccentric: boiling hot water from the cold tap, no water at all from the hot. I walked across the great bridge back into town, rewarded by a floodlit view of the west gate of the ramparts and, in the centre, by orange trees heavily loaded with fruit. Badajoz is generally disappointing. Despite its fortress and the customary remains of far-off, warring times you find in frontier towns, there was little in the stones and mortar to give the twentieth-century visitor a *frisson* of the past.

In a narrow street a gipsy-looking busker was singing to his guitar during the *paseo*. He noticed a beautiful, probably foreign, blonde girl in a striking purple hat standing in a shop doorway. She affected not be listening to him at all but rather to be looking intently at goods on display in the window. Anybody could tell that she was staring, rapt, at the singer's reflection in the plate-glass. He would blow a blast on a duck call to indicate the end of one song and the beginning of the next. This had a comical effect, coming between one sad love song and another; but the girl was too embarrassed to turn and face the gipsy and laugh as everybody else did. Taking a fancy to her, he struck a minor chord and began improvising a song the meaning of whose words everybody (except the exotic girl of course) could readily understand. It was about a lovely Nordic girl in a purple hat who found herself one summer's evening in a Spanish city, knowing nobody but, being lonely and homesick, yearning for a love affair. In spirit it wasn't unlike a medieval lyric for the lute: funny in the cirumstances, yet sincere and effective.

Back at the hotel I sang for my supper by telling the chef about the gipsy and the girl. Delighted with the yarn, he served me himself with a tender cut of rump steak and a bit of Roncal cheese: a meal I enjoyed all the more on account of an impromptu floor-show. In a corner of the restaurant, two little children played 'Quixote and Dulcinea' – the Spanish version of 'Mothers and Fathers'.

My route next day led past tobacco fields and strips of oats and barley. Along uncultivated stretches of land great, graceful broom shrubs flourished. They were lovely and de!   , about to break into flower. At the verge, tall spikes of f   ..   arched over under their own weight. Then fig orchards and olive groves began. I noticed what was done when an old or diseased olive tree was chopped down: the gnarled old stump was set on fire. After the first brisk flames it smouldered away, dying as it had grown, slowly, collapsing at last into its final ash. One such stump I had passed several days before, miles from anywhere, was still releasing a little of its sweet-smelling smoke.

Of all sub-tropical flora proclaiming that one had crossed the border into Andalusia, the prickly pear, *higuera chumba*, is surely the most memorable. It looks as the word *chumba* sounds to me: comical and clumsy. I'm not given to anthropomorphizing plants; but this one does seem forever to be trying to scramble over dry-stone walls and knocking them down in the attempt. Once over, it falls into even more of a turmoil. Not knowing which way to go next, it tries playing leap-frog over itself in all directions at once. If the mournful grace of olive trees makes you sigh, then prickly pear will make you laugh again. Both belong down in that part of the country.

Transitions are seldom gradual in Spain. At the very line dividing Badajoz province in Extremadura from Huelva in Andalusia, not only did the flora change. On the road, abruptly pot-holed, corrugated and strangely cambered, somebody had just run over a huge lizard. I stopped to examine it. I didn't care to touch it even with the point of my shoe: but did so gingerly and found the flesh still yielding. It was twenty inches long from snout to tail-tip, the size and shape of a young alligator. The head was large, the colours apple-green and greeny-yellow, with a little cerulean blue where back and belly joined. The decoration on its back – whorls and a myriad dots – was like the feather patterns on old-fashioned golfing shoes and Paisley ties. It was a strange beast indeed, compelling close scrutiny; a faintly disturbing one, to be left to the marauding kites.

Not far on the road brought gipsy encampments, the smell of woodsmoke, mountain woods full of the fresh green leaves of chestnuts and poplars, and the songs of many nightingales. I came to the small town of Aracena, white, quiet, elegant: a cool place built in tiers high up in the midst of leafy countryside. Girls on their way home from school were practising on their castanets. From my whitewashed room in an eighteenth-century house I could see, at the hilltop, ruins of the Knights Templar castle. What I wanted to see was far beneath this, deep under the hill's immeasurable tons of rock: the Maravillas caves.

Maravillas means 'marvels', a word travellers are wary of: but justified here. Underground rivers forming the caves have produced an astonishing series of many-shaped formations coloured by oxides of iron and copper in contrast with the pure white of calcite crystal. There is no system in Britain to rival this one in beauty or scale.

The visitor is regaled with few of those fanciful, teeth-grating pieces of whimsy by which, in caverns such as Wookey Hole, amorphous lumps of ordinary stalagmite are claimed to resemble persons, or this thing or that thing. In Aracena, the 'Virgin and Child' formation was unnervingly like a piece of realistic sculpture. The 'Snow Well', the 'Sultana's Bath' and the 'Emerald Lake' were chambers aptly named. It was the proliferation and variety of individual shapes and forms that amazed most. There were folds of drapery, organ pipes, corals and moss; bunches of tobacco leaves hanging to dry; there were piled-up plates of offal – brains and chitterlings, tripe, slidings of liver and kidneys; there were all manner of fungi – gilled mushrooms, *langues de boeuf*; there were oozings of icing sugar, florets of cauliflower and white broccoli; Hindu temple carvings and walls by Gaudí; magical white grottos, their roofs reflected in the clear, still water; and some that looked, in their reflections, like a sierra seen from ten thousand feet up in the sky. One stretch of corridor was gloriously rude, one of Nature's pieces of extravagant pornography; it made the nuns in our party fall about: ever so many big, pallid, circumcised penises hanging limp (if one can say limp of stone) from walls and ceiling – accurate even to the extent of having heads of darker hue than the stems. Throughout, the lighting was tasteful and tactful, bringing out the best of the natural coloration – shades I couldn't remember having seen before, such as a rusty orange tint glowing unearthly through translucent, milky-white crystal, an ethereal blue as of a half-melted snowman, the pheasant-coloured veins of a Tibetan column.

The next day I made an excursion to another, but this time man-made, vast hole in the ground: the Rio Tinto opencast pyrites and copper mines to the south. From the road you can't see the bottom of the crater the company has scraped out. You can only guess how deep it might be from the evidence of terraced roads up which laden trucks (monstrously large, but

141

toys seen from that distance) toil from an unimaginably hot and dusty hell. The countryside here has been despoiled on a scale difficult to be calm about: a landscape less lunar than Martian, so predominant is the colour red. (There are other, unnatural-looking, colours too: chemical greys and blues, a sickly orange, the purple of permanganate of potash.) The river Tinto itself is still, to the west, the healthy, rich red its name suggests; but near the mine and at the bleak-sounding nearby village of La Dehesa there are only pools of dead water: cadaver-skin lilac or off-white poisonous stagnancies where, if you inserted your toe, you'd expect to see the flesh eaten away as in a bath of concentrated acid.

Everywhere around there were deserted houses and abandoned workings and mining gear. Slap in the middle of La Dehesa was a cemetery with old mines up to its very walls. Very few trees – pines and a strange, solitary palm – made a living from the bare surface soil. Even odder than the palm tree was the passing herd of goats that had – as far as I could see – nothing whatever to eat. In the middle of the waste land – a touch of Nottingham, this – somebody had built his loft of homing pigeons. Mesmerized, I watched two immense endless belts at work. One was depositing red spoil, the other, blue. The machinery and trunks must surely have had drivers: but I saw not a living soul. In Nerva, the local mining town, graffiti bore testimony to the unrest existing in the community. We Want Work said one wall, No To Unemployment another. Fuerza Nueva characteristically declared itself (with a fascist knack for wooing workers) on the side of the miners; whose union, on an adjacent stretch of masonry, declared Down With Contractors Responsible For Unemployment in the Mines. Later, back in Aracena, I saw that shares in Explosiva de Rio Tinto had gone up that day from 9.00 to 10.50.

Depressed by ugliness and hopelessness, I treated myself to a goodish, if curate's-egg, dinner. This comprised a cocktel de mariscos no better than the awful 'prawn cocktail' you'd be fobbed off with in Bognor Regis; then a magnificent delicias de solomillo, chunks of prime sirloin bonded with cubes of Manchego cheese so that the dish looked skewered, like a kebab. At an adjacent table, a man with an English undertaker's cough ate an odd meal of chicken soup containing cheese slices, followed by a soft-boiled egg perched on an old-fashioned inkwell.

Much cheered, afterwards I strolled among the acacias and stone benches where couples canoodled. (A quaint word, 'canoodle', but one that needs fetching out of retirement for its suggestion of the bygone kind of flirting and gallantry that still occurs in public places in Andalusia after the lamps are lit.) There was a pick-up game of four-a-side football in progress in the centre of the square. I happened to be in the right position at the right time to collect the tennis ball and execute a nifty pass. The small exertion left me gasping. Evil air I'd breathed at Rio Tinto after the damp air of the Maravillas caves had given me a touch of catarrh. To cut the phlegm, I made a cheap and effective toddy: three fingers of Soberano brandy, a spoon-twist of local honey and the juice of several lemons which, when I bought them in the market, still had twigs and leaves adhering.

I was driving south on the lonely road to Huelva. Having inadvertently left my passport and the car documents in my room, I felt anxious: suppose I met a police road block? Twenty kilometres from Zalamea, stopping for coffee, I was dismayed to discover four *guardias* lounging in the bar. *Guardias* travel in pairs called mockingly and quite without affection, *parejas*, 'married couples'. Through the side window of the inn I saw their car and motorcycles sneakily concealed in a shrubbery. I reconciled myself to interrogation. I'd always been treated by Spanish policemen with the kind of helpfulness and courtesy once associated with the British bobby: but in my experience lounging coppers anywhere are bored coppers, only too anxious to be officious. And when coppers anywhere talk to each other as these were talking, about 'the public', loudly, with undisguised contempt, confidence wanes.

'This old idiot came out of a side road – right, Pepe?'
'Right!'
'A peasant. Load of hay in the back of his van.'
'Right!'
'Not looking left or right.'
'Not looking.'
'We could see he'd been drinking. So we stopped him.'
'Stopped him.'
'He got out—'
'And threw up all over his boots!'

143

'*Hombre!* I ask you! The public are mad!'

'Mad! Tell them about that blonde.'

'Which one?'

'With the big – *you know!*'

'Oh, *her.*'

'No, *him!*'

'That's right! A *trasvestia*. Had us both fooled at first. The public! Mad! All mad, I tell you.'

So they continued, the four of them well aware I was listening. They were delighted with their shared wit, their world weariness and their aloofness from the rest of mankind. The little room in the *venta* felt crammed as a wartime arsenal with their assorted parked weaponry. With the reckless optimism of a new boy in a playground full of bullies, I believed that if I kept my head down and did not speak I might escape their attentions. But when I made for the door I heard:

'Where are you heading for, *señor*?'

It was the one with the pencil moustache and the half-smoked, extinguished Ducado who spoke: the one who had insisted the public were all mad.

'Huelva,' I said. 'Just a day trip. Then I'm coming back to Aracena. I'm staying in Aracena. All my belongings are in Aracena.' I felt as burningly guilty as a drug-pedlar or a gun-runner caught redhanded. 'How's the road between here and Huelva?' I continued, guessing how suspicious my ingratiating smile must appear to him. He surely knew I wasn't carrying any personal identification or documentation – a serious business in Spain. He gave me a hard look.

'Terrible as far as Zalamea. Then it's all right.'

'Thanks. Goodbye, *caballeros*.'

I was halfway through the door, hurrah.

'One moment, *señor*.'

'Yes?'

'A word of warning. There are brigands along this road.' His companions tittered and hissed through their teeth.

'Brigands?'

'Don't worry about a thing. If you're stopped and made to wait – well, one loud bang then it's all over.'

I closed the door, hearing laughter. I drove on thinking harsh thoughts about the desperate archness of constabulary

144

humour. Then, turning a corner in bottom gear on the steeply twisting, rocky road, I found myself suddenly surrounded by a stubbly gang of outlaws in check shirts and broad-belted corduroys. One of them put his face to the windscreen. I had no option but to halt.

I wound down the window an inch.

'What's going on?'

'You can't pass, señor.'

'Of course I can. Let me through.'

'Not yet, señor.'

I lit a cigarette and felt awful. I counted eight of them. They prowled all round my little Fiat, commenting upon its right-hand-drive, its tinted glass, its exotic numberplate. The ringleader then banged on the window and mimed that I should get out. I shook my head. He mimed that I should wind the window down a little more. I did so, another bare inch. He put his mouth to the gap.

'The *caballero* is perhaps a foreigner?'

'Yes.'

'Then it's useless to explain what's going to happen.'

'When?'

'Maybe ten minutes. Why not get out?'

'I'm all right where I am, thanks.'

He shrugged. Three or four of them had a muttered conference across the bonnet. Now and again they looked at me and grinned not unkindly. Now I was glad to have left my documents behind; but how I wished I'd also forgotten to bring my currency and traveller's cheques. I finished my cigarette and was about to light another. But then there was an almighty explosion and the sky ahead, just over the brow, was full of stones and pebbles and dust flying. The Rio Tinto Mining Company of course, dynamiting.

'Now you may pass,' said the brigand chief.

The last few miles to Huelva, I listened to Radio Seville. Like many local radio stations, this one specialized in self-consciously (ie, for the most part bogus) regional culture, with 'poets' and 'musicians' crowding avidly into the studio to say portentous things about the fancied importance of their sense of identity. I endured, with dismay, a new and saccharine pop-song version of Granados' *Noche andaluza, de luna llena*, and was only just in time to switch off before another sub-musical

145

group began to demonstrate what it had done for a poem by Juan Ramón Jiménez.

In Huelva (where Jiménez was born in 1881) genuine Andalusian culture and identity were happily still in good heart. Men in Cordoban hats trundled loads in and out of the bustling fish market. The bars they used for a quick glass had girls wailing snatches of *flamenco* as they shelled peas in the kitchen or tipped buckets of water away in the street. I had a *caná* of dry sherry with a *ración* of fried squid; then walked down to the docks.

It was true: sun, air – the very feel and fragrance of all things here in the far south of Spain – were a special benison indefinably different from the way they were elsewhere. I sought the shade of an avenue of palms; their fronds lightly caressed the crown of my head as I passed under them. On the quayside the *guardias* had a helicopter: in this case pilot and co-pilot made up the customary *pareja*. Juxtaposed with this twentieth-century high-tech was a wonderful, old, ramshackle, over-head railway; partly dismantled where it had once crossed the road, but the rest left to rust and flake away in its own good time. On every side was the smell of fresh and rotting fish and fruit.

A few kilometres away was Punta Umbria, from which the great navigators and *conquistadores* set out on their intrepid adventures westwards. I gazed at it across the water from a beach between Las Antillas and the Isla Cristina. I had stopped along a spoilt, bungaloid stretch of dunes, marram grass and pines, very hot indeed, grateful to wash my face and hands in the refreshful Atlantic. From here, turning inland near the Portuguese frontier, I went first through vineyards and orange and fig groves; then through the kind of desperate, dusty-earth fields that might well have made a man want to sail out in search of somewhere – anywhere – else. On the other, eastern, side of Huelva, the coast road leads past Palos de la Frontera (from where Columbus set sail) towards the Coto Doñana nature reserve. Set within the basin of the Guadalquivir and stretching a good part of the way north-east to Seville, the National Park is the largest wild area left in Western Europe. Wild and untamed it may be a few miles inland, but the coast itself is horribly raped: not quite as horribly as it is eastwards from Estepona, of course, but still colonised and

146

vulgarized beyond redemption. In Matalascañas, a new non-place without identity or character, huge Germans at terrace tables ate and drank hugely and listened to huge brass band music so loud you'd fancy the multitudinous flamingos browsing in the *marismas* would have no option but to flinch as one and take off in a single flock for a quieter place, any place, far away. I rested my eyes contemplating some stunted umbrella pines, trees which, as they age, twist into shapes reminiscent of those impossible stances achieved by girl gymnasts from Romania. These near Torre de la Higuera were rich, cool, green, wonderfully rounded.

A visit to the Coto Doñana ought to be very heaven for naturalists – particularly bird watchers. But I wonder if it is so. Granted, the national park is famed for being the largest area without roads in Western Europe; its swamps, lagoons, cork-oak forests, pinewoods and sand dunes provide splendid habitats for lynx, mongoose, flamingos, eagles, vultures, hawks, falcons, countless migratory woodland birds and waterbirds: but the fauna you find on arriving at the main entrance is daunting. Vast flocks, or swarms, of schoolchildren are having boisterous picnics among the trees, falling further and further from the control of haggard teachers as they wait their turn to be taken by Land Rover or high-sided lorry on the four-hour safari. In the well-appointed reception building you can buy the usual kitsch associated with such places: tea trays and tea towels adorned with transfer pictures of owls and such. There are books to be had on mammals, reptiles, birds, insects, butterflies and trees: but none on wild flowers (reflecting the indifference of Spaniards to the abundance and variety of their flora). Outside, paths marked with rustic poles lead after about a third of a mile to a row of creosote-smelling huts from which you can, by pushing open a trap-door in the wall, observe the birds. All very Peter Scott. Not for me, though; nor, I daresay, for anyone whose delight in nature is essentially a matter of unpremeditated encounter; a pleasure not to be shared with several (let alone many) others; one which cannot be had by intruding upon the privacy, therefore the dignity, of the wild creatures. No: the only alternative to true wilderness is the zoo. This in-between stuff is for checkers-off of names on lists, carriers of photographic paraphernalia, dull experts. They're welcome to it.

Unpremeditated and memorable were three encounters, Nature-with-Man, I had on the way back to Aracena. On a lonely stretch a day's hike from Puebla de Guzmán (in which village I had seen a bar called 'Kunta Kinte'), I turned a corner to see a shepherd whose flock had not quite all crossed the road. I slowed. He threw first stones and then his heavy stick with almighty force at the stragglers to make them hurry. I edged along, said *adiós*, looked into his ancient, staring, suspicious eyes as I passed. I saw him in my driving-mirror as he bent to pick up his stick and shout towards heaven. A few miles further on I stopped for a wan young fellow who needed a lift along the road towards San Telmo. We drove through vast eucalyptus plantations. 'These trees,' he said. 'Look at them. They've not been here long. They are all that will grow. *Look at them*. So many eucalyptus trees. Nothing, nobody, can live here. This is where I get out, señor.' There was a barely discernible track leading into a thicket. I watched him until he was engulfed by trees. He was the saddest-looking man I was ever to see in Spain. Something of his depression stayed with me until, high in the Sierra de Aracena, I stopped for a restful smoke outside a cottage where a man was watering his plot. It was the time of evening when old men and very young girls and boys return with donkeys loaded up with fodder, the lush leaves and grasses of early summer. All round the cottage was a splendid garden of shrub roses and climbing roses, exact lines of onions and broad beans, an orchard of quince, apples, pears and oranges. I got out and expressed my admiration. The man put down his watering-can and nodded, gratified. 'I wish I could grow this in my garden in England,' I said, pointing to a fleshy shrub with carmine flowers, the wild oleander you see everywhere in Andalusia. 'Oh – that,' he said. 'The *adelfa*. It grows uninvited. It hopped over the wall into my *huerta* from the forest one night! But I think it's so beautiful I've decided to let it stay – at least, until I need the space. *Vate con Dios.*'

Before leaving Aracena and the high, cool, westernmost part of the province of Huelva, I went to a most interesting bull-fight: a *novillada* in which nine animals were killed by nine different *toreros*, two of whom, *rejoneadores*, fought on horseback before killing on foot. Unusual though they may be even to aficionados, these small, remote, country-town and

148

village bullfights – seldom seen by tourists and without a prominent place in the literature of tauromachy outside Spain – are of the greatest importance to the art, being the base of a pyramid whose peak is the full-blown *corrida* taking place in Madrid and the great provincial cities. The matadors are mostly promising beginners from the schools of bullfighting, gaining experience. Neither they nor their more seasoned teams (or *cuadrillas*) wear the gorgeous suit of lights customarily associated with their trade; instead they dress in the more sombre garb known as *traje corto* – short black jacket, grey or black trousers and white shirt much as worn by flamenco performers. Also, ordinary cloth caps (in the absence of the broad-brimmed Cordoban hat) are the order of the day: so that, when the participants enter the ring at the start of the evening's proceedings, they look for all the world like a group of traders arriving for a stock fair.

The entrance fee is less than a quarter of what you'd normally pay to see a bullfight – though at 800 pesetas for a seat in the shade, or 600 for one in the sun, certainly not cheap for the average unemployed *andaluz* peasant. Two of the nine *espadas*, Espartaco (Chico) and Campuzano (Chico), were the much younger brothers of famous and distinguished *toreros*. The latter's eldest brother, the much-revered Tomás, was otherwise engaged that day; but another brother, José, accompanied the boy into the ring to act as his servant, steadying him when he vomited from nerves and anxiety, folding his *muleta*, handing him his sword, stage-whispering advice from the *barrerea*, cutting the ears the crowd awarded him, carrying him afterwards with pride and dignity, shoulder-high for his *vuelta*, an already truly courageous, diminutive, veritable chip off the old Campuzano family block. In the ring, grass and thistles grew in vigorous patches; and when the spectacle was over they would continue to grow undisturbed for another year. The little local band played with all their might and main, undismayed by notes sharp or flat or downright false. Farmers and their ladies in from even more rural localities made knowing remarks about the horsemanship displayed in the two bouts of *rejoneo*. One of the riders, having been awarded the trophy of a tail, twirled it round his head and sent it flying like a *bola* to his mother in the crowd: the grisly, bloody, but most acceptable basis of a sticky *olla* next day. From start to finish there was something engagingly old-fashioned about the whole affair and the atmosphere it generated. Despite the tractor used for the *arrastre*, despite the lamentable marching band of red-cloaked and mini-skirted, kazoo-playing, baton-twirling, silver-cardboard-hatted, pre-pubescent girls, it might all have been happening in the time of Goya.

Of the eight provinces of Andalusia, Huelva in the far west is the one least corrupted by outside influences, the one most likely to maintain its integrity. People get on with their lives and pursue old customs unself-consciously. The least *típico*, they are therefore the most typical folk of Andalusia. Every year the great, rugged processions of gaily painted caravans set off to converge upon El Rocío across the Marismas to celebrate at the shrine of the miraculous Virgin of the Dew. The subject of numerous television documentaries and such, the long march of the *romería* is still motivated by compulsions more ancient than the meretricious ones of the media.

Many of the pilgrims to El Rocío come from the Triana district of Seville, on the 'wrong' side of the Guadalquivir, once (but no longer) a predominantly gipsy quarter. Seville is of course the capital of the eponymous province adjacent to Huelva. The Sevillanos have their own Virgin, whose formal title is Nuestra Señora de la Esperanza but who is always called, familiarly yet with due reverence, la Macarena. I had high hopes of seeing her; indeed, of visiting all the well known and well documented tourist attractions. I knew them by heart, so often had I visited the place as an armchair traveller at home with my Michelin Green Guide. I knew where the cathedral was, where the Alcázar, the Giralda, the old tobacco factory, the Bull Ring, the María Luisa Park, the celebrated thoroughfares such as the Sierpes and the exquisitely named Paseo de las Delicias. Seville is one of those cities, like Paris and New York, which you seem to know intimately from films, novels, music and poetry, long before you go there. But the moment I crossed the Triana Bridge I sensed that Seville was about to become a name the very mention of which would henceforth give me the shudders.

Shudders, yet also nervous laughter. My arrival coincided with that of an enormous military convoy which held up all traffic attempting to approach, or leave, the junction of roads on the left bank side of the bridge. Tanks, armoured cars and other sinister, nameless, camouflaged vehicles were wedged nose-to-tail with civilian cars, vans and lorries. The stench of diesel fumes was appalling, as was the roar of engines. A caterpillar track repeatedly glimpsed in my side mirror seemed forever about to crunch my little Fiat: there was a thrumming and a throbbing felt through the very road surface. There was no escape: for in front of me was a huge khaki truck. In front of *that* was one of those small and monstrously noisy three-wheeler delivery pick-ups of which there are mercifully fewer these days. This one had become over-heated and its stalled engine now refused to start, thus holding up three parts of the convoy, the manoeuvres of – who knows? – perhaps a major NATO exercise. *Guardias* and Military Policemen gathered, remonstrated, gesticulated, shouted and bawled above the uproar. The three-wheeler, loaded with cauliflowers, was rocked on its springs. Then the driver got out. He was a vast man, easily twenty-five stone but short. And he had one of those wooden peg-legs, exactly like those of pirates in boys' adventure books, on which to hop an impromptu ballet of frustration and seething anger as his van, shedding many cauli's, was manhandled by the unsmiling, uniformed men to the side of the road.

Seville is bedevilled by a one-way circulatory system which has the unacquainted driver flung centripetally away from where he would like to be. No sooner free from the Spanish Army, I was the victim of merciless squadrons of *taxistas* and other, equally remorseless, indigenous drivers who, without fail, forced me into lanes I did not wish to be in. Each time I saw with relief and joy that I had contrived to head yet again towards the Giralda, some Jehu in a Seat with a defective exhaust pipe would ease me toward yet another suburb of ugly apartments. The word *giralda*, meaning a weather-vane, implies constant turnings round and round according to the caprice of unmanageable forces. Off I shot northwards towards the *barrio* of La Macarena; westwards I was propelled over the river towards Triana. I tried entering again by way of the San Telmo Bridge; then whoosh, I was all but shunted on to the NIV towards Madrid. There was nowhere to stop, not even for a moment. Each time I went this way or that past the cathedral, I remembered the famous sentence reputed to have been uttered by its Chapter in 1401 when the mosque was destroyed. 'Let us build a cathedral so immense that everyone on beholding it will take us for madmen.' I could only suppose that a similar sentiment was held about their ghastly blue-print by later City Fathers responsible for the one-way system regulating Seville's traffic. I shed all pleasantly romantic thoughts about the place, remembering the horror stories I had heard about the growing problems here of muggings, robberies and violent attacks upon tourists. My right-hand drive car, with its English *matriculacíon* and its cargo of luggage, was all too valuable. One day, I thought, I'd come back by plane or train. Meanwhile, the crazy carousel having cast me this time southwards, I let myself be swirled like the city's waste down the road towards Cádiz.

But the day's troubles had scarcely begun. Most of them still lay in wait for me in Utrera.

I thought it might be an ideal place to stop: a medium-size town with some Roman remains worth looking at. However, it seemed at first that Utrera possessed no hotels. I tracked down a *casa de huespedes*; but I guessed the establishment would probably provide only cold water, oblige me to eat in and offer rates disadvantageous to one requiring only an overnight stay. I wandered about, tired, wretched, self-pitying, pining for the luxury of a hot bath and somewhere to relax as I wished. I had a pleasant surprise by coming across a school of flamenco dancing through whose open windows I was able to listen and watch for a few minutes without seeming to be intrusively nosy. The room was packed with children about ten years old accompanied by their mothers. The girls wore traditional Andalusian gipsy dresses, long and layered, white and polka-dotted; their hair was beautifully dressed and they all wore earrings and make-up. The instructor, a dark, thin, knife-fighting type in his thirties, put a tape of *sevillanas* on his cassette player and began shouting instructions as the miniature couples began to gyrate with graceful arms aloft like underwater seaweed. At any other time I would have wished to remain at that window for a long while: but I was weary and needed somewhere to hang my hat. 'We're not well off for accommodation here,' the traffic warden said. 'Nobody ever comes here, you see.' But then he told me about a road house the other side of the railway line.

Every traveller's instinct told me that I was in for a hard time. I should, no matter how exhausted, have continued towards Jerez. But what I did was to drive to the *venta*, carry my bags into a loud and unattractively scruffy bar and begin the first of several mutually hostile confrontations with the waiter.

The *camarero* was rushed off his feet, attending to a vociferous crowd of thirsty home-goers from work: but not too rushed to be incapable of favouring me with a prolonged glare of purest disdain. I asked if there was a vacant room. He went out to a back room to enquire. He returned, but ignoring me, continued to serve even uninsistent drinkers. 'Well?' I said. 'Yes,' he said, 'there is a room.' He poured another round of *cañas*. 'How much?' I said. 'Fifteen hundred,' he said. The place was a dump: not even mentioned in the *Guía de Hoteles* (the official publication of the *Dirección General de Empresas y Actividades Turísticas*, which lists pretty well every habitable hirable room in Spain), let alone in the red Michelin. For fifteen hundred, in those days, you could get a comfortable double room with *baño completo* in a well-appointed, two-star hotel or three-star *hostal*. I knew, somewhere beyond the pain of headache and the giddiness of exhaustion, that I was being ripped off. 'I'll take it,' I heard myself say. A key on a ring with a bendy cardboard fob was thrown on to the counter. I saw my passport being placed on a shelf of dusty old lottery tickets, within casual reach of anyone sitting at the bar. I wrestled my bags up some urine-scented steps.

The hotel industry in Spain is stringently controlled by the Secretary of State for Tourism. On every bedroom door there ought to be found a notice in three, sometimes four, languages plainly stating the Ministry's sanctioned price for the room in the high, middle and low seasons. My bedroom door was innocent of such a notice. I turned on the red tap to run myself a bath. While waiting, I discovered that the loo was dirty; that there was no glass except for a cracked, cloudy-plastic thing; that there was no bung for the washbasin; that there was no ashtray; that the sheets had not been ironed (indeed, to judge by some faint lipstick smears, they had probably not been changed since the former, very likely fleeting, occupants left); and – almost the worst indictment I can make of any hotel room – the pillows were not only encased in turquoise nylon but were stuffed with that rebarbative, orangey, shredded sponge-foam material, several bits of which now readily spilled out into my hand like entrails from a Taiwanese teddy-bear. Checking my bath water, I discovered the red tap was running stone-cold. I had a cold bath, and it *was* cold.

In situations such as this – when I am tired, frustrated, feeling I'm being put upon – I transmogrify into Mr Pooter with the magical ease of Clark Kent turning into Superman. My sense of humour deserts me, as does my sense of the ridiculous. Riding a fast high horse down the piss-stinking staircase, I dismounted and stood upon my dignity at the counter. The *camarero* listened with contempt as I began shouting a catalogue of dissatisfactions. I asked for, but was not given, an *hoja de reclamación*, the official complaints form which by law should be available on demand to hotel and restaurant clients. When I had done, he told me with infuriating calmness that despite my assertion to the contrary, there was, indeed, hot water. I followed him upstairs. He entered the bathroom. Hot water, and it *was* hot, poured, abundant and steaming, from – the blue tap . . .

A minor but recurring frailty of mine is a capacity thus to lose winning games by a single, maverick point. I ought to have the common sense to towel down at once, pack my racquet and shuffle off court. Instead, perversely I insist upon serving for another set: which for certain will contain a humiliating final rally. So, downstairs again after a warmish bath (most of the hot water having being wasted during the demonstration), I asked for a *fino* and, smiling in a conciliatory manner, offered drinks to the *camarero* and his newly-arrived colleague. The offer was refused: love-fifteen. I left a sizeable tip for the communal *bote* which could not but be accepted: fifteen-all. On the offensive once more, I wagged a finger and pointed out that I wasn't your ordinary tourist but was in Spain to do a job of work: thirty-fifteen; that I was, in fact, an ordinary working bloke like them: forty-fifteen. I'd cracked it! I had a passable dinner in the *comedor* of soup, salad, a bit of pork steak and some good bread and wine. Then, after several slugs from my travelling Soberano bottle (in one of two replacement plastic glasses I found on the bathroom shelf), I fought for a while with the awful pillow and eventually fell asleep.

In the morning, not even contemplating having breakfast in the *venta*, I paid my bill, which, for room and dinner, was fifty pesetas less than the fifteen hundred originally quoted for the room alone. They had obviously capitulated, fearful that I might go and report them: if not to the Ministry of Tourism then at least to the *alcalde* of Utrera.

I felt much better. Having deservedly won the match hands down, I was in a sunny, magnanimous mood. Had this indeed been a game of tennis, I would have spritely leapt the net, shaken hands with my (however unsporting) opponent and tapped the umpire on the knee. Cheerfully I drove away, enjoying the petty malice of having 'forgotten' to leave my room key. And I had covered several kilometres before I noticed (game, set, match and championship to them) that, during the night, my off-side wing mirror had been wrenched, presumably with considerable strength and violence, off.

What infuriated me about this episode was that such an experience, rare in this usually courteous and obliging country, could have been avoided had I acted more circumspectly.

Not that I could have done much to dispel the generalized anti-British feeling I heard expressed in the *venta* bar and, on occasion, elsewhere. Spanish emotions were still unsettled then by the conduct and outcome of the Falklands War. And I could understand only too well the strength of feeling against Mrs Thatcher and her ignominious little campaign; my own sympathies could be summed up in two words: *Malvinas argentinas*. Being a Briton, I had to take a share of my country's *mala fama*; but fair enough, I concluded, if all I had to suffer on that account was the loss of the odd wing mirror.

By the time I reached Jerez de la Frontera, my anger had partly abated. The town, with handsome avenues of rustling palms for the thoroughfare of countless elegantly groomed horses, was both a sight for sore eyes and a balm for ruffled nerves. At the outskirts, the huge *bodegas* of Domecq, Harvey, Terry and Humbert looked less like repositories of fortified wine than hangars for fleets of Jumbo jets. A heady scent lay on the air, and warmth poured down like a soothing lotion upon the skin: Andalusian sunlight being to English sunlight as *oloroso* is to flat mild ale. The influence of England – of

155

old Anglo-Hispanic families of vintners and merchant shippers, of England's traditional and unquenchable taste for sherry – is immediately and most powerfully sensed, and, in this instance at least, it is an influence entirely benign and desirable, of equal mutual benefit to our two countries.

Shortly after, I saw lovely, ancient Cádiz ablaze in whiteness on a long rock ledge across the bay. A grand, bastioned city, Cádiz has existed as a trading centre for three millennia. First it was in the hands of the Phoenicians, then of the Carthaginians, then of the Romans, then of the Visigoths, then of the Moors. You look at Cádiz and see, from the gaunt stone of its upper ramparts down to the brightly-coloured plastic pavilions along its holiday beaches, an encapsulation of Spain's long history and of her changing relationship with the outside world; of exploration and exploitation, rise and fall, fame and infamy, prosperity and ruin. Here, English influence has been of a different kind from that in Jerez. First it was baleful and bloody: Sir Francis Drake set fire to Philip II's Armada anchored in the harbour four centuries ago. Subsequent English adventurers made repeated attacks. English naval power, for many years, brought nothing but bad to Cádiz. On the other hand, Nelson was to blockade the harbour in 1800 and overcome Napoleon off Trafalgar, a few miles down the coast, in 1805. Looking down on Cabo Trafalgar through thin sea-fret from a lofty perch in Vejer, I felt glad, proud even, that our great admiral and the Duke of Wellington did what they did in Spanish waters and on Spanish territory to rid Europe of a tyrant. Had I been a Spaniard in those early years of the nineteenth century, I think I could have been grateful to certain Englishmen: Napoleon needed ousting. But after rounding the Point of Tarifa, where Atlantic and Mediterranean meet and you catch your first glimpse of Gibraltar, it's easy to sense and sympathize with the slow-burning rancour the Spanish nation feels about the continuing British proprietorship of the Rock – particularly since the establishment of NATO and the demonstrable strategic unimportance in the nuclear age of control of the Straits. I gazed across the marvellous Bay of Algeciras at Gibraltar. Wild horses wouldn't have dragged me there. I imagined the bored and boorish servicemen and their terrible wives I'd encountered on leave in England, for whom 'Gib' meant little more than duty-free fags and booze, red pillar-boxes and swarthy local men sweating in British bobbies' helmets. Before long, oh dear, there would be similar types on leave from Fortress Falklands. I thought of the sinking of the Belgrano; remembered with a sigh what D. H. Lawrence had felt after needlessly throwing a stone at the snake by his water-trough – a pettiness.

CHAPTER NINE

Touts clamour round in Algeciras, trying to sell you tickets for the hydrofoil crossing to Africa. Not a few of their clients are reputedly transsexuals *en route* to Tangier for the operation to have their penises off: well, I wouldn't know.

Beyond San Roque and La Línea the Costa del Sol begins with the first heavy crop of bungalows, chalets and villas: not all that bad but a clear intimation of worse to come. Then Estepona; and, after Estepona, the various egregious developments, horrors and excrescences, of Marbella, Fuengirola, and Torremolinos before the next actual place, Málaga.

Estepona could be worse than it is: before long, no doubt it will be. Within an hour of arriving I was short-changed and over-charged; but I found agreeable chums in my hotel *conserje* and his three-legged dog. In the Civil War the man had fought with the Republicans, right up to the end, in Cartagena; all he did now, all day long, was read history books and hand out keys. The town – that part lying back from the promenade – still has some residual identity and integrity as, say, Hastings does; and it is almost as dull. On the front there's a good copper-bronze statue of two fishermen. They have their back to the sea – as if to symbolize the natives' rejection of their traditional calling in favour of the infinitely more lucrative one of catering to the holiday-maker. They turn their eyes northwards, skywards, towards the hills: whence cometh, in aircraft from Luton and Gatwick, their salvation. The only fishing I saw was some desultory rod-casting from the mole: a trio of blokes from Dagenham hauling in wads of weed, as they might just as effectively have done from the harbour arm in Shoreham-by-Sea. The beach did not look inviting. The sand was a curious dark grey. Bulldozing was in progress; a quantity of large asbestos pipes lay about, flaking and crumbling to killer dust. Flaking and crumbling too were

158

the droves of English and German pensioners in the seafront cafés. It might have been Torquay in the Thirties, genteel old folk taking scones and tea at five in the afternoon. This was nice, endearing, apt. But there were grotesque visions, too: a pair of antique ladies in bathing costumes walking from the beach, their wrecked bodies like tortured creatures by Goya, with pitted, gouged and marbled skin, varicose veins and unthinkable, nameless sagging bits slackly swinging between chest and navel each step they took; and a fat crone (Belgian: she had a flag sewn on her Bermuda shorts), dead drunk at breakfast-time and sprawling across a bed of pelargoniums, her pink shoulders and chest all a-bubble with heat blisters.

The resorts differ startlingly from each other. After staid, lumpen, bourgeois Estepona you come to snooty, exclusive Marbella: thousands of residences and *louche* private clubs half-hidden by pines and prowled by Dobermans which would tear off your arm as soon as look at you. Money, much of it (as is common knowledge) criminally or sub-criminally come by, reeks in Marbella. Its vulgarity of ostentation, not to mention of taste, is far, far more offensive than that of cheap-and-cheerful Torremolinos. In Torry at least they make no bones about having a raucous good time, with plenty of grub, booze and a fresh bit of the other each night: save up for a year, blow it all in a fortnight, don't begrudge the next man his laughs, live and let live. In Marbella the fat cats parade their wealth by means, paradoxically, of semi-concealment, epitomized by the Merc with the black-tinted windows. It gets to be known that a round of golf here will set you back £75. There's a sense of quiet pride among the denizens when word goes round that a wanted thug whose stock in trade is the sawn-off shotgun is about to buy a vacant plot.

Fuengirola is a kind of cross between Marbella and Torremolinos. Enormous slabs of concrete stand cheek-by jowl the length of the front: but there are many private apartment blocks among the package-deal hotels. The holiday visitor here sees nothing more of Spain than a few metres of beach and some asphalt. The curved bay, lined by so many high-rise buildings, precludes glimpses of the hinterland. In its way, Fuengirola is quite smart: not with the *chic* of a Riviera town to be sure, but it certainly has more style than the depressed, down-at-heel seaside towns of Britain. Here and in Torremolinos nothing of a real town need visibly exist save that which serves the short-stay resident. You'd be hard pressed to find a shop to sell you a tube of Vim or a reel of cotton; commerce is geared to the tourist trade between the fringe of the sea and the hotel foyer. The beaches are funny, regulated, totalitarian. Everybody lies on regimented rows of mattresses under awnings admitting dappled sunlight. Pathetic little lubricious men, their feet burning on the blisteringly hot sand, hop about on the sly to inspect the multitudinous bare bosoms. The latter rather make one laugh, in bulk quantity rapidly losing their titillation quotient and becoming (at any rate, to the artist's eye) images variously of pieces of fruit, earphones, desk bells, distant domes, slip cushions, drawer handles or what you will. Too many ageing, undelectable and flabby-floppy women bare themselves on the Costa del Sol beaches; and pleasant though it undeniably is, erotically and aesthetically, to gaze now and then at the naked breasts of firm young women, one is, if with a reluctant sigh, glad that the truly desirable and nubile ones are as often as not those who keep themselves partially covered.

What most depresses the spirit along this stretch of coast is not urban, so much as suburban, growth. Where between towns there are not already flats, hotels, villas, apartments and such then there are hoardings in Spanish, English, German and French advertising them: for sale, for rent, for time sharing; parcels of land, land already built upon, land partially developed. Here and there you might pass a remnant of a field still in the hands of a peasant farmer who has either stubbornly refused to sell up or who is cannily waiting for land values to rise even further before making his killing. So you'll see a few straggly tomato vines growing up wigwams of canes (as runner beans do in Worcestershire) surrealistically among the swanky chalets. A pair of oxen wearing woolly hats like tea-cosies will lumber along pulling a plough beside a brand-new tennis court. Irrelevant dry rivers carry their drought down to the sea.

My front numberplate got broken in a car-wash in Torre-molinos. I sought advice from a traffic *guardia*. He wrote down the address of a firm that would fix me up. The pro-forma he used was couched in the kind of formal language that might have been used when giving instructions to travellers three centuries ago, ending with the desire of the Chief Constable of the province that God grant me many years of life. This was more my Spain. I drove through Málaga, then past a series of Moorish towers that reminded me of the Martello towers along the southern coast of Kent. I had a meal of six broiled sardines and a half-bottle of dry sherry in a smoky beach *merendero* near Torre del Mar, where most of the customers were local people not British. Heading gratefully inland, I thought hard thoughts about my fellow-countrymen abroad: how lacking in style, dignity and grace compared with Spaniards; how ungainly, clumsy and frumpish; how frequently they abused their spoiled children; how overwhelmingly superior they considered themselves; how indisputably right they thought they were about Gibraltar and the Falklands.

After a short distance I came to flocks of sheep and goats, to white villages and hamlets; to lovely mountain scenery with broom in sublime golden flower; to wayside oleanders and fields of ripening barley. At Colmenar I hoped to find a *fonda*: but there was none. Instead, before continuing to Antequera, I had a coffee in a bar full of old chaps playing dice and dominoes. There was a *porrón* of wine on the counter, seemingly for anyone's free use. It took a long while and many shouts before deaf old María could be persuaded to come and take my money.

One of the great pleasures of wandering in Spain is that of arriving, as I now did at the end of May, in a small town, Antequera, about to begin its *fiesta* or *feria*. 'Come back in August,' people said. 'The summer fair's much more impressive. This spring one's more for the *peques*.' The local paper confirmed this: the week's programme, published by decree of the *alcalde*, was crammed with juvenile tournaments and competitions in tennis, table-tennis, athletics, football, basketball, handball, go-karting, volleyball, chess, karate, cycling, shooting, painting, and aeromodelling. On the Wednesday there was to be a bullfight, a *novillada* with picadors; and all week long the live-stock market would be in progress on the grounds next to the Capuchinos Esplanade. There was also to be held, on the last evening, the finals of a *cante flamenco* contest sponsored by the Savings Bank. The largest pre-fair advertisement carried by the newspaper was one placed by the Holy Cross department store, for 'exclusive dresses and elegant suits'; it was addressed to *novias* and *novios*, sweethearts and lovers. The second largest had been placed by a certain Doctor Juan Luís Rigual Pueyo; it informed not only youngsters in love but the public at large that he specialized in treating obesity.

I took a room at the edge of town, no distance from some cyclopean prehistoric dolmens and looked towards El Torcal, the strange-shaped mountain which, with its bizarre rock chaos, dominated this part of the province of Málaga. Along the road came a great flock of unattended goats. Opposite was a kind of upper footpath leading past first-floor windows. Purposefully the goats followed their leader up the stairs from the street. I watched them stream along and disappear along the route which no doubt generation upon generation of their ancestors had taken before them. Soon after the goats had gone, a procession of mothers and daughters began coming along the same path, as no doubt generation upon generation of their ancestors had done too. In long, flouncing polka-dot dresses, their hair piled high and adorned with combs and flowers, they were making their way to the fairground at the top of town. And after a dinner of three slabs of pork *a la plancha* – and not without a fleeting recollection of Dr Pueyo's advertisement – that's where, as it was getting dark, I went too.

I've always loved fairs. This one had the usual rides, including a ghost train, *tren de fantasmas*, at one opening of which two men with cushion-ended sticks buffeted the riders as they came round and round. I went on the Ferris wheel for an owl's-eye view of the dazzlingly-lit stalls selling chunks of coconut, fresh-fried potato crisps, *chocolate con churros* and dozens of varieties of sweets: hard nougat and licorice, toffee brittle, sugar almonds, soft *turrón* from Jijona. Beautiful young and very young women, now united with their fathers and brothers, moved like *tableaux vivants* or animated bouquets between marquee and marquee, pavilion and pavilion. All was pleasant, good-natured fun, without so much as a hint of the rowdiness and latent violence one sometimes senses at English fairs.

The sound of guitars playing a *sevillana*, that most thrilling of all dance music, drew me to the largest marquee. Inside I found a long bar and, at each end, a raised wooden stage

162

on which couples of all ages were dancing. The girls in their layered dresses claimed the eye first, of course; but then one noticed the grace, fervour and commitment with which the dance was being performed by middle-aged and older people – plump folk not necessarily even in best Sunday clothes, let alone traditional *andaluz* costume. A fellow who, in jeans and yellow working shirt, partnered his skinny, worn wife, was in my view the champion of the evening. The stylized movements of his feet, the expressiveness of his arms (upraised, on the chest or behind his waist), the sinuosity of his fingers, his short bursts of heel-drumming or *taconeo*, were all done with such bravura that I wanted, again and again, to applaud. The *sevillana* is a narrative dance telling a story of two lovers meeting, their initial attraction, their flirtation, their courtship, their growing desire and passion. The couple never quite touch; yet seem to be held close and all but touching by an invisible rope. They share a dramatic tension of restraint and unrestraint. The entire sequence, stage after stage of a never-changing tale unfolding between briefest intervals of linking guitar and *cante hondo*, is charged with the frankest sexuality but enacted with the propriety of ritual: movements of hip and thigh; downward or sideways glances; the advancing and withdrawing steps; the striking of attitudes as the woman first beckons and then repulses her man; the grimaces of pain or feigned distaste before the sudden, final, flashing smile of pleasure as the final chord is struck and the dance is over.

Staying in my *hostal* was an Italian ex-army officer, tall, thin, in his seventies. I had shared a table with him at dinner. He had fought in the Civil War near Antequera and now, nearly half a century on, was making a nostalgic tour of the battle fields. 'Which side were you on?' I asked him. 'The correct side,' he said. At the *feria* he bustled about with his movie camera, chivvying, uttering peremptory orders, making territorial claims to the best vantage points from which to film. When the children's *sevillana* competition began, he tried to order me off my chair. I stayed put. The music started up. Five-year-old tots and wisps took the stage and raised their arms. 'The correct side,' I remembered him saying. 'Yes, I was a captain. And I had three men shot near here. For insubordination.'

The *novillada* proved worth seeing, not worth paying to see. The following day I stood alone in the middle of the elegant *plaza de toros* in Ronda where throughout the eighteenth century the Romeros – father, son and grandson – devised and developed the rules of modern bullfighting. The ring, though compact and intimate, was an enormous expanse to share with a bull; but with an involuntary shudder once again I perfectly understood why a young man would want to do such a foolhardy thing for a living.

Ronda is altogether a thrilling place to be: not even the coachloads of gawpers up for the day from the coast can detract from the effects of gazing over the parapet of the Puente Nuevo, far down into the *tajo* or ravine dividing one half of the town from the other. The *frisson* of imagining war prisoners and criminals being hurled into that rocky chasm! Intimations of sudden, plunging death can be ghoulishly enjoyed, too, at the Chorro gorges, halfway between Ronda and Antequera. Here there is a sheer cliff 1,300 feet high where the river has sliced through limestone with the apparent ease of a wire through cheese. Anyone with the stomach and the head for it can follow the so called King's Path, *El Camino del Rey*, to the vertiginous very centre of the gorge and imagine what it would be like to do the journey (as a king reputedly once did) on horseback.

I drove back towards the southernmost tip of Europe through the Serranía de Ronda. The terrain, much pitted and eroded and littered with stones and rocks, has often the air of having been laid waste by armies of vengeful giants. You scarcely believe that there are human habitations not far way, so deserted and desolate does it feel. A jacaranda in glorious full blue flower or a stray pomegranate in carmine blossom will betray a *cortijo*, a farmhouse; a grove of lemon trees on a precipitous slope announces a huddlement of labourers' huts: you relish a moment's reassurance before the next long and lonelier stretch.

By unfrequented roads I came down from those bleak heights and found that, the sea-fret having for once lifted, I could see the mountains behind the Barbary coast of Africa. Time falls away when you gaze across water at another continent. Now I was in not Spain but Biblical Tarshish, not Andalusia but Moorish *al-Andalus*. The name of Tarifa, that white, African-looking town in the province of Cádiz, denoted no longer an import tax, tariff, but a cape: Trafalgar, since earliest memory that most English of names, of course means Cape of the Cave, *Tarif-al-Ghar*. Here, east and west meets; sailors – ancient navigators on their way to the New World or contemporary sail-boarders bent on pleasure – named the wind from the rising sun *levante* and the wind from the setting sun *poniente*.

I headed inland again: past rocky steppes overrun by prickly pear and aloes, and prairies of sunflowers, veldts of thin pasture where longhorn cattle nibbled round patches of crimson vetch. Arcos de la Frontera, on an amazingly dramatic rock spike and all but circled by the Guadalete River far below, was a tourist-free version of Ronda. A bright-eyed, grimy little boy, about ten years old, began to spout historical facts about the town at me the moment I got out of the car. He might have been an urchin from the alleys of Marrakesh. He would not desist. On and on he went, non-stop, parrot-fashion, until I gave him a handful of change to go away. But after five minutes he came back with an ice-cream. When he had finished it he spouted on, only to leave when I said he had told me more about Arcos than anyone could wish to know. 'In that case, *señor*,' he said gravely, 'so long as you know, in addition to all else I have told you, that the west façade of Santa María is a fine example of the Plateresque, you are left with no option but to move on and learn about somewhere else.'

Carmona lies between Sevilla and Écija, the two hottest cities in Spain. To reach it I had to pass once again through Utrera, where I would more willingly have lain all night in the gutter with the mangiest pariah dogs then go back to the blighted *venta*.

On its isolated height, Carmona is first glimpsed from a great distance. For a long while I drove across baking vastnesses of cereal plains without seeming to get nearer. At last I reached the city walls, entered by the Moorish gateway, climbed as far as I could go. The road culminated at the courtyard of the *parador nacional* Alcázar del Rey don Pedro, a wonderfully appointed four-star hotel now occupying the site of one of three Arab fortresses the town once possessed. King Pedro the First who built it as his sumptuous palace no doubt earned his nickname 'the Cruel' in his lifetime; but he earns the gratitude of every tired, dusty latter-day traveller arriving during the raging heat of early evening to find a room available in this blessed oasis.

I have stayed in not a few *paradores*. Each has been comfortable, excellent value for money; some, however – for all their splendid architecture and décor – have been oddly lacking in individual character: the deadening hand of state-controlled uniformity does as much as Hilton or Trust House Forte to disperse whatever is unique or idiosyncratic for the sake of some flavourless house-style. This is not the case in Carmona. It is worth the price of a double room (roughly half the price of a bland box in a British three-star) if only for the chance, after bathing away the rigours of a long day of Andalusian frying-pan heat, to nurse a long drink in the arcaded patio. Here, as if for the first time in one's life, one learns what coolness is. The *toldo*, or awning, is drawn across the inner space at first-floor height to make a deep and welcome shade; the central fountain is playing and its water tumbles refreshfully back into its ample basin; the potted palms and ferns and ivies and succulents have dark-green leaves that look moist and shining; the blue and white *azulejos*, the stone pillars, the black, wrought-ironwork furniture and sconces – all are inviting surfaces to touch or think of touching: entering that patio is like splashing in the watercress shallows of a chalk stream.

Then, as the fiercest heat abates a little, you venture outside once more to gaze across the enormous plains you have crossed to get here. This is one of the great sights of Spain: flat expanses of wheat broken by patches of verdure, the puny roads straight and white and soft-edged as newly-made vapour trails left by aircraft. You feel as lordly as Scipio must have felt when, two centuries before Christ, he overcame the armies of both Hasdrubal the Carthaginian and Massinissa the Numidian under the wall on which you stand. And when the light fades and you become part of the city's silhouette of domes, ramparts, spires and towers, then – and not before – you go and dine on gazpacho and roast lamb in the great vaulted hall. Tomorrow, strengthened as much by the stunning vista as by a robust dinner, you will feel up to spending a grisly hour among the cypresses of the Roman Necropolis before moving on.

*   *   *

As a boy in the sixth form, I read a play by Lope de Vega called *Fuenteovejuna* in a delicious miniature volume, Cambridge-blue-bound and printed on rice-paper. (There were three other Lope plays in the postage-stamp size book; such economy of space inclined me towards believing that the dramatist had indeed composed 1,500 *comedias*, as some literary historians claimed.) In the far north of the province of Córdoba I found myself entering the little town – scarcely more than an overgrown village – of Fuente Ovejuna at the busy midday hour when the streets are full of cooking smells and the shutters rattle down and the yellow school bus brings the children home. In the play, all the citizens conspire to assassinate the tyrannical *Comendador* of Calatrava. The prosecuting judge, in an attempt to discover the name of the murderer, has many of the inhabitants tortured; but each interrogation follows the same pattern:

'Who killed the Knight Commander?'
'Fuenteovejuna, my Lord.'
'And who is Fuenteovejuna?'
'Everybody, one and all.'

The place was workaday; scruffy at the outskirts, homely and with comfortable, shady corners within; and with ample evidence that 'one and all' had at least the bare necessities of life. Further along the N432, however, you come to harsher and much more uncompromising settlements: Peñarroya, full of deserted works buildings and several tall, gloomy, industrial chimneys dangerously dilapidated amidst scrubby fields; and open-cast mining villages like San Antonio, where the land has been violated, exhausted, left to lie bleeding. Much has been angrily said and written about the poverty of agricultural labourers in Andalusia – and rightly, for generations of absentee landlords have treated them abominably down the centuries. But the plight of miners and factory hands, when the earth is spent of mineral resources and they and their places of work are abruptly abandoned, seems all the more poignant. You can hold body and soul together where stuff will grow and wild creatures can pick a living: but you can't eat the spillage of waste tips or drink rusty and chemically poisoned water. You could well imagine a small community of pitmen hereabouts in their despair collectively deciding to murder their ex-employer just as Fuenteovejuna did their unfeeling *Comendador*. This is still a country of volatile passions, where just such an outcome seems ever possible.

What the people of Córdoba had just done, seeking to ease *their* situation, was to elect a communist mayor and council. All over the city there were large posters depicting the new *alcalde* calling upon his citizens to work hard and play hard. It's an exhilarating place, Córdoba: a modern, forward-looking provincial capital of the new, democratic Spain which has also been in its time a Roman capital (of Baetica) and the seat of the mighty Caliphate during seven centuries of Moorish occupation before the Christian reconquest. For a long while, too, the city had a thriving Jewish community. In the quarter still known as the *Judería* (though the Jews were shamefully expelled from Spain nearly five hundred years ago), there still survives, near a good, seated statue of the philosopher Maimonides, a fourteenth-century synagogue; a simple, plain, wholesome, profoundly moving building: endearingly small, not used for worship, yet generating no less of an atmosphere of holiness than either the sumptuously golden sacred *mihrab* at the heart of Córdoba's celebrated mosque or the holy of holies of any richly-endowed church anywhere in Spain.

You sense here in Córdoba the inevitable excitement generated whenever wildly differing cultures meet head-on. They won't necessarily mix (much better, in fact, if they don't), but, flint struck against flint, they strike sparks off each other and briefly illuminate the darkness of barbarity. Walk towards the town over the traffic-tormented Roman bridge; pause by the vast Arab waterwheels and the ruined mills before entering, via the courtyard of orange-trees, the Mezquita; then, in that ineffably beautiful, infinite forest of slender trunks bearing a red and white canopy of round arches, discover – delightful absurdity – a Christian cathedral slap-bang in the centre! For once in one's travels the word 'unique' is accurate; you are, as rarely before, overwhelmingly grateful simply to share in the human condition, humbly thankful merely to be where you are and to have the privilege of seeing something wonderful while it endures. A visit here, whatever one's faith, is in itself a purification and a lifting-up of the heart. Latent in the subdued light is enlightenment; and in the juxtaposition of mosque and Christian fane (the former built partly with columns from even older, pagan, edifices) and in the fact that these stand cheek by jowl with a miraculously surviving synagogue, there is a wise parable.

More antediluvian even than these marvels, the Guadalquivir passes between the blunt cutwaters of the bridge: a river hostile, as inland as this, to vessels except those of shallowest draught. It has fallen from the high sierra and threaded the great ranches and forests; now it will flow through *campiña*, country of tilled fields, wheat plains and orchards. Just above the bridge, little islands have arisen from the siltings, colonized by scrub and small trees giving the strongest impression of a scene ever the same yet always ever so slightly changing, as running water itself is. It is a good place to rest the eyes as you lean against a balustrade in the failing light: so might Roman Seneca have done; and Averroës in the twelfth century, his mind upon Aristotle; and so might the poet Góngora, half a millennium later, as he composed his intricate, baroque verses.

I stayed in a *cortijo* in the suburb of El Brillante, north of the railway line. The inner patio was enclosed by walls and flights of steps and balconies dazzlingly whitewashed and enchantingly decorated with flowers in hanging pots and baskets, this kind of gardening being perhaps above all other arts and crafts – even above bullfighting, tooled leatherwork and silver filigree – what the *Cordobés* has a natural flair for. Like any craft, this one demands much knowledge and technique; like any art, it demands taste, a sense of proportion, an eye for form, colour, mass, composition and – perhaps most importantly – restraint; and it has to be regretfully admitted that, among the patio gardeners of Córdoba, this last quality is sometimes found wanting. (This said, I'd add that over-exuberance is one of the better faults of certain artists.) The patios of Córdoba, were there no other attractions in the city, would themselves bring visitors from afar. With artless negligence, handsome front doors are left half-open along the narrow alleys of the old quarter; nobody minds if you step just inside to admire. Some of the patios are noble, patrician, symmetrical, graced with statuary and a richness of tiles and hand-painted pottery; others are humble, in the peasant taste, wayward, capricious, with terra-cotta pots and crude plaques in primary colours and a sticky glaze depicting Virgin and Child. Many have vaulted arcades, most contrive to blend sunlight and shadow, all have in common their flora and some

169

source of water. It was the Moors' genius for bringing water to where no water was, their quest to slake deserts and to introduce verdure and colour to the parched earth that created these lovely cool corners. Here, *in parvo*, we see what they did on a greater scale in Granada, in the grounds of the Alhambra and the gardens of the Generalife; here, each time you see a fountain playing in the light or hear a hose left to splash across gleaming *azulejos* or a child's watering-can to fill beneath an overflowing basin, you may easily comprehend the very obsession that led to the irrigation of the great *huertas* of Valencia producing their several crops of fruit or vegetables a year. With a patio the object is to create not food to eat but sustenance for the eye and the ear: a place of natural and man-made beauty. White limewash walls set off the displays of bloom and foliage. The more aristocratic the patio, the more discreet its hues and uninsistent its flowers: cool greens, yellows, feather-leafed ferns and the smaller-blossomed species of clematis. The more homely the patio, the more rampant of habit and strident of colour: scarlet and crimson and all manner of clashing pinks and startlingly bright blues; fleshly and pungent pelargoniums, carnations, trailing lobelias, trellised roses in such abundance you'd think they were suds and foam from a dye works rumbling over a cascade. Apart from the sounds of water – splashings, gushings, tinklings, oozings, tricklings, drippings and bubblings – your patio should also offer the liquid music of a sweet songbird, a canary or a linnet, its cage partly concealed among the ferns on an upper window-sill or gently swinging on a slender gold chain from an eave beneath the pantiles. And at night your senses will perceive it all in different terms: for the lamps will pick out surfaces the sun neglects, like the rim of a jar or the underside of a certain tremulous leaf; and from the darkness within the fronds of a palm tree moths will start to fly; under your hand you will feel the warmth of the day caught in the capstone of a pier; and, if you're lucky, one of the chinks in the ivied wall will be home for a fidgety cricket.

After dinner, Córdoba changes character, subtly and seductively. By daylight it is, for all its gaiety of flowers, an essentially formal place: you look at it from across the river and somehow detect a gravitas – almost like that of Castile – in the very skyline. At night all softens. Walk between the

Guadalquivir and the tactfully floodlit Alcázar, then back to the ancient, alley-riddled core of the *Judería* and you will hear happy impromptu singing, sometimes accompanied and sometimes not, but you will also hear music to make your hair stand on end with its passionate, anguished beauty: for Córdoba never quite forgets that it is 'a serious place on serious earth'.

Nowhere in Córdoba is this more strongly felt than in the Museum of Bullfighting. This is not only a collection of the ephemera of the spectacle – in particular of *carteles* of bullfights long ago – but also a kind of shrine to the many great matadors of Córdoba: Lagartijo, Guerrita, Machaquito and, the greatest of them all, Manuel Rodriguez Sánchez – Manolete – for whom the city seems to be in perpetual mourning. (There is a fine, powerful statue of him near the parish church of Santa Marina.) The head and hide of the enormous animal that killed him adorn the walls; there are paintings, busts, photographs and recumbent effigies celebrating him; there are contemporary documents, accounts, newspaper reports and such, all eerily giving the impression that Manolete was a messiah who might yet, if his memory is kept alive in this pantheon, return to delight all those aficionados, who have kept the faith. In its way this museum of bullfighting memorabilia (some would say – and they'd be wrong – of kitsch) can leave one, strangely, with thoughts about eternal values no less profound than those prompted in the synagogue, the mosque or the cathedral; and anyone who perversely continues to believe that bullfighting is merely a cruel and barbaric blood sport on a par with foxhunting ought to spend a ruminative hour here.

The landscape of the province of Jaén (at least, that of the Morena, Segura and Cazorla ranges and of the terrain surrounding the eponymous capital city) is as massive, irregular and daunting as any in Spain. Overwhelmingly it is the reddish-earth olive plantations which impinge upon one's consciousness for hours after one has driven past olives, their remorseless geometries of dots and lines infinitely stretching away in all directions over the uneven topography. Someone has estimated that there are 150 million olive trees in the province: there could be twice as many, but perhaps the most

171

significant of statistics is that all those trees are owned by only a handful of people.

There was a procession taking place in the streets of Jaén when I arrived. It was led by fifteen-foot high *gigantes* representing Ferdinand and Isabel, *los reyes católicos*, followed by giant Moors with silver crescent moons on their breasts. (These giants are less often found in Andalusia than in central and northern Spain, where they are regularly prominent during a town's *fiesta* and are often kept during the rest of the year – as in Burgos, for example – in their own abiding-place in cathedral or parish church.) Behind these came the inevitable battalion of *cabeduzos* or big-heads – grotesque, monstrous, often startlingly life-like when representing human types such as a top-hatted negro or a jockey in riding-cap and silks. Most of the big-heads here were Walt Disney creations: Mickey Mouse, the Three Little Pigs and the Big Bad Wolf, incongruous figures to follow the rulers of Aragon and Castile perhaps, but colourful and whimsical and appropriate to what was – one now realized – predominantly a children's occasion. Musical bands followed, and all the youth groups, the church organizations, the white-socked and high-hatted baton twirlers, the boy scouts in berets and the dancing schools, on builder's lorries, represented by half-a-dozen *mojo* and *maja* diminutive boys and girls.

Being in Jaén was nowhere near as stimulating as being a couple of miles outside it. From the car park of the parador (housed in the *Castillo Sta Catalina* high on its hill to the west) there is a panoramic view over the city and beyond towards the distant sierra. Just below you, the city packs a scrum of tight streets round a cathedral which had seemed huge and ugly and disproportionate but which, from this height, now looks right – imposingly grand. Behind an encirclement of modern, high-rise buildings, the tangerine earth and silvery green groves lead the eye to a vague and misty blueness where maybe there are no more olives. So stunned can you be by so much grandeur, you may not be aware of the hoopoe resting close at hand until it suddenly flies up before you.

The stone hereabouts is a delicate, early-spring tint of yellow, the yellow of a narcissus petal but not of its eye. I went on to Úbeda and Baeza, a Tweedle-dum and Tweedle-dee pair of towns (though the latter is only half the size of its twin)

172

separated – and this is rare in Spain – by only a few kilometres. In the church of Sta María there were some remarkable *pasos* stored in the side chapels, and in a patio adjacent
there was a strange medlar tree; and an elderly couple who
seemed to be guardians of the place apparently lived in a kind
of apartment set into a massive wall. My wife, who had joined
me for a few days at this time, casually said to me – as though
she might have been passing a remark about the weather –
'I've just seen a ghost.' I knew, and I was calm about it, that
she had indeed seen a ghost. And it was not until many months
later, back in England, that I remembered the incident and
asked her what her ghost had been like: tall, bearded, white-
robed, she said without hesitation, and at the very edge of
vision and walking away from her, and when she turned her
head he had simply vanished.

But the dog had not. All afternoon a mongrel of independent
means, with a ribcage like a xylophone and ears sawtooth-
edged, had been trailing us through the strees of Úbeda. If
we window-shopped we would see his reflection in the glass;
when we had a coffee he would attend upon us at the café
terrace; each time we thought of a ruse to throw him off the
scent he outwitted us and we would come across him lying in
ambush. We had long passed through the spectrum of emotions
such a situation imposes: we had found him engaging,
amusing, affectionate, loyal, a sticker, a bit of a pest, a damned
nuisance, a worry, and a really serious problem. Now, in the
cloisters of Santa María de los Reales Alcázares, here he was
yet again: and I would swear he was laughing. He scratched
at his fleas and licked his private parts and moved off, clearly
wishing us to follow. We went in a different direction, hoping
to get back to our hotel without the benefit of his company;
but he headed us off, looking pained and accusatory. It would
be best, we decided, to take no notice at all of him. Let him
become bored, let him, by the constant attrition of feigned
indifference, get the hint. He was a very thin animal, wiry –
and nobody's fool, I realized, despite his face being that of
a comic grotesque. I took pity, unpremeditatedly blessing the
hungry creature in my heart as the Ancient Mariner did the
slimy thing with legs. 'I'm going to find a butcher's shop,' I
said aloud and within his hearing, 'and I'm going to buy him
a bagful of bones.' But all the butchers' shops were shut by

then. We bought ourselves a sticky cake and he had a bit of that instead. In the morning, when we carried our luggage out to the street, there he was. Like so many Spanish dogs, he was a character, one I would often bring to mind in the years to come. I started the car and moved off; and I fancied I saw him in my mirror trotting behind and still visible when I reached the Granada road and accelerated away.

What, new, can be said about the Alhambra? Coming face-to-face with God, who would attempt to write a character-sketch of Him? The task of finding words for the Alhambra is too overwhelming. It is as near to the perfection of the Garden of Eden as one is ever likely to come on earth; and surely Paradise is indescribable except in the plain terms of the Book of Genesis. I had expected to dislike the buildings: I thought I should be facetious about their femininity, what with that famous flamingo-pink outer stone and the interiors too fussy by half and full of all that fidgety Arabic fiddlededee. I would consider them purely as horticultural ornaments, I thought: as so many fancy gazebos and summer-houses – mere conservatories and arbours and meretricious pavilions such as they are running up in plastic these days for garden centres just off the Kingston-by-pass. But I soon realized that I had been foolish beyond belief to think I could come and sneer at the Alhambra. If it is one of the greatest tourist cynosures of the world – let alone of Spain – why, this is hardly surprising. The Alcazaba, the Casa Real and the Generalife occupy the best possible site in the best possible climate. There is an unfailing supply of water from the diverted river Darro to irrigate the various levels under cultivation.

The Catholic monarchs Ferdinand and Isabel, when they occupied the buildings after the reconquest, had the good taste and judgement not to change them radically; with a light touch they did some restoration, to be sure, but essentially the fabric of the palace was not interfered with. And even their grandson, the Emperor Charles V, was unable to destroy the effect by plonking down his grandiloquent Renaissance pile between the fortress and the Casa Real. (Ironically this heavy-handed formal gesture, though through no artifice of his, successfully emphasizes the grace and gentleness of form of everything else.) No other series of gardens and buildings I know can

174

absorb so many visitors so serenely as the Alhambra. The vast open spaces of, say, Kew or Versailles have their tranquillity shattered the moment the gates open and the first strident coach party is let in. Here though, there is something which civilizes and tames the hordes, however beastly: perhaps it is the very intricacy of the design, the impossibility of playing at chasing games in and out of such a complex system of pathways, patios, arbours, avenues, pools, waterfalls, sunken *allées*, pergolas, clipped dwarf box-hedges, trellises, staircases, love-seats and sequestering trees. Others may find the palaces intolerably overrun; but the admittedly large crowds of tourists did not impinge upon my repose when I was there. Some visitors positively added to the joy of the place, in particular a young nun enjoying a day out with her parents and siblings. Her habit and wimple made a perfect black and white foil for every flower-bed or shrubbery she passed.

When darkness begins to close, you sit in a little gravel court on the Albaicín hill across the Darro and watch the stone of the Generalife and the Casa Real drain the last colour from the sunset. The lamps come on among the greenery to create a play of light and shadow if there's a little wind. And then you walk down to Granada past lovely villas, *carmenes*, your head so full of flights of fancy and myrtles and statuary and fountains and reflections and roses and palms and pots and urns and willows and water-lilies and cypress and lemon trees and cascading blossoms you feel that you too must get one of those silly stickers for your car's back window stating, complete with red heart, '*I love the Alhambra*'.

CHAPTER TEN

After so much richness, I yearned for plain fare: a bit of bread and cheese instead of Christmas cake. Skirting the edge of the Sierra Nevada – snowcapped even in summer – I descended into Andalusia's easternmost province of Almería. The city of Almería is by the seaside. Smart, teeming with fashionably-dressed and well-heeled people at the *paseo* hour, it gives no hint at all of the bizarre landscape a little way inland. This is of the kind beloved by science-fiction addicts: a weird desert with utterly bare cones or pyramids of pitted sandstone, blindingly white and monstrously littered across the terrain. There is no visible sign of living water: dried-up river beds, twisted and agonized, look like lengths of spent cordage angrily flung down. The heat is unbearable and the light is such that you can see a fly's eye a mile away. 'Like something in a film,' the visitor murmurs as he gazes at a landscape evoking variously the moon, Mars, the Sahara and Death Valley. And he is right, for this has been the location for dozens of paella westerns as well as for *Lawrence of Arabia*. When I stopped for a picnic lunch I watched a plastic cup marked BBC being blown about like tumbleweed by skips and catches over the sand.

In a village market I had bought a bag of red cherries and some peaches which were very juicy and ripe as could be. Greedily savaging one, I broke my denture and, flustered, accidentally spilled the olive oil from a sardine tin over my trousers. Low in spirits, I drove to Albacete, where I found a friend in Jesus: don Jesús Calvo, a semi-permanent resident of the hotel where I took a room. He was about forty, fair-haired, of slight build, with a thin, handsome though slightly twisted face. Within minutes of my arrival he was telephoning, on my behalf, a dentist and a dry cleaners.

'But why should an Englishman want to come to an ugly city like Albacete?' he said.

176

'The obvious place to come. Here there are people who can fix anything for you in no time at all.'

'Where there are sewers,' he said, broadly smiling, 'there are rats. *Venga* – why Albacete?'

'When I was a boy at school, one of the chapters in my Spanish text-book began, *You can't pass through Albacete without buying a penknife.* I've always wanted a penknife. So here I am at last.'

'*No se puede pasar por Albacete sin comprar une navaja.* Absolutely correct. You must visit my good friend Gómez, the best *cuchillero* in town. I myself shall conduct you to his shop. Where there are sewers—'

'There are rats.'

English-speaking visitors to Albacete were not as rare as Jesús implied, it seemed. On the door of my room was a notice reading: *It is forbidden to transport or use things that show fire hazard. No smoking at the bed or to throw cigarette stubs into the paper buckets or through out the windows. Wear the ashtrays!*

The dental surgeon's name was Dr González Vázquez. His receptionist listened patiently while I explained my problem: that I'd broken off the front left incisor from my denture and perhaps what I needed was not a *médico* but a *mecánico*. She told me, in front of a crowd of people in the waiting room, to show her the plate. 'Take it out. *Sáquesela.*' A youth and a black widow looked on dispassionately as, not without difficulty, I did as asked. I also produced from my wallet the detached incisor wrapped in blotting-paper. It was not long before the dentist attended to me. 'This denture was made by an amateur,' he said. 'The broken tooth must have been badly protruding.' He was quite right; it had been jutting out like an old donkey's, having had to be mended twice before. I looked round at his splendid consulting-room. His equipment was the last word in modernity – here in a remote corner of Spain where, not so long ago, patients would have had to submit to the most painful, primitive treatment. I thought of my own dentist's distincly inferior facilities (in prosperous West Sussex at that) and felt sorrow – even shame – that I had to show the good Dr Vázquez an example of such bad British workmanship. 'And yet your health service,' he said, 'was once the envy of Europe. *Vaya*, if I take a wax impression

177

now, *caballero*, you can collect your denture the day after tomorrow at one-thirty.'

Back in the hotel bar, gummily I had a long conversation with don Jesús. He came there to live for a while every year. His *novia*, Mari-Victoria, lectured in philology at the university. I asked him what his profession was. He was cagey. After a pause and a cough and the ruminative lighting of a cigarette (he chain-smoked), 'What I do,' he said, 'is think. I didn't have much primary education. I left school young and for a time I was apprenticed to my father, a blacksmith.' From time to time he dropped dark hints about himself, obviously enjoying the mystery with which he surrounded himself. Perhaps he was a lawyer (Spain is full of qualified, non-practising, indolent lawyers); perhaps he was a newspaperman; perhaps he was both – a legal journalist; perhaps it was true that, having published seditious articles in the provincial Press upon the restoration of the monarchy, his passport had been confiscated; perhaps it was even true that he had been involved in a fist fight with the police and had been summarily convicted and imprisoned. I did not mind whether or not the whole truth was vouchsafed to me. With a man like Jesús, what is interesting is his own, projected, version of himself. His face was much creased with laughter lines: the laughter of a cynicism he was quick to deny. His favourite phrase – with which he would open sentences, close them, fill the gaps between – was, *Que nadie so engañe*, 'Don't anybody kid themselves,' or, 'Make no mistake'. I saw no reason to disbelieve that he was originally from Asturias in the mountainous north: he was after all blond, fair-skinned and blue-eyed as many Asturianos are. 'We are the only true Spaniards,' he said proudly, pointing out that the Kingdom of Asturias was the only one not conquered by the Moors. '*Los Asturianos y los demás*, Asturians and the rest'.

Jesús spent most of his time in the hotel bar, leaning at the counter or perched on his high stool, constantly fidgeting, flicking his ash, jingling his small change, darting glances all about him like a watchful chameleon. It became credible to me, as the days went by, that thinking and speaking his thoughts could indeed be all that a man like Jesús did with his life: for he liked nothing better than holding forth with anybody on every conceivable political, economic, historical, religious, linguistic, literary and philosophical topic. His *tertulia* would be joined by other residents, the passing trade, local drinkers and certain members of the hotel staff. The latter were possessed of quite remarkable scholarship. The desk clerk Satu, bespectacled and in his late twenties, had a degree from Spain's Open University – the *Universidad a Distancia* – and was forever crossing swords with Jesús on matters of law and language.

An elderly German couple, having just arrived in Reception after a hot, exhausting drive from Madrid, was regaled with a brilliant exegesis of the seminal works of Chomsky before they were able to sign the book and receive their key. Satu, like many another well-educated Spaniard, was a wizard on the theory of language but a duffer as a practising linguist. His spoken English, execrable, made me wince. I guessed that it was he who had composed the notice on my bedroom door. Careful not to offend his dignity by questioning his erudition – almost as important as machismo to a literate Spanish male – I managed to get him to suggest I re-write it.

Over dinner, Jesús was inclined to talk about more earthy matters: he could be lyrical about summer salads in the remoter *pueblos* he knew: the good olive-oil, firm tomatoes, bread made from the best flour, lettuces, peppers and cucumbers bespangled with water-drops, crispest rings or chunks of pure white onions. Also he loved to expatiate upon where the hidden springs of rivers were and *arroyos* that last flowed as long ago as 1952. He suffered terribly from a duodenal ulcer; every so often he would have to leave the table, his face more twisted than usual, to fetch medicine or to endure a spasm alone. During one such absence I asked López, the waiter, what don Jesús really did for a living. López, though perpetually harried by Jesús and forever having to scuttle after this or that during every meal, was obviously very fond of him and could not be drawn to say more than, 'He has private means and keeps himself to himself.' I admired López for a tactful and loyal reply that gently chided my curiosity. He was a short man, married, father of a large family, with an eye for the ladies: but whenever respectable strangers patronized the dining-room, he and Jesús, *pour épater le bourgeois*, would make a loud pretence, with outrageously camp behaviour, that López was gay.

179

'What do you think about Spanish women?' Jesús asked me, returning with a glass of chalky jollop and a small duffle-bag.

'Exquisite.'

'*Nada de nada.* Swedish, Dutch, German women – they're the ones most Spanish men go for, *que nadie se engañe.* But they know nothing. Bread, López, fetch more bread at once. *Las rubias*, blondes! The difference, you see, Eduardo? That's all it is. Superficial attraction of opposites. Englishmen like Spanish women just because they're dark, *morenas*. López, bring me an ice-cream. Brazilian women? *Que nadie se engañe*, dirty but delectable. Best of all? Argentinians. Very *cariñosas*. They say delicious things in bed. Spanish women put out the light and *nada de nada*. What is your opinion, López?'

'Don't ask *me* about women! I'm a *maricón*! Let's talk about boys instead,' said López.

He giggled and nodded towards a large man sitting with his back to us at a nearby table. By his neck one could tell he was enraged. Jesús picked up the duffle-bag and withdrew a pair of vivid blue ladies' slippers, a present (he whispered) for Mari-Victoria. 'López,' he said aloud, 'You are to come to my room at midnight, wearing these.' The large man turned his head as Jesús proffered the slippers and kissed López gallantly on the tip of his elbow. 'I have also bought us this,' he said, producing the rest of Mari-Victoria's present, a tube of hand-cream. The large man turned away, eased his collar and concentrated on the menu. I picked up the tube and translated aloud the French label. '*Que nadie se engañe*, it sounds much sexier in French,' said Jesús. 'If the instructions had been in Spanish, there'd have been none of that naughty innuendo about using the stuff on your *hands*!'

We went back to the bar, leaving the poor large man to ruminate on the decadence of Spain since the advent of democracy and to enjoy his *pollo al ajillo* as best he could.

There was a second waiter called López – Fructuoso López, no relation. Jesús enjoyed needling Fructuoso, an aficionado, about his knowledge of bullfighting. There was to be a *becerrada* in Albacete which I intended to go to (a *becerrada* is a bullfight without picadors for young hopefuls and *becerros*, bull calves). Fructuoso maintained that the improver matadors would clear 25,000 pesetas for their evening's work; he knew for a fact that this was so – for had he not eavesdropped, at the time of the last *becerrada*, when the bullfighters were staying in the hotel?

'*Nada de nada*. Once they've paid for the services of their *cuadrilla*, their food, transport and accommodation expenses, they're well out of pocket, make no mistake. Make no mistake. Make no mistake, Fructuoso, those young *toreros* would earn more doing your job. Pour me a *caña* at once.'

Jesús began picking his teeth. This was more comical than offensive: as a gesture to conventional politeness and gentility he concealed the whole lower part of his face with both hands, little finger cocked and trembling in the attitude of a harmonica virtuoso. When he had done, he helped himself to a *tapa* of *moje*, a Murcian salad not unlike cold ratatouille with the addition of oily flakes of bonito.

'Small wonder you've got an ulcer.'

'*Nada*. Now, Eduardo, you say you're very interested in the bulls. Tomorrow's Saturday. Would you like to go to the ring and see the *escuela taurina*?'

'Is the Pope a Catholic?'

'Eleven o'clock. We'll watch the lads, *los chavales*, training. Albacete's famous for bullfighting. Probably the greatest *corrida* ever was held here. And I was present! The matadors were Diego Puerta, Miguelín and Carnicerito Úbeda and the bulls were provided by El Conde de la Corte. He was a son of Albacete. He'd saved his six best animals for his home town. Eleven ears were cut that day, eleven ears and three tails! Think of it! There'll never be another like that one, make no mistake. One journalist wrote that now he could go to his grave knowing he'd seen something unsurpassable. We all came reeling out of the plaza delirious, *que nadie se engañe*. I can't remember when it took place. Eight years ago, was it? Fifteen years ago? But when it was doesn't matter. Miracles don't happen in real time.'

On our way to the ring next morning, Jesús pointed out a much-faded painted sign on the lower floor of a house that had been the Republicans' Press headquarters in the Civil War. Since 1936, naturally, the sign had often been whitewashed over and some of the letters had chipped and flaked; but SERVICIOS DE PRENSA REPUBLICANA BRIGADAS INTERNACIONALES was still quite distinct.

'Where we are standing, so I've been told by Señor Moraga,

the *cronista*, a bomb fell and a woman was killed by shrapnel. It destroyed one house entirely. But *vaya*, I'll show you some different words on a different wall!'

There was a plaque, above the SOL entrance to the bullring, reading:

El Exmo Ayuntamiento de Albacete
Al Matador de Toros
JUAN MONTERO NAVARRO
10-9-1928 – 10-8-1971

The plaza could have accommodated about 10,000 people. It had been rebuilt in the early Twenties to a strongly Moorish design. In the ring, spread about in twos and threes and sometimes singly, were a couple of dozen boys aged between ten and eighteen – and some tiny tots, too – doing various exercises. Most wore tee-shirts, football shorts and kickers or trainers as worn by English lads having a kick-about in a recreation ground; one, for all the warmth of the mid-morning sun, was in a parka. The maestro, a former *banderillero* called Mariano de la Viña, looked in his blue tracksuit for all the world like a British comprehensive school sports master; until, that is, you saw him move: not with gross athleticism, coarse and brutal, but with the elegance, and grace, economy but vast latent strength of a classically trained dancer. He got his pupils into pairs in order to rehearse passes: one boy being the matador, complete with cape; and the other, carrying aloft a large set of horns, imitating uncannily the movements and rhythms of a bull.

'That lad there – the gipsy,' said Jesús. 'What a fighter! But he's frightened, a coward. *Caca en el pantalón.*'

'But you have to be afraid, don't you? No fear, no imagination. No imagination, no valour. You can't have a fearless hero, can you? If ever I get in a ring with a real bull – and I fully intend to before this summer's out – I hope to be scared out of my wits.'

Two youngsters were practising the *quite*, the procedure by which members of a *cuadrilla* will divert a bull's attention from a fallen matador, or from the picador's horse, and then lure it away. The 'bull' had his back to the *torero*, as if getting its horns under the horse's belly; the *capa* was agitated at the side

182

of the bull's head. The bull, in its own good time catching sight of the cloth, turned and moved. A *verónica*; and the *quite* was accomplished.

The maestro upbraided some lazy boys who had sat down. '*Entrenados*,' he urged them. 'Get training.' He shook his head a little sadly. 'The *chavales* won't put their heart and soul into it this morning,' he said, coming over to us. We shook hands, and, while we chatted, he continued to instruct a little fat boy in khaki shorts, sandals and striped shirt – as unlikely a candidate for tauromachy as one could imagine. He demonstrated how to take the eye-hook from the *palo* so that the stick could then be slotted through the *capa*, whose cloth could then be pulled taut with the eye-hook replaced. The stick was about two feet long, with a metal point, the shaft cleverly carved like a little totem pole. The fat boy did some rudimentary passes, *naturales*, trying but failing to arch his tubby little body. The maestro showed him over and over again how better to place his feet, how better to position the *capa*; but the boy, it was plain, never was going to learn because his body would not arch. In the centre of the ring a tall boy, all alone, was confronting an imaginary bull; watching it, advancing upon it crabwise, giving his *muleta* a flutter or the merest twitch, seeing the beast charge, bringing the cloth up over the bull's head as it passed. It was done superbly; one could 'see' the bull by the very movement of the boy's body. The fat boy trod on his own feet, trying to emulate what he had seen. Sadder than this, two middle-aged and portly men began padding around the perimeter of the arena, jogging, trotting, sprinting, alarming us by going bright red in the face.

'Some would-be *toreros* don't ever know when to give up,' said Jesús. 'You can't blame a roly-poly ten-year-old. But as for these ancient *tíos*! And you too, Eduardo, must give up this nonsense about intending to enter the ring with a bull. Apart from any other consideration, matadors are not allowed to wear glasses as you do. That's the law. Contact lenses are permitted but not *gafas*. Also it is forbidden to wear a moustache.'

'I have no ambition to be a *matador de toros*, Jesús. All I want to do is know what it's like to be face-to-face with a *toro bravo*. As for the moustache, I didn't start to grow it until I arrived in Albacete. It was something to do while I waited for my teeth to be repaired. I'll grow some long side-burns instead and look like a *bandolero*.' A lorry arrived with the *becerros*, so everybody had to vacate the ring. This was another of the odd laws of bullfighting. 'We must come back this evening and have a look at them,' said Jesús. 'Meanwhile, a glass of *fino*.'

Albacete is – by Spanish standards – an ugly city: but it is full of delightful people and beautiful corners. It suffered badly during the Civil War when part of the cathedral was destroyed by fire. Jesús took me to the *cuchillería* of his friend Gómez; then excused himself with a comic, erotic pantomime suggesting that he had an assignation with his *novia*.

The city's steel is not as famous abroad as that of Toledo; but much of the merchandise on sale in Toledo is produced here. Albacete is famous for its handsome fighting weapons: swords, flick-knives, clasp-knives, throwing-knives, sword-sticks; for the varied tools of the bullfighter's trade like the *estoque* as well as the *espada*; for scimitars, sabres, daggers and bayonets; for stilettos, épées and open razors; for blades to cut throats or to slide between ribs. Gómez' stock of such items was large, lovely, wickedly dangerous. Merely to contemplate them might make a man a murderer: though they were safely locked up in their cases, they made me tremble. I bought a battery of kitchen-ware to take home: some place settings – which turned out to be second-rate; but also some solid knives with hardwood handles with which to carve joints, chip bread, chop parsley, slice onions, slit liver, cleave chops, snip bacon rind or decapitate fowl. And, of course, I bought myself a penknife, one that would be legal in England. Later, when we were looking down into the corral at one of the bull claves, Jesús, unimpressed, said I might as well have my experience with a fighting bull there and then. 'Show this one that little penknife of yours and he'll run nonstop from here to La Coruña.' In the next pen there was a *manso* – a tame, castrated bullock, put with the others to keep them calm. It had a loud, clanking bell round its neck. 'Better not show *him* your knife, though, Eduardo. *Mansos* don't forgive men with knives. *Que nadie se engañe!* Tomorrow you must come to the *sorteo*, when the draw is made to see which fighter gets which bull. I'll go to the *becerrada* of course, but forgive me if I don't accompany you to the *sorteo*. Urgent matters I must attend to – understand?' He put on the machismo act again.

'Say no more. When am I to be privileged to meet her?'

Mari-Victoria came to the bar for an *aperitivo*. Proud, shy, Jesús introduced us. She was a liberated brunette, vivacious, witty, mocking, her rimless octagonal spectacles in no way diminishing her attractiveness. Though she spoke good English, she was reticent about speaking it in front of Jesús. She had been to summer language schools in Cambridge and knew my old college. She complimented me on a prose book of mine which I had given to Jesús. Now he presented me with a copy of *La familia de Pascual Duarte*, which he signed and inscribed with a fulsome message. We were both fans of the author, Camilo José Cela, whose works had been the subject of one of our more prolonged discussions into the small hours.

While Mari-Victoria and I chatted, I became aware of Jesús (unbeknownst to his *novia*) candidly sizing up the members of a wedding-party now beginning to arrive for the marriage feast: in particular, several youngish, unaccompanied (though not necessarily single) women of quite extraordinary beauty. When bride and groom arrived and it was time for Mari-Victoria to leave for her class, Jesús and I went upstairs for an unwontedly early dinner. Guileless as a schoolboy positioning himself by a plate of buns, Jesús chose a table in full view of that occupied by the wedding guests. One thirty-year-old beauty had dense tresses of black wavy hair, immense dark eyes, voluptuous lips, and the movements of her fingers and shoulders as she caressed the stem of her glass were both elegant and sensuous. She transmitted flirtatious messages in body language to all corners of the room, but mostly in the direction of our table. Jesús affected not to take any notice of her. López and I knew at once what was going on, though, and the situation became funnier and funnier as Jesús tried to maintain his usual bantering conversation with us while being by turns encouraged, aroused and disconcerted by the temptress. She was ablaze with her sexuality; in her white and navy-blue organdie dress she was beautiful, disturbing and dangerous as a brand-new presentation box of duelling knives, open and available to handle. Jesús, distrait, had two cigarettes burning. I watched his face, side-long. Every now and again she had been making microseconds of eye-contact with him; gradually these contacts were becoming of longer and longer

185

duration: entire seconds; two or three seconds, several seconds; also even franker, more insolent, more burning and more brazen.

When the party was over and the couple had left, the guests all retired to the *salón de música* in the basement, where a *discoteca* was soon in full swing. In the bar I chaffed Jesús when he excused himself on the grounds that he had a little writing to do.

'Whatever would Mari-Victoria say if she knew you'd been getting the old come-on from a pile of note-paper?' said López, lisping and mincing and grinning hugely. Jesús was discomfited.

'Mari-Victoria and I have an open relationship. We are free and we place no restrictions upon one another. By God – look at the time. I'd better phone her, quick!'

I was buttonholed at the counter by one of the guests, an enormous, healthy, powerful country lad from the Baleares. I understood little of what he said, for his Catalán was unfathomable to me and he was the better part drunk. He would have been about thirty-five, with stubble like swarf and eyelids to crack walnuts. He started to get stroppy, saying he'd been charged twice by the waiter Fructuoso for a round of drinks. Everybody knew this could not be so: Fructuoso was methodical and as honest a young man as you'd find anywhere. It was distressing: the kind of flare-up that's common enough in English pubs but exceedingly rare in Spain. Bystanders – strangers and fellow guests – were making a low hissing sound signifying disapprobation. I went out for a short walk; and by the time I got back he was being loudly belligerent and offering violence to anybody who contradicted him or who tried to calm him down. 'Can't hold his wine,' Satu whispered to me. The man switched from Catalán to Castilian. He made more noise, more threats; but – as is more often than not the case – no actual blow was struck. 'This isn't the end of it,' the fellow bawled. 'You are all thieves. You have cheated me. This scene will be continued.' And he charged outside, pursued by several outraged members of his family. He could be heard wallowing in the dark and echoing street, unrestrainable and wild as a water buffalo.

'Where's Jesús?' I asked Satu. 'He'd have enjoyed this.'

'On the sofa, in the half-dark, in the vestibule.'

'With—'

'The fellow's wife, yes.'

It was two in the morning. I went to bed, read some pages of *La familia de Pascual Duarte* and, at twenty past two, looked from my window down into the street. A taxi had just arrived and the driver was holding the rear door open, revealing a large and familiar male occupant. Jesús and the lady came out of the hotel. As decorously as could be he kissed her hand, helped her into the car, said goodnight, shut the door and came back inside. Mischievously, I rehearsed how I would twit him in the morning on failing to land his catch.

However, he was not visible at breakfast or in the bar at mid-morning. I went to the *sorteo* alone as planned. About a hundred men and boys watched as the five bullocks were prodded this way and that through a kind of maze into separate pens. The allocation of beast to bullfighter was done by a raffle, bits of paper being drawn from a hat. The corral was behind the plaza, next to the slaughter-house and the chapel. Viewing was from openings in the first floor, with much jostling for position and mutterings and gruntings of knowledgeable opinion. In the ring itself the sand was being smoothened. A grey stallion wearing a decorated straw hat was towing a ten-foot spar of timber which the driver rode like a sledge. Round and round they went in diminishing concentric circles until all was level and in good order. Back in the hotel – still no sign of Jesús – a youthful matador arrived with his *cuadrilla*, one of whom carried a bundle of white-papered *banderillas*. I had an excellent lunch of *potaje* followed by baked hake and a pudding of apricots, alone.

All afternoon I worked. It rained heavily for a while and I feared the *becerrada* might be called off. At seven o'clock, disconsolately I went downstairs and was just in time to see José A. Carretero from Madrid – second on the day's bill – pass through the bar with his *cuadrilla*, all dressed in their suits of lights. These always look very odd anywhere but in the ring.

There was no chance of any sunshine. It was as bleak as a February day in Huddersfield as I took my cheap seat in the SOL enclosure with the *afición*. A strong wind was blowing. Foolishly I had not put on a jacket, so I shivered in my flimsy shirt. Satu and his girlfriend sought me out. They kindly gave me a cold beer. I asked Satu if he'd seen Jesús.

187

'Fleetingly. He looked very sheepish. He said he wouldn't be coming to the *becerrada* after all. He sends his apologies to you. I think he's going round to Mari-Victoria's, if you know what I mean.'

'Best place to be, weather like this.'

A young *alguacil* on a spirited grey led the procession of five *cuadrillas* into the ring. There were perhaps 1,500 spectators, no more. The wind was too strong, interfering with the cape work of the first *espada*, a young fellow I'd seen under instruction in the *escuela taurina* the day before. He had been wearing beach shorts then. Now, though utterly transformed by his suit of lights, he had lost his authority: he was flustered and he had drawn a bad bull. He had no option but to kill quickly and clumsily. The second, the *Madrileño* I'd seen in the hotel, was much more accomplished. He placed his white banderillas well, his *faena* began with fourteen consecutive *naturales* and, although he killed ineptly, he was generously applauded. The third and fourth were comic and embarrassing affairs; but the fifth bull, fast and scamperingly nimble on the hoof as a piglet, was fought with grace and style and the crowd, anxious to go home and get warm, awarded an ear. Miserable, I decided to leave Albacete early next morning. Maybe I'd unwittingly offended Jesús. Maybe I'd laughed too loud when López had made his joke about note-paper giving him the old come-on.

I had been repeatedly pressed by don Francisco, one of the hotel bar's regular lunch-time customers, to visit his 'English pub' in the middle of town. I phoned don Francisco as he had suggested. He collected me in his Mercedes. The 'pub' was characterless; a bar of the kind rapidly, alas, coming into vogue throughout Spain: Scandinavian softwoods, black vinyl and chrome furniture, 'lighting' providing a ludicrously faint lambency, ashtrays apparently hacked from the living quartz, glass tables, a couple of shelves of different brands of Scotch whisky and pink plastic swizzle-sticks topped with parasols or parakeets. It had that kind of spurious comfort hostile to both conversation and ordinary, civilized well-being. Don Francisco had named the establishment for his son, anglicizing Luís into Lewis. The place had been burgled a few days before: an air-vent specially opened by an early-evening 'customer' having been used to effect a late-night entry. Don

Francisco had received a tip-off that a repeat performance was planned for that night. We sat at the padded bar in the gloom for a very long time, drinking a good single malt. I felt I could not – as an invited guest and the only occupant of the bar apart from the proprietor and his staff – leave until after the arrival of a few customers. At last, a young couple that I could scarcely discern entered and sat down in the far corner. Don Francisco scribbled and passed to me a note which, by match-light, I read: *These are the ones. Shortly I'll telephone for the police.* I took this as my excuse to leave. Within minutes I was back at the hotel.

Jesús was wearing a hurt expression. '*Hombre*, where have you been? Wait till you hear of my adventures! Don't anybody kid themselves!'

'Don't *anybody* kid themselves,' I said. 'The lady left with her husband in a taxi at two-twenty. She'd been less randy than tiddly at the reception. I am sure you acted with the gallantry of a true Asturian *caballero*. However, you were sorely tempted. So afterwards you felt guilty and you've spent most of today being nice to Mari-Victoria. Something like that. I understand how it is!'

'Eduardo, you know about the human heart.'

'Maybe. But listen, Jesús, I really have to continue on my way tomorrow. I'd love to stay in Albacete for ever, but I can't. I'm going to leave before breakfast, so I'll say goodbye now. Okay?'

He was a little maudlin drunk. He clasped me by the elbows and, though he was broadly smiling, his eyes glistened.

'*Un abrazo!*'

'I'll send you a postcard now and again, Jesús. You won't forget *el Inglés*?'

'Never. Never. *Que nadie se engañe! Que nadie se engañc!*'

CHAPTER ELEVEN

Africa does not (and never did) begin at the Pyrenees: approaching Elche from the north-west, however, coming from the harsh aridities of the plain of Albacete in Castilla-La Mancha to the abundantly fertile, irrigated *huerta* country of the Comunidad de Valencia, you do have the strongest impression of one continent ending and another about to begin.

There is more to this visually than the increasing numbers of date palms glimpsed from the road. After gaunt hilltop fortresses like those of Chinchilla de Monte Aragón, Almansa, Sax and Villena, you come to a patently gentler territory in a much more benign climate; a mild, domestic, agrarian ambience rather than a beleaguered, martial one. Here, where seven centuries of Arab occupation have bequeathed the benefits of the ploughshare more obviously than the miseries of the sword, you sense Man would surely prosper if only nature and neighbour were co-operated with rather than constantly resented and railed against.

Elche is an oddity. There are almost as many palm trees as people. The old city of white, cubist houses grew up amidst the famous grove – or was it the other way around? – and at first you see the place in the way you become aware of an itinerants' encampment: as a higgledy-piggledy effect of low, flat-roofed dwellings half-hidden among the trunks. Something peculiar seems to be going on: how can 125,000 people be accommodated there? You come off a stretch of scruffy bypass, curious and anxious.

It began to torrent with rain when I arrived. Everywhere in the world has its characteristic smell during the first seconds of a rainstorm. In Elche steam billowed up from hot pavements, and in the city centre there was a sudden, pungent, un-European, primeval smell. All went strangely quiet, too, as though some primitive god of the waters had to be propitiated. After twenty minutes there was blinding sunshine among the long rods of rain, turning them into vertical lasers; and then the rain ceased and the steam thickened and there was an equatorial stickiness to be breathed.

The strangely-named river Vinalopó, carried through a gigantic concrete channel, serves as the main artery of a complex irrigation system that is weird to behold. By way of one of its nine bridges I went to a renowned garden, the Huerto del Cura, while the trees were still dripping on to the puddled pathways. This is an unsettling place: full of the vivid, riotous colours (precisely those of parrots) of exotic plants associated more readily with jungles – or deserts – than a formal town garden. There are some peculiar juxtapositions. Cheek by jowl with beds of suburban salvias or love-lies-bleeding, cacti sprout like spiky, hard, upright vegetable marrows, or like malicious artichokes, or like angered porcupines, or like monstrous pin-cushions bedecked (if flowering) with bows of orange taffeta. There is an oblong lily-pool presided over by a replica of the ancient and most peculiar stone bust of La Dama de Elche. (The original, found towards the end of the nineteenth century in nearby La Alcudia, is displayed in Madrid.) She wears a head-dress like two ammonites connected to a cone and her expression is inscrutable, in the manner of sphinx or Giaconda. Bizarre, too, is the most celebrated palm of all in Elche: the Imperial Palm with its seven trunks all springing from one a little above ground level. Before I left I was accosted, among the carob trees, by a Bible-toting religious maniac. He was stubbly, unkempt and wild of eye as he rhapsodized about the beauties of nature. 'You must hope that heaven will be like this,' he said; but he could not have been more wrong, I thought, if I were to have the likes of him for company.

Like people, date-palms divide by sex. Female trees produce the fruits (rather second-rate ones, these of Elche) while the males have their blanched fronds harvested and distributed all over Spain not only for the religious processions of Palm Sunday but also for the protection they are supposed to afford buildings against being struck by lightning. The best specimens I saw were in the Municipal Park. They were ravishingly beautiful; the more so because pure white doves nest in the bracts left when the fronds have been cut. Several trees wear

191

round their necks chains with nameplates. These celebrate famous local worthies; an agreeable custom, it seems to me: how gratifying to have a tree named for you – and much more flattering to bigwigs, I imagine, than the conventional commissioned civic bust or statue.

In the park there were tropical and sub-tropical species whose names I did not know. In particular there was one growing among carobs and bananas, a blue-flowered ornamental tree that I immensely admired; a sort of jacaranda, maybe it was. Its leaf was not unlike that of wisteria; and, as with a wisteria, the blossoms emerged before the leaf. But the flowers were not trailing racemes: more like large Canterbury-bells. Rain had knocked many to the ground. Two old ladies sitting nearby (on a bench made from the trunk of a palm) looked friendly and jolly. I struck up a conversation.

'Can you tell me what this is called, señoras?' I asked. I picked up one of the flowers.

'I call it campanita,' said one. 'But don't ask me. I'm no expert on anything, señor, let alone botany.'

'She used to be quite an expert on certain subjects – didn't you, María?' said her companion; and they both cackled and shrieked and pinched each other. They must have been in their eighties. I could tell by their eyes and complexion that one had been fair and the other, María, dark. I made some small talk about the park, the town, the cost of living, the fact that I was travelling to every corner of Spain. And whatever I said, their answers were full of innocent double-entendre. They were flirting with me mercilessly.

'What do you think of Spanish women?'

I made some kind of gallant answer calculated to charm.

'What do you prefer – blondes or brunettes?' In the circumstances, of course, no answer could have been tactful.

'I married a blonde,' I said.

'I was a blonde,' said María's friend with a smirk.

'Ah,' said María, 'but they don't have morenas in his country!'

'You must come back in the middle of August for the fiestas,' said her friend. 'It's lovely here then. First the Mystery Play in the basilica. And then all the decorations are put up and there's lots of singing and laughing and the coloured lights are so pretty. Yes – come back in August.' She had the smile of a young girl.

'The men are allowed to give any of the ladies they fancy the glad eye during the August *fiesta*,' said María. 'We've all you need here in Elche. Don't bother going off all over the country. Stay here. But if you really have to go, come back in August. We'll still be here!'

I walked back beside the river past vivid lilies and lovers intertwined like ivy. That night I ate a whole leg of roast suckling pig – afterwards I couldn't sleep, which served me right. Someone was playing Beethoven's *Pastoral Symphony* on his record-player; he played it three times over; and it had never sounded as apt as it did in the humid dark of that odd Eden, Elche.

I hankered after the sea. Not stopping for the palm grove at Orihuela or the cathedral at Murcia (whose façade reminded me, irresistibly, of the confectioner's art), I scurried down to the ancient port of Cartagena. As its name suggests, this was a Carthaginian deep-water haven. The Romans developed the town. After a long period of disregard by the Moors and the Christian conquerors, it was rediscovered by Philip II and Charles III, who, recognizing its strategic and commercial importance, fortified it and created an arsenal within the walls. So for well over two thousand years Cartagena has been both a commercial and a military harbour. Few places are as powerful as naval dockyards for evoking a sense of history. The smells of the quayside are much as they have always been; gulls still scream and a sense of relief and shelter pervades after perhaps many weeks of the menace and loneliness of open sea. You gaze across the water at the high country of Cartagena's embracing promontories and hinterland and realize that what you see is essentially the same as hundreds of Phoenician sailors saw. A courtesy-visiting French warship, the *Triton*, had not long tied up when I arrived. I was disappointed to have just missed the kind of fracas which I imagine must have occurred here on occasion since the times of the Carthaginians: a seaman had insulted and abused a prostitute in a café and had been hauled off to jail. 'There was no need for the man to slang her just because of her trade,' grumbled the waiter. '*Putas* have their dignity, like anyone else.'

Just east, there is a stretch of ruined mining country; and

to the north of La Unión (a town of two communities, dividing between those who use the soft 's' and those who use the hard) are some incongruous-looking windmills with baggy canvas sails. I came to a spoiled, overblown seaside resort village, Torrevieja, where there was a large permanent colony of expatriates, mainly Belgians. I was immediately fleeced: charged twice the normal price, in a nasty bar, for a bottle of beer and a *tapa* of *boquerones*. In the cafés gentlemen Belgians were preyed upon by card sharps, lady Belgians by improver Don Juans. It was one of those ugly, funny and sad places where the prevailing mood is one of a desperate gaiety born of despair. The Costa Blanca, the Golfo de Valencia littoral, then the Costa del Azahar (the 'Orange-blossom Coast') are indeed a string of towns and villages by turns predominantly ugly, sad and funny – though Alicante surprisingly still conserves much of its character and beauty, despite its summer crowding and tawdry, high-rise slabs. I drove the whole coast to Castellón de la Plana and was left with few memories of any of it anywhere – save farcically irredeemable Benidorm, a parody of Torremolinos, Fuengirola and Marbella rolled into one.

North of Castellón I sampled *autopista* driving for a few kilometres, from one *enlace*, or link, to the next. You take your ticket as you enter the motorway and you pay when you leave for as far as you've done. It was expensive, the stage I did costing 90 pesetas. The road surface was curly-ribbed, as though about to be re-asphalted, but permanently so. Along the central reservation oleanders grew; and the hard shoulder resembled a high-tide mark with countless festoons of black, shredded, lorry-tyre retreads like dried bladder-wrack; crumbled plastic bottles like wads of yellowy whelk-eggs; abandoned pallets like flotsam from a recent shipwreck.

What you do remember about the Levantine coast is the continuous *huerta*: millions of oranges, tangerines and lemons; the olives and carobs and almonds; also the convolvulus, violet-flowering, growing against walls and around the doors of farmhouses – particularly striking by morning or evening light and when it mixes with bougainvillea. As I approached Peñíscola along a narrowing lane I saw a very old woman in widow's black gathering up windfall apricots and peaches.

Peñíscola, the 'City in the Sea', was very much to my taste.

Sitting on its rock, topped by its castle, more impressive than St Michael's Mount but less dramatic (and less commercialized) than Le Mont St Michel, it separates two beaches: a place where Spaniards go for their holidays, not yet spoiled (I'd give it five years). It is a quirky place where you can park your car on the sand if you feel like it and light a bonfire by the water's edge to broil a bit of fish. Square dwellings (some of them, regrettably, souvenir shops) line tight lanes leading to the top. In the harbour nets are being mended on board, and you really can go all aboard the *Swallow (La Golondrina)* for a trip on the briny, as in the days before the package deal.

I was sitting quietly on a lower rampart when a tiny little lady asked me to take photographs of her with her cheap, plastic camera. She was excessively petite; could have been any age between twenty and forty. While tidying her jet-black hair and smoothing the creases from her skirt, she volunteered the information that she came from a South American republic, that she worked as a nursemaid and domestic for the family of that country's consul in Paris, that the family was on vacation in Peñíscola, that she was having her weekly two hours off, that she was desperately unhappy in her job and longed to get out, that she had no money however and therefore no option but to serve out the term of her contract, that the children of the family were a trial, that the mother did nothing all day but smoke, and, oh yes that the photographs were to send to her parents, friends and boyfriend, her *chico*, back home. She posed gravely, the sombre stone of the *Castillo* as background. Of Indian descent, she would have looked apt if dressed in *poncho* or *sarape*, in feathers and beads and one of those bowler hats, sitting on a mule and smoking a pipe or chewing coca. 'Smile,' I said, and she did, holding up the brim of her straw sun-hat and swaggering jauntily. What I captured would have told the folks back home precisely how she felt: her grin brave but hinting at a despair born from virtual imprisonment, semi-slavery, deep wretchedness. Would have – but after taking the camera back from me, she dropped it on the edge of a step; and the plastic case was a dozen black shards.

She was not one to weep. What she wanted was for me to put her in my car and drive her away to Madrid and buy her a plane ticket to La Paz, or Quito, or wherever. She had taught herself to shed words not tears to relieve her misery and bemoan her situation. I felt pity but not compassion. I bought her a lemon *granizado* and listened to her for half an hour until the slush in the glass became warm water and she gave me up as a bad job and had to hurry, Cinderella-like, back to the consul's summer villa to see to his awful children's needs.

Halfway to Benicarló, I found a spot on the beach nobody else wanted and spent the afternoon swimming. The Mediterranean looked calm enough: as usual though, its deceptive little waves slapped fast and savage like the hands of a petulant masseur. Refreshed, I was in a mood to move inland again. However, I discovered I had lost my keys; and having changed in the car, I now found myself standing at the top of the beach in only my swimming trunks, carrying a towel and a, by now, three-quarters empty litre of *tinto*. Luckily, I had a spare set of keys in the car and I'd left the driver's side window open a fraction of an inch. Thumb and forefinger quickly aching, I fiddled in vain at the interior knob with a long spike of broken fruit box and a length of split cane from the gutter. I felt a criminal: worse, an inept criminal. A sympathetic group of teenagers cycled up, at once becoming unsympathetic when I asked jokingly if they knew how to rob cars. Ten minutes later, a Land Rover containing a *pareja* and a half of guardias came along. I flagged them down and explained what had happened. Friendly and concerned, they assured me that soon a *policia municipal* would pass by. They waited the three minutes until he came. All four policemen inspected the small gap at the top of the window and agreed it should not be too difficult to open the door with the aid of a piece of wire. The *municipal* said I should stay beside my car; that a bus would be along in no time at all; that it would stop; that the driver would present me with a piece of wire which he (the policeman) would have handed to him. He saluted my semi-nakedness and off he went towards Peñíscola. Off, too, went the *guardias*.

To while away the time until the bus came along, I made a miniature lasso of the draw-string of my swimming trunks, lowered it behind the glass, guided it towards the catch with the piece of soft cane. And at the precise moment when the *municipal* drew up in his car (he'd been just too late to catch the bus driver: I'd seen the bus go by) my door yawned open. Clearly, it was time to head inland again.

The Zaragoza road, climbing up hairpin bends into mountain country, soon brought me to Morella. The town looks stunning: the shape of an irregular cone – a limpet, a squat Dalek – with orange and white buildings rising in tiers towards the castle on its lofty rock. Its spread skirts, hemmed with bastioned walls, brush a strangely terraced landscape of frightening immensity. Morella is in the province of Castellón: but the abundant *huerta* now feels a continent away; it is also in the upper Maestrazgo, an area straddling parts of both Aragon and Valencia, whose villages were fortified by the Knights of Montesa in their long struggle against the Moors. Linguistically, the Maestrazgo is a real mongrel. In Morella itself the people speak a dialect mix of *valenciano, catalán* and *castellano*; in villages not thirty kilometres away in different directions the language is pure *valenciano*, pure *catalán*, pure *castellano*. Morella, like many another frontier town, feels fiercely independent, tough and sinewy. The fabric looks well cared for – but from genuine affection, not mercenary kowtowing to the tourist, not faked-up and smelling of museums. (All exhibits are for sale, incidentally, in Morella's idiosyncratic museum of miscellaneous junk.)

When I arrived, two men were stretching out fifty yards of big firecrackers – in aid, I supposed, of the advertised *fiesta*. The *hostal* bar was crowded and deafening with domino players banging down tiles and raucously betting for high stakes – until, after about ten minutes, the crackers went off, echoing and re-echoing in the constricted street like the opening salvos of a military offensive, to welcome a bridal car all decked out with gay white ribbons and flounces. The domino players all trooped outside; one had a face, beneath his beret, the shape of an ace of spades inverted. The bride peered out; and though I'd never of course seen her in my life, I guessed that she, like all brides, looked better than she had ever looked before; better, I thought, than she ever would again, except when pregnant: which, I saw when she stepped out, she very obviously already was.

For three pounds fifty a night I had a double room and shower; and, from my balcony, a panoramic view (itself worth five pounds a look) across countless miles of astonishing landscape. Dinner comprised three local specialities: *sopa morellana*, a kind of consommé under a raft of tiny, feather-light, flour-and-water dumplings; *ternasco al horno*, an entire shoulder of lamb on the mini-ploughshare bone, with beans and carrots; and *cuajada* (or, in *valenciano, collà*), a sweet curd of cow's milk with distilled herbs.

The following morning, I made the ascent of terraced streets leading inexorably and through lovely arcades towards the *castillo*. On the way up I could not but step inside a superb Gothic church containing quite the most spectacular and original spiral staircase and balustrade, the stonework delicately carved with Biblical scenes, that I have ever seen. A little higher, past two cannon left behind from the Civil War and some horses grazing in a meadow by an endearingly small bullring, I reached the castle entrance. 'How much?' I asked the custodian. 'Whatever you like,' he said, '*la voluntad*.' So I gave fifty pesetas and received an official looking, numbered, unpriced ticket. First passing through the ruins of a monastery, the Real Convento de San Francisco, I reached the summit and had it all entirely to myself. Below, I could see men putting up flags and bunting for the *fiesta*; a little way off a man was unloading fodder from his donkey's pannier; in the far distance the rugged sierras of Aragon stretched, rippling, across the horizon. I'll go there right now, I thought. It was early enough for a day trip to see more of the Maestrazgo; so, deciding I could easily be back in time for the evening's festivities, that's what I did.

I passed through a series of delectable villages, after Forcall, by way of the remote-feeling Bergantes valley, the churches with blue-tile domes and (in Zorita) with little spires atop the domes. It became a jagged upland country, with saw-toothed lines of mountain against the sky. I gasped as a golden oriole flew close in front of my windscreen. My old map, with a line of small crosses indicating that the road surface might be bad, was in this respect not out of date. After Zorita I came to the extraordinary sanctuary of Nuestra Señora de la Balma; you glance up suddenly to see first the chapel then its outbuildings from left to right set into the rockface and you sense that there has been human habitation here for many centuries. When you investigate, you learn you are not wrong. The evidence of smoke-encrusted cave ceilings would be proof enough, but beyond this there is an atmosphere of timelessness and of holiness well-nigh palpable upon this wooded, cliff-side hermit's perch. The Virgin and Child, in jewel-encrusted garments, are in a railed-off gilt chapel in the darkest part of a cave reached by way of a tunnel. (You bend as you go, like a miner on his way to the coal-face.) The walls are festooned with grisly *ex-votos*: waxen limbs and heads (this Virgin is successful with intercessions to do with mental illness); bunches of large candles, like white exotic fruit; first communion dresses in plastic covers; pathetic little pieces of sewing and embroidery; and most disturbing – photographs of the long-ago sick and dying.

Approaching Mas de las Matas, I recalled the Channel Four television documentary series about the Spanish Civil War. In one sequence, three old anarchists from the village – a carpenter, a teacher and a peasant farmer – reminisced about the summer of 1936. Then, they had achieved the ancient dream, they said, of a collective society without profit or property. Money was abolished. The community took over all means of production. The village tradesmen joined in voluntarily; and all known right-wingers were forced to join. The only people allowed to keep their property were those left-wingers who were not anarchists. It was touching to watch the old men's faces as they spoke: their expressions were wistful, nostalgic, not without a tinge of bitterness, not without a touch of vestigial youthful idealism. The peasant farmer told how his family had been in tears when he took all their sheep and money to the Collective, and how, the harvest having been delayed, they worked day and night until all was safely gathered in. There had been snags, the men ruefully admitted. Because everything was free, everybody wanted to drink coffee and smoke cigarettes. A rationing scheme had to be devised in order to share out fairly commodities brought in from outside; not just coffee and tobacco but sugar, rice and meat, to each of which everyone was entitled to a hundred grammes a day. People needed time to adjust to the idea of a collective society, one of them said. The barbers took their chairs and their tools to a large shop that was found for them. Their work was done mainly when the labourers came back from the fields. Some people said they were lazy, spending all day doing next to nothing. It had to be explained that the barbers went on working until gone ten o'clock at night.

Maddeningly, though I remembered the substance of what the old men had said, I had forgotten their names. It would have been grand to track them down and tell them, perhaps over a drink, how impressive their performance on British television had been – and how brave I thought their experiment was, of almost my life-time ago. As it was, I entered a crowded bar and chanced to meet the *alcalde* of Mas de las Matas, Alfredo Monforte, and his chum, Eugenio Añón. They were members of the *Grupo de Estudios Masinos*, an archives and local history society.

'Wonderul,' I said. 'Then you're the very ones who can tell me the names of the old fellows who were in the Channel Four documentary, talking about the Collective of summer 1936. It may even be that they're here right now in this bar.'

'No such film was made here,' said the Mayor.

'Oh, but there was.' I described the sequence.

'I would have known – not that I was Mayor at the time you are speaking about, *señor*. It must have been a montage those film people made.'

'No, it wasn't a montage. I've worked in films and I know a montage when I see one.'

'Some people came here writing notes for a book.'

I imagined director, producer and production secretary, complete with clipboard, on the recce trip. 'Three old chaps on a bench or a low wall overlooking the village,' I said. 'You could see it was Mas de las Matas. The houses, the church with the high tower – all plain as anything. They turned round and pointed.'

'A montage.'

I began to have a nagging worry. Suppose he was right? Suppose I had been hoodwinked by a filmic trick? But suppose, too, that a mayor, possibly hostile to left-wing views, preferred to pretend, for political reasons, that such a film had not been made? To prompt a telling response, I enthused gushingly about the Collective. 'Perhaps the rest of the world may still have something to learn from what happened here?' I said.

'Pah! The Collective was an utter disaster. It was all very well in theory, but the reality was different. That first crop, after they'd set up the Collective, was a farce. Nobody worked as hard as they'd had to before. And I'll tell you something else: the hens stopped laying and the cows stopped giving milk!'

This was not, I felt, the first time he'd made the joke about hens and cows. 'As Mayor, what party do you represent?'

'No party. I am for all the people. Co-operation is the great thing. Tomorrow I go to Teruel for a meeting of mayors, to see what we can do for all our people.'

'But presumably you must have some political affiliation in order to get elected?'

'Anti-communist.'

'Independent?'

'Independent.'

'In Britain, "Independent" usually means "Conservative," ' I said. ' "Keep politics out of local government: vote Conservative." ' It sounded as jaded a *mot* as the Mayor's, about hens and cows.

He was not such a bad chap, I decided. I wondered what he did for a living. He became cautious, his answer suggesting that he did a bit of buying and selling of this and that. He kindly gave me a copy of the booklet on Mas de las Matas which he and his local history group had compiled (and for which he had been several times, he said, to the National Museum in Madrid to do his research).

Walking together towards the *plaza mayor*, we were hailed by an oldish man, big, with a face like that of former Archbishop of Canterbury Ramsey. He stood, in blue shirt, old grey trousers and bumpers, on the step of his handsome, ample, eighteenth-century house: don Joaquín Villalba, a retired teacher. He invited us in. A door off the entrance hall led to the cellar, a lovely, muddly old glory-hole. On a bench were two casks, marked *vino de Joaquín*. I accepted a glass from the larger one. It was very strong, sweet red. Usually I do not care for sweet wine, but this was superb. I had a sample from the small cask; even stronger. The three of us made ourselves comfortable on makeshift benches of planks set upon upturned buckets. Don Joaquín produced a biscuit tin. It had once contained Scottish shortcake. He made much of this, having spent an enjoyable holiday in London and Edinburgh. Inside, there was not shortcake but a small tin, this one containing

dice-sized cubes of *serrano* ham to chew on while we drank.
I had the impression that our host often entertained in this
way.

'Come and look at this.'

He led us out of the cellar, up to the ground floor, along a
passageway, to a room containing a vast, cobwebby corner
cupboard which proved – as he threw open the door – to
be crammed from floor to ceiling with dozens of single-malt
whiskies and Spanish brandies *de marca*. He grinned, inviting
comment.

'Quite amazing, don Joaquín.'

He looked gratified. He smiled at the Mayor. By admiring
his collection, I had passed the test.

'Come with me. *Mi casa, su casa.*'

We trooped up a wide wooden staircase to a pleasant dark-
brown room, dingy but comfortable. I was presented to his
wife, a comfortable lady who must once have been very
beautiful. They had not long got back from Teruel, she told
me. On the table were a great bunch of red carnations and
a box of chocolate toffees. Two young women, the daughters,
schoolteachers both, came in; were introduced; left. In a great
oaken sideboard, don Joaquín had even more whiskies. He
opened cupboards: even more. There were groups of bottles,
platoons and sections, standing in ranks or at ease under
tables, behind whatnots, in carboard boxes. 'It's an interesting
hobby and gives me something to do out here in the country,'
he said. This was their summer residence; home was in
Zaragoza, but Mas de las Matas was their beloved birth-place.
He loved to garden, as well as look after his whiskies. He had
just bought a new mattock, which he brandished in the dark-
brown room like a warrior on a battle-field. 'You make me
think about my garden,' I said. 'The strawberries will be ready
now.' At this, he went out to the kitchen and brought me a
bowl of strawberries.

All afternoon his hospitality continued like this: whole-
hearted; and unpredictable as the bounce of a rugby ball.
'You'll appreciate a good cigar?' he said, offering me a choice
of three sizeable ones of Cuban origin. 'Or perhaps a cigarette?'
Four packets of different brands of Virginia-tobacco, King-size,
filter-tips appeared from the table drawer. 'Now you must try
some *Gran Duque de Alba*. There is no better *coñac* in Spain.'

202

He poured it into an exquisite, 200-year-old eyeglass.

'Tell the Englishman about the Collective,' said the Mayor, who was drinking ordinary J & B.

'A fiasco,' said don Joaquín.

The Mayor looked at me, triumphant. 'Communists say all men are equal – right?'

'Right,' I said.

'That lady was made to wait hand and foot on the Red *junta* that ruled the Collective. In this very house, that happened.' The señora nodded but said nothing.

When, finally, I was able to leave, the Mayor accompanied me to the *plaza mayor*, where I had left my car. I said how much I admired the church and its remarkable tower.

'Come and see this.'

Inside, he showed me the pillar where the Reds planted their dynamite. All had been perfectly restored. The façade, too, had survived the Civil War. Outside, he indicated a statue which the Reds had tried in vain to pull down with a rope. I saw a crack in the fabric of the west wall. 'Nothing to do with the War. A hundred years old, that crack. We're trying to get the church declared a National Monument. If we do, we'll qualify for financial assistance from the Ministry of Culture.'

They are good husbandmen hereabouts; every ripening fruit on the peach trees was wearing its own protective paper bag. Above one small peach orchard I saw the very hill where the old men had been filmed. What was I to believe? In Spain, patently honest and likeable folk of opposite political persuasions are still giving patently sincere and yet totally conflicting accounts of the same events in the Civil War; and it is very often impossible to know whom to credit. I remembered something being said in the television documentary about six right-wingers being murdered just outside Mas de las Matas by an armed terrorist gang that drove around Aragon killing the rich and the religious. The local Collective committee, however, had done their best to prevent the killings. Nothing surprising in this: I could not bring myself to believe that anybody I knew of, or had come across, in Mas de las Matas could kill anybody. But I wondered whether they ever gathered together – at *fiesta* time, maybe: those three old men of the Anarchist Collective, don Joaquín and his wife and daughters; the Mayor and his archivist friend with the curious name of Anón?

Back in Morella it was getting towards dusk. A flight of racing pigeons (dyed startlingly viridian or rose-pink, like the day-old chicks I had seen weeks before in Cáceres market) wheeled overhead the moment after I had finished reading a mayoral *bando*, or proclamation, declaring that all sporting pigeons not registered with the society of *Columbicultura* would be shot.

I found a leaflet of the *programa de actos* of the evening's festivities in the San Juan quarter of the town, where my *hostal* was situated. I was too late, alas, for the children's sports and the open-air supper. At eleven o'clock, after Rosary and Mass, there was to be a bonfire followed by a dance; and this would continue until the small hours, concluding with barbecued *chorizos* (in the local dialect, *torrá de xoriços*): more a parish *verbena* than a *fiesta*.

Towns built in tiers may be climbed either by way of streets hairpinning or corkscrewing up and round or – more direct but daunting – by steep flights of steps which can be painfully uncomfortable underfoot. Those of the *barrio* of San Juan are mercifully gentle, each step of a manageable rise and width so that you do not have to keep shuffling or skipping from one to the next. I timed my after-dinner ascent, under some young plane trees, to coincide with the beginning of Mass. Beside the church was a small square. At the entrance to a lane leading away, the bonfire had been prepared, and against the church wall, between its two doors, a stage had been erected. The band was preparing itself: the customary tedious musicians' ritual of mikes, amplifiers and sound levels. Mass itself was a low-key affair, with a full house of all ages. In the front pew, four burly chaps sat in readiness to shoulder the *paso*. Many of the men in the congregation were holding large candles; and the children had small ones in paper windshields. A little boy of four discountenanced me as I knelt by stroking my belly through the back of his pew. After the prayers, his mother indulged him with winks and kisses and little jokes and paid no further attention whatever to the service. The priest gave a sermon, the first words of which were (as the band began warming up) 'We shall be brief.' It was about the life of John the Baptist, about no man being able to serve two masters and there being no ifs and buts in being a follower of Christ. We reached the point where you are enjoined to say hello to your neighbour. I shook hands with the ancient man next to me, not knowing what say. '*Viva en paz, hermano,*' I said; and it seemed to suit. We shuffled outside. The candles were lit, lovely in the dark yard. The band were still messing about with boxes of electrical tricks: but when they saw that everyone had come out of the church they got down from the rostrum and took their places, *sans* instruments, in the procession. The men with their large candles lined up with the boys behind them with their small ones; then came the women and girls with theirs. The *paso* of St John the Baptist emerged, its husky bearers slightly ridiculous in funny, apocopated, lacy-fringed surplices. The procession moved off to tour the *barrio*, climbing the steps, pausing at the landings both for breath and for the *paso* to be seen by the housebound. I had a coffee and, unable to put the day's conundrums out of mind, talked to an old fellow in a bar about the Civil War. He had been in Madrid for the duration, driving a lorry. Life had been hard, he said, but at least he'd lived to tell the tale – which was more than he could say for his brother. He'd been in Morella when it was bombed by the Nationalists, the International Brigade being in occupation at the time. Water under the bridge, *lo pasado pasado*. Enjoy what's left of life – that was his only motto. We went together back down the steps to the *plazuela* by the church. The bonfire was well alight and the band had begun to play: two trumpets, two sax (one doubling on clarinet), guitar, keyboard, tom-tom, drums, cowbell, tambourine and vocalist, calling themseves 'The Orchestra of the People'. Apart from the odd paso doble and local (Valencian) song, they specialized in South-American music, mambos and cha-cha-chas. Splendid musicians they were (the reedmen in particular: like reedmen the world over; smooth, middle-aged types in rimless spectacles, smart about the collar), and the exuberant singer had a strong, true voice. Dancing began at once, the tinies and the old 'uns leading the way in a rudimentary gallop. Perched on some railings apart, I watched a huge man approach from up the hill with his diminutive mother. The band was rendering a folk-song that had to do with a hat full of sow's blood. The huge man, blissful with drink, got mildly ticked off for bawling out the chorus.

'Conceived during an air raid,' my old companion from the bar said. He laughed; but I could not be sure whether he was joking or, in all sincerity, retailing one more Civil War legend. I decided against stopping for my xoriço, needing a good night's sleep before moving on to Catalonia.

CHAPTER TWELVE

There was one more meal to be eaten – lunch – before I left the Maestrazgo. I reached Valderrobres in the province of Teruel and was stopped in my tracks at the hump-backed bridge over the river Matarrana: for the town, by some *trompe l'oeil* effect of perspective, appears to be painted on to a theatrical backdrop. Pure Aragon the overhanging eaves, the colour-washed plaster (yellow, orange, brown, the remembered, rinsed, blue-bag blue of laundry water); Aragon too its old-fashioned feel. The *fonda* was virtually untouched by the twentieth century. Its dining-room had a sink with a brass tap where you could wash your hands, drink from your knuckles or fill your *cantimplora* before you went your way. There were old prints on the nicotined walls and the plain chairs were rickety and homely. Tables were set round the perimeter of the room (as at the Travellers' Club) so that everybody could talk matily (as does not necessarily happen at the Travellers' Club) to everybody else: lorry drivers, young bank clerks, commercial reps, wandering nondescripts such as myself. We were attended by a middle-aged man so thin (perhaps he was tubercular) I could not understand how he stayed alive. His voice was weak, too, and everything he picked up – a teaspoon, even – seemed too heavy for him to manage. In a *fonda* you take pot luck. Everyone had a whole loaf and a full bottle or *porrón* of wine brought to him by the thin man: a loaf borne by his two hands looked ponderous as a Cyclopean stone; a *porrón*, like an amphora. He brought each of us a tureen of soup, two eggs *mahonesa*, three hunks of rabbit, a banana and a luscious peach: all for less than two pounds – and served on spotless linen.

From Valderrobres you pass serrated, chalk-white mountains, orchards of filberts, olives and almonds; you come to the Ebro, to the town of Tortosa; and now you are in Catalonia.

And here, before you cross the river, is another scene to stop you in your tracks: the site of the Battle of the Ebro. In the summer and autumn of 1938 the Republican troops, having successfully pushed across the bridge with the intention of attacking the Nationalist army advancing on Valencia, were unable to move any further forward and, by constant attrition, lost 150,000 men in the trenches. In the middle of the river you see, on your left as you drive across following the direction of the Republicans' retreat, the appalling memorial erected by Franco *A Los Combatientes Que Hallaron La Gloria*: that is, to those combatants only who died fighting for him. From a concrete base two nasty iron spikes arise, like Ku Klux Klan cowls, one bearing an eagle. It looks a very tawdry monument now, rusting away into the fish-teeming water. At the edge of Tortosa I saw a large graffito reading *VIVAN LAS FUERZAS DEL ORDEN*. This and many more messages of support for law and order had been written not (as Franco's ghost might understandably assume at first) by neo-fascists but, ironically, by those wanting anti-democratic military *golpistas* to be severely dealt with. Spain is a different country now.

Different, in some respects, beyond recognition. The last time I had been in Tarragona had been in the late Fifties, long before democracy and the proliferation of cars, the restoration of the monarchy and free speech. Also, long before the influx of what I found in the Rambla Nova at the *paseo* hour when I arrived: many of the dregs, degenerates and druggy, middle-class drop-outs of Europe, particularly from Germany and Holland. On this evidence, the city was well on the way to becoming a kind of Mediterranean Amsterdam, a warmer Hamburg: sad. Tarragona must surely have the worst water in Spain, being undrinkable, musty, red, of a hardness impervious to soap. The following morning I drank beer with my breakfast bread (the coffee was tainted) and left at once on the northward coast road by which, a quarter of a century before, I had arrived from Barcelona. What I remembered was a pot-holed and cratered surface, no camber, little traffic, no white lines and extensive stretches without any buildings whatsoever. What I now discovered was a good highway under my wheels but at the cost of a blight of ribbon-development and commercialization. South of El Vendrell is the Roman triumphal arch, the Arco de Bara. When last I saw it this ancient monument of a mighty civilization had been standing in splendid, faintly absurd but apt isolation, like the vast and trunkless legs of Ozymandias or a stuffed elephant somebody had carelessly mislaid. Now it stood on its own tidy island of tended oleanders, surrounded by flags of all nations and by chalets and pylons like an advertising hoarding. *Eheu*: the Via Augusta reduced to the rebarbative charm of the North Circular Road!

I turned inland again at El Vendrell (Casals was born here) and was soon entering fertile fruit and cereal country: carobs and almonds in orchards lower down, maize in the upland fields. In Tárrega I bought a melon the size of a junior rugby ball and I ate and drank it all in one go at the roadside for lunch. By this time I had picked up a few words of Catalan. When actually *in* Catalonia, I had to think of it as Catalunya not Cataluña. Here, a *bocadillo* was an *entrepan* (though a sandwich was a *sandwitz*). The written language was often easy enough to understand: but it looked distinctly odd, a new Romance idiom invented by a committee of disaffected Esperanto freaks. *Reforçament del ferm i correcció d'ondulacións*, said a road sign. I bumped along over uncorrected undulations through Agramunt and as far as Artesa de Segre, with the Pyrenean foothills to the north beginning to loom. Before long I should find myself in a chalet-and-yodelling country at the limits of Spain: 'beautiful' landscape for calendars, but not my favourite kind and I did not want to go there yet. I pulled up in Artesa de Segre outside an *hostal* where a lame old man, portly, with a fair complexion, was tending his hanging baskets. The town looked uncomplicated and unpicturesque, just the sort of unimpinging and undistracting place in which to hole up for a day or two, get some work done, wash socks, write letters.

Jubilación is the Spanish for 'retirement'. The word always brings a smile to my lips: I imagine an elderly man, the seconds having ticked away of the final minute of a lifetime of work, throwing his hat high up in the air and shouting Whoopee! in jubilation. The lame old man with the plants – who turned out to be the owner of the *hostal* – wore the kind of wide-brimmed straw hat that might have been designed specifically for throwing into the air. I told him that one of his spikier specimens was called 'mother-in-law's tongue' in

English. He was delighted with this; and each time we met after that he was to chuckle and repeat the words, *lengua de la suegra, lengua de la suegra!* He showed me his small *huerta* at the back: a neatly regimented parade of salad vegetables and melons. 'Of course,' he said, 'what with my leg, I can't do as much as I'd like.' Some of his produce appeared on the dinner table that night: lacy-leafed lettuce, radishes sculpted into flowers with crimson petals and white stamens. The excellent Noguera wine I drank, *Verge del Pla* was made in the town, too.

In the nondescript town square – no more than a triangular island where the main road curved and a minor one broke away – there were a few benches where *jubilados* liked to sit and natter and watch the world go by. One of them, Modesto Brunet, became my temporary chum. He was seventy-seven years old; a short, wiry asthmatic. We would move from one bench to another during our several encounters at different times of the day so that he could have the benefit of stray breezes from any of the limbs of the Y of streets. There was a round stone seat, too, with a column rising from it: I could sit one side of the column, enjoying the shade, while he sat in full sun. Striking up our first conversation, I began by apologizing for not speaking Catalan. 'You have to get up early in the morning if you want to learn Catalan,' he said in Castilian. 'Do you know how to say, in Catalan, *En ninguna cabeza cabe que Dios debe diez?*'

'No, Modesto.'

'*En cap cap cap que Deu deu deu!* That's good, isn't it?' He was delighted with this linguistic oddity and insisted on writing it down for me on a page from his tiny notebook. 'I'm fond of words,' he went on. 'I started to write a little when I retired. Nothing serious, you understand, just to pass the time. I paint, too . . . well, when I was a kid I wasn't bad at drawing. Then for sixty years I had to work and never had the chance. You see that building? At last they're getting round to doing it up. It's going to be a cultural centre – a little theatre and gallery and so on. Anyway, that was the school in my day. One master, several classes – and he was seventy-five years old, though he didn't look it! He taught us to do good handwriting, I'll say that. Line after line of strokes we had to do, *palitos*, little sticks, to learn to control the pen. Come to think of it, he had to be a good teacher. You couldn't go up into the next standard unless you passed in the three rules. Apart from those subjects, we did drawing and singing and, every so often, we had to dance and sing in public. There was a friar who helped out, too, but he buggered off to get married – oh, don't get me going on about priests and friars! Yes, the old school got bombed in the War and stayed in ruins all these years.'

'Did Artesa de Segre get it bad during the Civil War?'

'A lot of suffering. People gunned down without mercy. I'd been a shoemaker until the War. When the Nationalists won I had to flee to France. Afterwards I did a bit of black marketeering, *estraperlo*. Hats mainly, but a bit of all sorts. *Venga!* There's not a village for many miles around where I'm not made welcome to this day! Bread was supposed to cost one peseta a loaf, but the Franco régime made people round here pay twelve – out of spite, you understand, because we Catalan people created our own independent state. Well, we've got the *Generalitat de Catalunya* now. That's something, a degree of autonomy. Mind you, first and foremost I think of myself as a Spaniard, a son of Spain. The PSOE isn't anywhere near radical enough to be what I'd consider socialist. True socialism will come to the country one day. Not in my lifetime but in ten, fifteen years maybe, if the world is spared. We're in a difficult period of transition, *mire*. But at least you can say that we're all equal in this neck of the woods. None of that stupid class nonsense. Round here it doesn't matter a fig what a man is, or what he owns, or what his father was. Equal – that's us.'

I thought of the young farm labourer who routinely drove his John Deere tractor on the forecourt of the smart *hostal* and parked among the potted orange trees and assorted Mercs and Seats and who, having cleaned himself up, ate a four-course lunch off fine napery: not often you saw such a thing in England. On his tractor windscreen was a sticker *Playboy's Discoteca, Las Palmas* with the usual rabbit head and one ear flopping.

'Well, Modesto,' I said, 'the working people here seem to be materially better off. And the quality of life is improving.'

'Quality of life? Don't you believe it. In the days when I was a shoemaker we made good things well and sold them cheaply.

211

Now they make bad things badly and sell them dear. Once, chicken tasted of chicken. Not now. Pork has lost its flavour, too. And most of the meat you get is injected with water to make it weigh heavier. Blame the rich industrialists! We get exploited, they take the money. Not that I'm interested in having more money. I've got all I need and nobody round here would see me go in want. My only complaint is against the cold weather. All winter I have to stay indoors because of my asthma. It's nice for me when the summer comes round again and I can sit outside like this and talk. Come back again this evening and you'll be able to meet the members of our *Sinofuese* Club.'

One of the waiters in the *hostal* was about to leave for Barcelona to see the League Cup Final. There was *mucha emoción para el Barcelona*, he assured me, even in this fairly distant country town in the province of Lérida, or Lleida, as he called it. Black market tickets were fetching up to 12,000 pesetas, he said (about £60). Modesto, I thought, might do worse than to come out of retirement whenever *el Barça* had a big match on. I said as much when I saw him later. There were two other old men with him on the bench; and an old lady, who remained standing.

'These friends are my treasure, Eduardo,' he said. 'The pensioners' Club – the *Sinofuese* as we call ourselves.' He introduced us: María, with brooch and blue-rinse; Pau, with big cheekbones and shining eyes.

'Why *Sinofuese*?' I asked. (*Si no fuese* means 'If it wasn't for.')

'Well – take old Pau. He was a ploughman. Saved hard all his life to buy his own *finca* a few kilometres away. He owns two tractors and there are four cars in his family. He's got lots of pigs grazing out there, in beautiful countryside. He loves it. He'd go there every day *si no fuese*.'

'Wasn't for what?'

'My shoulders playing me up,' said Pau. 'Rheumatism. I'm not too clever on my feet, either.'

'And Pepe – he was a taxi-driver all his life. Always had to cart other people wherever they wanted to go. Now he could afford to have his own car and go touring—'

'If it wasn't for being partially paralysed down my right side.'

'And I would take María dancing,' said Modesto, 'if it wasn't for my asthma.'

'He was a wonderful dancer when he was a young man,' María said. 'You should have seen us.' She did a brief, jiggling, solo, on-the-spot dance, her elbows jutting high. 'He was a lad for the ladies,' she said. 'And still would be—'

'Si no fuese,' he said, with a lascivious grin.

I had to continue my travels. Next time I saw him, Modesto gave me a sealed envelope containing some of his drawings. 'Don't open it now, Eduardo. They're only cartoons, chistes. Not much good, but they'll remind you of me when you get back to England.' They were in crayon and pencil on scraps of paper torn from magazines and packaging. The situations depicted – marital infidelity, gross appetites, prisoners in solitary confinement – were lively, Rabelaisian and as funny as most cartoons carried by the Spanish Press. Perhaps the captions needed a little light subbing and perhaps there was too much cluttering detail; but I have no doubt that Modesto, promising draughtsman turned shoemaker and black market-eer, could have made it as a professional cartoonist si no fuese.

Money, shamefully but unashamedly, is now the chief product of Andorra. The duty-free stores are vast warehouses of tobacco, liquor, perfume, luxury goods and plug-in appliances: cathedrals of capitalism, fanes to covetousness, shrines to greed, temples to materialism. The Andorrans have come a long way since the days when they relied on bringing out a new series of ever more vulgar pictorial postage stamps from time to time in order to scratch a living; and they have come light-years from the time when their six communes depended on land they could terrace and animals they could graze.

Many years ago I did some camping sauvage with my family on a mountainside just off the N20, south of Ax-les-Thermes. We gathered great basins full of blueberries and wild rasp-berries and mashed them up with cream to make wild-fruit fool; then we gorged ourselves silly, watching enormous grasshoppers leap about in the herbs and grasses. We knew we were near to paradise. Across the chasm, a mere five-minute glide for an eagle through the bluish evening haze, were the peaks of Andorra. I'll go there one day, I thought. It looked deserted, untouched since creation, territory impos-sible to enter except at a sharply acute angle. The reality, I discovered now, was that you queued in a long raft of cars in order to get into the capital town, Andorra la Vella; that you queued longer in order to park; and that you queued longer still in order to leave. The police, in maroon-coloured jackets and peaked caps, reminded me of bygone cinema commissionaires. Even without the crowds and their ugly-with-wanting faces, even without the long perspectives of shelves of booze, I would have disliked the town – as I disliked anywhere hemmed in claustrophobically by sheer mountain-sides. Some streets never see the sun; others are glimpsed by sunlight for a few minutes a day in summertime. What you have to do to feel unconfined in Andorra is escape by hair-pinning upwards, to the *cortons*, high pastures, where pale horses and cattle wander at will and, like the frontier with France, cross and re-cross the road at its highest point.

Up there in the fresh breeze you become aware of an Andorra which will have to find other means to survive and prosper when the EEC finally puts a stop to its cynical 'plastic-bag' economy. Since Spain became a member of the Common Market, Andorra has been an isolated little island (not much bigger than the Isle of Wight) of feudalism and *laissez-faire* business arrangements, with no taxation for brass-plate companies two-thirds owned by Andorrans. For centuries the tiny principality supplemented a peasant farming income by the hard graft of smuggling: man and mule crossing the mountains to and fro by night. Heavy lorries on a firm road surface changed all that. The Andorrans became complacent and lazy: all they had to do was import goods from France and store them for as short a time as possible in their aircraft-hangar-size supermarkets before selling at a profit to Spaniards whose customs men turned a blind eye to car-loads and coach-loads of day-tripping small-time smuggling entrepreneurs. Perhaps the Andorrans will develop their ski slopes; perhaps they will create a little legitimate light industry: else for sure it will be back to postage stamps and mules by darkness.

Some French trippers, on their return, were being given a hard time by their *douaniers*. I raced along to Puigcerda to re-enter Spain at the first possible opportunity; then climbed six thousand feet to descend, much relieved, into Ribes de Freser (whose name suggests another fruit mish-mash: black-currants and strawberries).

The hotel here was endearingly run-down: no hot water (*en*

214

reparación) and the table-cloths not ironed; but the torrenting river sounded lovely below my room and the butch, trouser-suited waitress was not overtly man-hating and the *dueña*, giving me a good handful of plums off her tree, fell about at the thought that in Spain they import seed potatoes from England in order to grow them, harvest them and export them. Back to England.

Mountain scenery such as you pass through by way of Olot towards Gerona is, while undeniably picturesque, immediately forgettable. At Banyules I circled a nice blue lake where I fed the fish a too hastily bought loaf of the kind of worthy, hard black bread whose unprepossessing looks betoken a peasant wholesomeness which might sell like hot (and, no doubt, wholemeal) cakes in a Home Counties health-food emporium. Then the coast road south from dull Blanes was as ghastly with insensitive development as could be imagined. I was growing, like the black bread, ever more stale and crusty. Impatient with Catalonia, I was yet nervously excited and anxious to arrive once again in her capital city of Barcelona.

The last few kilometres on from Mataró, I fell to reminiscing upon my last visit. This had been at the end of the hippie era. I had led a group of undelectable-looking American students for the first part of their 'January Term' there. I remembered taking some of them to a football match: not in the vast and wonderfully appointed stadium of el *Barça* but in the bleakly unsheltered and crumbling concrete terraces of the city's other (and much less glamorous) First Division Club. The wind that blew that Sunday afternoon down from the Pyrenees was one of the coldest I have ever known. Each *venta ambulante* selling liquor wore a kind of ammunition belt from which bottles dangled like immense grenades. The students and I kept one of them near us to dispense *copitas* of brandy throughout the match. To supplement the brief and meagre warmth of the spirits we jumped and danced and yelled 'Sin vergüenza' ('Shameless') whenever – thankfully often, in view of the cold – players on either side committed a foul. Earlier that day I had danced the *sardana*, the national folk dance of the Catalan people, outside the cathedral. Individuals, couples, small parties, would arrive from adjacent streets, place bags and bundles on the ground, then join on to the free end of a line of dancers or break a circle and so enlarge it. Music was provided by a surprisingly large uniformed band seated in rows, their backs to the cathedral, brass and deep woodwinds, mainly, providing a wierd music – part tragic, part witty, part cynical – for a dance like an intricate and altogether more solemn version of the *'Palais Glide'*. There were other Americans in Barcelona at the turn of that year than my group of students: hundreds of the crew of the enormous aircraft carrier, the *United States*, who roamed the Ramblas and the *barrio chino* all night long and who, when sentimental and sobering up, gathered under the statue of Columbus and speculated upon how many times his vessel, the *Santa María* (a replica of which was moored in the harbour nearby), might have been contained in theirs.

That New Year's Eve it had been much too chill for snow: but after midnight had struck, I don't know how many hundreds of thousands of artificial snowballs – little tissue paper bags containing tightly-packed white confetti – were thrown in the bars and the streets so that every surface was left as though overlaid with moonlight. Now, years later, entering the grim outer suburbs of Barcelona, though uncomfortably hot I shivered with remembered cold. In the distance, a gas tank exploded on a tower block roof: an immense sheet of flame and then a pall of blackest smoke rising high in the air. I would have stopped to watch what happened next – surely the entire building could be consumed by fire? – but the traffic was inexorable and unimpressed and all I could do was be carried along like a twig in a torrent. Not before I was as though beached in an underground car-park was I able to stop.

Barcelona is a superb city: an intoxicating mixture of the elegant and the sleazy, the respectable and the *louche*. These diverse elements – mutually tolerant – lie compactly between two broad avenues, the Diagonal and the Paralelo. Smack through the middle runs one of the liveliest and best-loved streets in the world, the Ramblas. Connecting the top end of the Paralelo with the bottom end of the Diagonal is the ample Gran Vía de les Corts Catalanes, with a bullring at each end. Within this great parallelogram, a number of smart boulevards such as the Via Layetana or the beautifully (and aptly) named Paseo de Gracia subdivide the space into manageable portions;

and every so often there is a focal point or a centre of interest to prevent one ever feeling disoriented. The railway stations are rationally located; the parks occur exactly where you need them; the Metro system is adequate (and in any case the plentiful taxis are cheap enough); the Montjuich and Tibidabo hills are handy for your refreshment. If you tire of the grid of nineteenth-and twentieth century streets, you can scuttle for the endearing, higgledy-piggledy Gothic Quarter. You can put on a suit or kick off your shoes, admire strictly traditional architecture or seek out yet another bit of over-the-top Gaudí as the mood takes you. I love the place dearly: not for the things that make me love the rest of Spain – Barcelona has more in common with Paris and Rome than with Madrid – but because it is true (and not belligerently so, like hateful New York) to itself, with its own brand of idiosyncrasies; hoping you'll like it but not too upset if you don't. There is absolutely no sense of this being Spain's second city – you'll hear no petty, provincial, small-minded whining as detected by visitors to Manchester or Birmingham. Barcelona, with its separate culture and language, is a people's capital, de facto metropolitan.

I found a doubtful but clean hotel in the centre. It had an art déco lift and, along its landings, several screens and glazed doors with net curtains behind which one imagined every kind of private behaviour occurring. 'You may come and go as you please at all hours of the day and night,' the hotelero said, 'and you may bring with you anyone you choose.' He was in his sixties, had a bullet wound in his left cheek and a dusting of dandruff over his purple shirt. He gave me a brass and steel key which must have weighed a pound and a half; then led me to a room containing little other than its enormous bed, a turn of the century wash-basin and a cupboard full of feather pillows behind which I discovered a considerable pile of Scandanavian pornographic magazines. I washed, changed, chained my document-case to a radiator and went out at once, pausing only to squinny through a rip in my host's lace curtain: he was dunking a biscuit in a glass of tea.

A change had come upon Barcelona since my previous visit. Then, there had been little sense of danger by daytime. If you went looking for (or at) low life by night in the dim bars and bodegas of the barrio chino or the other side of the harbour in Barceloneta, you knew you were taking at least some small

217

risk: but, during daylight hours, what was seen of lewdness at the assumed edge of violence was no threat to the idler. Now however, harm hung on the air like a rancid smell. At the lower end of the Ramblas the tattier whores had spilled from seedy streets and now they paraded in front of fashionable premises, watched by their pimps and fascinated Americans from the café terraces. Threading through to the *Correos* on my way to pick up my mail, in a doorway I came across a woman's handbag and most of its contents: comb and vanity case, diary and address book, a few letters. I went to a nearby police station and reported what I had seen; and was immediately bundled into a car and – to all intents and purposes under arrest – was taken back to the doorway where the bag and slightly fewer of its contents still were. Clearly under strong suspicion, I was made to give a complete report of the incident. My passport was examined, my shady hotel was phoned and I was advised not to leave Barcelona for at least another twelve hours. 'If you are a wise Englishman,' one of the cops said, 'you will stay away from this area of Barcelona.' Shaken by the experience, I came to the verge of hysterics, now realizing how I had made a wonderful howler in the police station: by the omission of a single letter 'i', one object I reported having found in the red-light district was not a woman's comb (*peine*), but a woman's penis (*pene*). Unable to stifle a loud snort of laughter, I attracted attention: and it only served me right, the snort coinciding with my making involuntary eye-contact with a presentable blonde, that I was immediately propositioned by her and asked, *sotto voce*, if I did indeed realize that 'she' was a *trasvestia*. I wished then, like anything, that the comb had still been in the doorway with the letters and the address book and the diary when the policemen had taken me back there.

The next morning I was given a warmly respectful greeting by the *hotelero* when I went out in search of breakfast. I strolled first in the Ciudadela park, where some men were playing a spectacular form of bowls in which metal discs the size of tea-plates were skimmed the length of a thirty-yard rink; and then I went to see whether any progress had been made lately on Gaudí's masterpiece, the Sagrada Familia. At the nearby Metro station, two girl backpackers from Canada ran out of the exit, raced to the corner of the block, glimpsed the

218

church, said simultaneously, 'Yippee, we seen it!' and, without breaking stride, pelted back to the Metro. Well, they had seen what there was to see: those outrageous spires like monstrous brandy-snaps, high into which one can climb by lift and steps among fantastical carvings. The carvings, though inspired by actual flora and fauna, in this context take on the properties of the creatures of dreams. If you have the energy to soldier on even higher beyond the altitude tolerance of the average tourist coach-party member, you find yourself cocooned, a vast embryo moth in cyclopean stone threads, getting on for three hundred feet above the earth. You overlook city and sea, oblivious to local noise; you feel you would like to stay there, enraptured, for a very long time. Perhaps the work (which has recently been restarted) will never reach completion: after Gaudí's untimely death (he got run over by a tram in 1926), no plans were found which could be used even as a rough guide to the ultimate vision of this most unpredictable of architects. On your way back to the centre of the Paseo de Gracia are two buildings which prove, if proof were needed, that Gaudí was an artist whose work could not possibly be continued or even guessed at by anybody else: the Casa Milá and the Casa Battló, luxury apartment blocks dating from early this century and which look like chunks of petrified ocean. Who else but Gaudí could have conceived such buildings as those – or those amazing artifacts designed for the Parque Güell? Coming down in the lift from my perch in the Sagrada Familia, I heard a Nebraskan matron murmur, of shapes and excrescences inspired by natural forms, 'Just like Walt Disney.' Depressingly, she meant this as a compliment: but the difference between Disney and Gaudí is the gulf between fancy and imagination, whimsy and passion, sentimentality and feeling. It was good to see builders' yards in the wide-open spaces between Gaudí's few completed fragments of his masterpiece. This was the best of all celebrations of him and a symbol of continuance and continuity: but I hope nobody in my lifetime gets very far with filling in the emptiness. When I next go back, I want it (like any place where I have been profoundly moved) to look and feel the same as it ever did.

In the Plaza de España a little while later I fell briefly out of love with Barcelona. The palm trees which had been so elegant and regal years before and which I had come specially to see had become scruffy and badly in need of replacement. The waiter, thinking he would please me, brought me an entire two litres of beer in a joke glass ('All gentlemen from Germany enjoy this'). Then an Italian woman with her large family at the next table discovered that her purse had just been snatched. And later, walking miserably in the Carrer del Tallers, I was buttonholed by a wretched, whining fellow who had been worked over by the police and who wanted me, 'a man with instruction', to take him to somebody in authority and plead his case. I had to shake him off as one would a persistent terrier. My *hotelero* (whom I had had to pay in advance) saw me neither come nor go. Within a quarter of an hour, taking deep breaths, I was on the road for Lleida (about which nothing can be said) and, beyond, Aragon.

CHAPTER THIRTEEN

South of Zaragoza, weary of main roads and not caring where
the way might lead, I struck off to the left and came soon to
a signpost indicating two small places whose names, though
vaguely familiar, rang but distant bells for me: Fuendetodos
and Belchite. The first proved to be the birth-place of Goya.
His simple, stone house was having its interior restored: I
was unable to enter or even to peep inside. The plaque on the
wall read:

IN THIS HUMBLE HOUSE
WAS BORN TO BE THE GLORY OF THE FATHERLAND
AND A PRODIGY OF ART
THE EMINENT PAINTER
FRANCISCO GOYA LUCIENTES
31 MARCH 1746 – 16 APRIL 1828
UNIVERSAL ADMIRATION PAID THIS TRIBUTE
TO HIS IMPERISHABLE MEMORY
ON APRIL 16 1913

On the parapet wall of a street on a higher level, was a bronze,
cubist sculpture of Goya's head, stark and tough, overlooking
the public wash-house. *Imperecedera memoria* were words
that would become increasingly poignant as the day wore on.

I drove a few kilometres futher eastwards and came to
Belchite. On one side of the road stood a trim, prim, new little
town nicely whitewashed and well-ordered; but on the other
side of the road – separated from the new development by
a rough tract of *terrain vague* where tractors were parked –
was the old town, the Belchite which Franco ordered to be
left exactly as it was – and for ever after – when the Civil
War ended. The name came back to me at once, Belchite being
a name always to associate with the horror, ignominy and

ultimate futility of war almost as much as Mons, Arnhem, Hiroshima or Guernica. But whereas those places have long since healed and greened over, Belchite remains just as it was the day it was destroyed half a century ago.

It was a chilling experience to walk its long main street of rubble. Every single house, of what must once have been a pretty Aragonese *pueblo*, was a shell of walls containing piles of dust and lath and plaster, broken bricks and tiles and smashed timbers which – on account of the dry climate – can scarcely have deteriorated since 1937. There is a pale blue lime-wash, ubiquitous in Aragon, which speckled the heaps of hardcore and rubbish in old Belchite. I found a piece of plaster which had been painted this colour and put it in my pocket to take home for a gruesome paperweight souvenir. It is on my desk, beside my left hand, as I write these words. It reminds me of the quality of stillness in that appalling, ruined place; of the silence, except for chattering sparrows and one lovely-voiced, unseen bird whose song I could not recognize. Yet it recalls, too, the imagined clamour of grenades exploding in every home, one by one, until the Republicans had won the strategically unimportant little town from the Nationalists. There can be little doubt why Franco chose Belchite rather than many another suitable candidate to be an imperishable memorial to the tragedy of Civil War: it had been picturesque, and it had been pointlessly destroyed by the vanquished. I walked on to where the streets opened at what had once, I guessed, been the main square. Here I paused, hearing the tintinnabulation of sheep bells – uncanny. I could see the perforated church tower from which larger bells must have pealed every day of the year without exception in the old days. Was my imagination playing me tricks? But then, from nowhere, a shepherd led his flock through. The street still served as a sheep-run as it had always done: and why not? There was not a blade of grass in sight, yet the animals nibbled at the rubble.

'Not much for them to eat,' I said.

'They find what they want. Not enough rain.'

'What happened here was a terrible thing.'

'A long time ago. There's a young fellow living in a house lower down. He's mended it enough to keep the weather out. Go and see.'

'No fear!'

The young clerk in the branch of the Banco de Zaragoza in the re-built Belchite told me that not many tourists ever went into his bank. Usually they jumped out of their cars or motor coaches, had a quick look through the main gate of the old town and then zoomed off. The Civil War was just history now that democracy had come to Spain: *lo pasado pasado*, the phrase I had heard before. But on a wall still standing adjacent to the former *plaza mayor*, I had discovered, after talking to the shepherd, two graffiti quite close to each other. The first, supportive of a prominent contemporary right-winger, read: *Aragón con Blas Piñar* and was accompanied by a crude depiction of the politician – reminiscent of a cartoon Mussolini – giving the fascist salute. The second, accompanied by a scrawled hammer-and-sickle, read simply: *Espana Roja*, Red Spain. I told the clerk this. 'Spain's trouble is,' he said, 'that certain memories can't ever perish!'

Later that day, six kilometres to the north of Teruel, I came across a third example of *imperecedera memoria*. This took the form of that brand-new Spanish phenomenon, a Republican War Memorial. Still raw-looking (it could never, of course, have been erected during Franco's time), it was a strange construction: white, cubist, suggesting a citadel, with odds and ends of stuck-on bits and pieces such as a pair of red clenched fists and black and red Anarchist flags. I found it moving: both for its unlettered and unofficial simplicity and for its having come into being so many years after the death of those it honours; eloquent testimony to the doggedness of those ultimate losers of the prolonged struggle for Teruel, the families of Loyalist survivors. In front of it, to attract the attention of passers-by, was a plain white cross with a notice reading: *These bodies teach lessons for all to learn: you may cut the flower but you won't kill the plant, and dictatorships are futile.* The notice was signed, *Your comrades and families.* The main inscription on the monument, *To our comrades who fell here in defence of liberty and democracy 1936-1939*, was perhaps less telling than certain other tributes both collective and personal. One thousand and five men shot by the Nationalists had their bodies thrown here into an artesian well eighty-four metres deep, almost filling it. A dwarf wall encircling the top of this well bears notices giving the plain facts of the *holocausto Teruel*; and here and there are pathetic individual memorials

such as that to Felix Lorente Doñate, who died on the first of
September 1936. His widow's fifty-year-old grief is expressed
as freshly and poignantly as if her husband had been killed
only the year before.

> I looked for you everywhere. How unjust that you should
> be here, at one with your suffering, having had to leave me
> and your four-year-old daughter on our own. We do
> not forget you, your wife Felicitas Hernández and your
> daughter Ángeles Lorente RIP.

An Anarchist's message to his mate reads:

> Here is the path of passion which you call death but which
> I call salvation, because I judge it by the horizons you
> opened and not by the ground in which you are buried.

All around there were tiny cairns of pebbles supporting
makeshift crosses. There were countless flowers – natural and
artificial – strewn by the wind up to a hundred yards from
the monument over the dusty land. To the north stretched a
dead straight road across a monotonous plain, furnace-hot
now but by all accounts killingly glacial in that long-ago winter
battle. To the south, beyond ploughed fields, was the little
provincial city of Teruel, which, though it was of scant
strategic importance to either side to take and hold, had been
– with quite incredible vehemence – attacked, and won, and
lost again by the Republicans. If only for the sake of their
morale, it had been vital for them to keep a firm grip on Teruel
during that period of the war. But tragically it slipped from
their grasp, like an exhausted drowner from his rescuer under
the ice, just as it began to seem to be saved. Teruel's name
lay heavy on my heart; and little did I guess, as I continued
on my mournful way there, that my spirits were about to be
lifted by quite the most joyous (and barbaric and pagan)
festival I have ever taken part in: the *Fiestas del Angel*.

Fueros – ancient rights or privileges – are jealously maintained in cities throughout Spain; and nowhere more so than
in the region of Aragon. It is one of Teruel's time-honoured
privileges that its citizens, the *Turolenses*, may run tethered
bulls through the city streets during the annual *vaquilla*

(amateur bullfight) festivities within the *Fiestas del Angel*. The Mayor, who delegates responsibility for public safety during this hair-raising jamboree to a number of *peñas*, bullfighting social clubs, had posted his proclamation a few days before:

> Be it known: That the *Fiestas Del Angel* taking place between the 1st and the 11th days of this month of July and during them the traditional *Vaquilla Del Angel*, I call upon that good civic common sense which has always been demonstrated by Turolenses to ensure that the festivities be thoroughly enjoyed with appropriately good public behaviour . . .

There then followed rules which were to be at all times stringently obeyed. Most of these were purely of parochial interest, to do with the reservation and allocation of seats in the bullring; two, however, which might have been proclaimed in a forum very many centuries before, forcibly claimed my attention:

> Five: It is prohibited for minors to take part in events involving tethered or horn-tipped bulls or *Toros De Fuego*.

> Seven: Ropes for tethering bulls are to be handled only by those authorized with distinctive arm-bands to do so.

Maybe *now* was to be my opportunity to fool around with fighting bulls, I thought! I could not begin to guess what a *toro de fuego* might be; but tethered bulls – or those with protectively tipped horns – might well provide excitement enough for a middle-aged, none-too-fit, inexperienced, frightened but incurably fascinated English aficionado. There were even to be full-blown bullruns for kiddies to take part in, a *vaquilla de los peques*, to be held (I learned from another poster) on the last morning of the *fiesta*. At ten thirty a heifer calf would be run from the bullring to the corral; from the corral, more *becerras* would then be run to the main square, the Plaza del Torico. And – as though even this weren't heady enough – there were to be free balloons and lollipops distributed in the market-place!

The *fiesta* had already been in progress for six days of minor events. I bought a handsome programme and found out what I had missed: the children's tetrathlon; the gymkhana; the crowning of the Beauty Queen; the judging and awarding of the Open Poetry Prize; two firework displays; several performances by a visiting dance troupe; three processions of giants and big-heads; a marionette show; a shooting exhibition; horse, go-kart and bicycle races; angling, basket-ball, handball and tug o' war competitions; a pelota knock-out championship; dancing in the streets; folklore presentations; an athletic sports meeting and a chamber concert – not to mention the daily *diana* or reveille at eight o'clock given by the Town Band doing the round of the streets! A breathless catalogue, yet the *Diario de Teruel* leader was complaining that only now, on the Thursday, were things really beginning to warm up; and indeed, continued the paper, perhaps the festivities started too early these days. Front-page photographs showed how deserted the centre of town had been at a normally busy hour the day before. The *Ayuntamiento*, or Town Council, was reneging on its obligation to provide the *Turolenses* with their entitlement of ten full days of *fiesta*!

By late morning many businesses were beginning to close, not to re-open before Tuesday. Some shop windows in the Plaza dal Torico were already shuttered and boarded up. I had a disastrous haircut and, with my spiky near-tonsure concealed under a white linen cap, I made some last-minute purchases so that I might make my imminent appearance with the bulls in suitable garb: white canvas trousers, red cummerbund sash with tassels, red neckerchief, and a pair of light, open-work leather shoes suitable (I hoped) not only for short bursts of sprinting in Spain but also for some dandyish personal display when I got home to England. Had I gone the whole hog, I should also have bought a kind of black blouson – not unlike the Oxford Commoner's gown – a garment, the salesman told me, which had become fashionable that year in Ibiza. Back in my hotel toom I tried on my rig and looked in the glass and felt suitably sheepish, glad there was nobody in Teruel who knew me. (Not, in all probability, that I would have been recognized: *fiesta* gear, worn by the majority of all ages, confers a grateful freedom of anonymity upon the wearer.)

That evening I wore it to an hilarious spectacle: a comic bullfight. The main protagonists were a versatile comedian called Toronto; a team of ten dwarfs; some chimpanzees; a buxom but beautiful woman singer of popular ballads and a band of drums and wind instruments. Now it would be foolish to try and pretend that a show in which human grotesques, parodied by a travesty of monkeys and aided and abetted by a knowing clown, put to death, after baiting them, three young dumb animals, could be anything other than the apotheosis of barbarity and bad taste. Anyone even attending such a performance should be ashamed; and anyone finding it the least bit funny ought to be ostracized as a moral and social leper and cast into outer darkness. Indeed, if tomorrow I became dictator of Spain, the first thing I should feel constrained to do would be to ban *all* bullfighting, whether comic or not – just as, were I dictator of Britain, I should be obliged to ban boxing and fox-hunting. That said, it really was a delightful and genuinely funny couple of hours on that Thursday evening in the Teruel bull ring: good-natured and good-humoured; and – for reasons I still cannot entirely understand – neither distasteful nor undignified for either human or non-human participants. As for cruelty and suffering, I observed none of the former and less of the latter than you would customarily see at a *corrida* or a *novillada*. The dwarf *toreros*, when actually engaged in fighting the bulls, did so in a serious and thoroughly professional bullfighting manner, with skill, agility and grace. When not fighting bulls but clowning, they were still as full of dignity and self-respect and *pundonor* as an egg is full of meat. If we laughed at them it was not because they were diminutive adult human beings but because they knew how to make us laugh at them without recourse to baseness. They did for a living what dwarfs have honourably done for a living down the centuries – and with gravitas. I honestly believe that nobody was left debased or demeaned. The chimpanzees were old hands at the game, too. They were clearly not terrified by the little charging bulls; they looked well fed, well looked after. Such shows are popular all over Spain. State laws, rigorously enforced, control what goes on in them; and I only regret that those laws do not protect the chimpanzees from being encouraged to smoke enormous green cigars during their act.

Teruel is an unprepossessing town: worth seeing but (from a

tourist's point of view at least) not really worth going to see. Among its few attractions are some miraculously surviving Mudéjar towers (these are truly superb: massive, intricate confections of brick and *azulejo* tiles), and the somewhat grisly mausoleum of the so-called 'Lovers of Teruel'. I had been in Teruel before, with my wife. We had stayed in the *parador* a little way outside the town, where it seemed that many Spanish honeymooners go – as American honeymooners go to Niagara Falls – drawn by the romantic legend of *los amantes*. The story, a woozy rigmarole not unlike that of Romeo and Juliet, was originally spun by Boccaccio in the fifteenth century and has often been retold by and to the gullible as though it were true. And even if it were – that Diego de Marcilla and Isabel de Segura died of heart-broken love for each other, that they were buried together in the chapel of the Santos Médicos in the church of San Pedro, that it was indeed *their* bodies which were exhumed in 1555 – none of it would impress me nearly as much as what still happens in the specially built necropolis today. Young newly-weds (but also groups of adipose and elderly foreign coach-gawpers) go down on their hands and knees in order to contemplate, behind a stone filigree, the mummified remains of the alleged pair. They look like enormous chrysalides, shudderingly awful and (I would have guessed) enough to guarantee at least a fortnight's impotence for even the lustiest of grooms. On the catafalque above are recumbent effigies of the lovers, their hands all but touching. There is much trumped-up pathos (not that the craftsmanship of the statuary is contemptible), but little of the feeling and none of the power of, say, the Arundel Tomb of Larkin's poem, the 'stone fidelity' that the stone knight and lady in Chichester cathedral have ultimately proved

> Our almost-instinct almost true:
> What will survive of us is love.

If the lovers of Teruel 'prove' anything it is that what tends to survive of us for several centuries is a sentimental version of a past affection; also (in a pure climate such as Aragon's) a membrane of skin like a bat's wing, tight over the bone. Perhaps nowhere more than in Teruel do both the Spanish lack of imagination and the Spanish obsession with the physical realities of death manifest themselves in one place so vividly. The guide recites the words; the myth is compounded and the visitor leaves, not bamboozled but with his humanity unwittingly diminished.

During my previous visit, I had noticed with great astonishment how the balustrade protecting the long drop into the chasm behind the bus station had been knocked over and left unrepaired. Now, an English person would at once envisage a small child falling to a ghastly, tumbling death among the bespattered rocks; but a Spaniard would not easily register such an event until there were documentary proof of its already having happened. Doubting Thomas would have made a good Spaniard.

The *torico* in the middle of the Plaza del Torico is a small black bull rather ludicrously supported by a tall (and partially fluted) stone column arising from a circular water trough. All but the sharp-eyed might miss it: but in this bull-obsessed, sub-heathen little city, this diminutive idol of the wild fighting beast is the cynosure of the annual *Fiesta del Angel*. Pressing in upon it, like an over-anxious congregation at the shrine, are the sides of the cramped, triangular square: mostly of five-storey buildings, creamy yellow with balconies and green slat blinds, standing upon a dark arcade of pillars not unlike the one (maybe it was one left over, surplus to builders' requirements) on which the *torico* stands. The buildings are not ancient: one, though baroque in style, bears the date 1912 on its façade; others are obviously much more recent than that (Teruel received heavy poundings from both sides during the Civil War); however, in this constricted area is sensed a long era of inward-looking, rabid, rigorously guarded ritual. A note in the programme made much of the welcome Teruel Festival extended to visitors from far and wide – and certainly I was at all times made to feel at home – but this, you felt, was a place which got on with being itself for as long as it liked: the rest of the world (and its opinions) could go to hell if its customs offended anyone.

The Friday *corrida* was a corker, full of memorable incident. Before it started, a wild rabbit somehow got inside the arena and made several circuits before it could be captured. Then one of the early bulls all but leapt the *barrera*. Another, after

229

the sword had gone in, ran a few paces backwards on its hind legs, jumped in the air and finally fell flat on its back, stone dead. The sixth bull was a bad one, lame, and everyone whistled until the President showed the green handkerchief for it to be withdrawn. Duly, in came three *mansos*, with bells around their necks, to accompany it out; and for a few moments the crowd was able to relax and make knowing, laughing remarks. Nobody was ready for the subsititute bull when he made his storming entrace from the *toril*. He was a real rogue. One of the *banderilleros* slipped when planting his darts and lay prone on his face while the bull put both horns into his back, first pushing then lifting him, inflicting a flesh wound in the shoulder. Then the matador, El Bayas from Tarazona (whose boisterous fan-club had travelled to watch him), came off even worse than his *banderillero*. Having put in the sword, he was gored in the eye. After falling, he got a second *cornada* in the right thigh and had to be carried from the ring. This meant that the senior matador of the three, the great José Antonio Campuzano, had the responsibility of finishing off the contest. Three times he struck – and seemed to strike accurately – with the *estoque*; and three times the indomitable bull rose again slowly like a Muslim from prayer before, still trying to cling to one last frail thread of life, it could do no more. It gushed blood from its nostrils, quivered in it flanks and – as though suddenly and unaccountably bored by the evening's proceedings – lay on its mucky side and expired.

Much later, when I went back to my hotel, I found Campuzano, the matador, finishing his after-dinner coffee on the terrace. He said goodbye to a group of people and then – bracelet, Gucci belt and shoes and hunk-of-gold-on-a-chain all aglint – he slid beside his manager into his enormous, elegant, pearl-grey Citroën. The car rose up slowly on its suspension, just as that sixth bull had risen up on its haunches. Then, a yellow-eyed beast, it charged at break-neck speed down the Calle de San Francisco towards the Madrid road. It was Nature imitating (if not Art) kitsch; it had been like a clip from an American soap opera. And (so it seemed) because it was I who had directed him as he steered backwards through a knot of parked vehicles and because it was I who – like an old acquaintance – had been the last to wish him *buen viaje* I got myself invited to occupy the seat he had vacated.

The invitation was extended by a burly and bearded character called José Hurtado Ríos. In his normal professional life he was a lawyer with the well-known Mapfre Vida insurance company in Barcelona; but he was in Teruel for a few days, accompanied by his lady (a cheroot-smoking, liberated blonde), in his capacity as a columnist for the French bullfight review, *Corrida*. He was a favourite son, *hijo predilecto*, he told me, of his native village of Tobarra, fifty kilometres south of Albacete. (During the next two hours or so, Señor Ríos was to grudge himself no opportunity of singing his own praises – particularly on the topic of his writings and especially the excellence of his poetry.) I asked him whether the wounds suffered by El Bayas had been as serious as they had looked from my *contrabarrera* seat.

'The wounds are clean. They've not done much for the morale of his two colleagues, though. They're both engaged to fight in Pamplona tomorrow.' The *Sanfermines* had just begun. The national Press carried long articles about the annual bull-running through the streets. Pamplona was, as usual, full of unimaginative idiots risking life and limb sprinting ahead of the early-morning stampede to the bullring. 'Nervous, you understand,' said Ríos, placing a forefinger on the side of his nose – as though this conclusion could have been reached only by the most knowledgeable and precipient of students of the art.

'Yes,' I said with a sigh. 'I do understand.'

'How could an Englishman understand about bulls?' murmured his lady.

I had been expecting the question to be posed sooner or later. 'Very well – let's get it over with,' I said. 'Come on – quiz me about bullfighting. If I pass the test, you may buy me a drink. If not, I buy you one. And leave.'

He quizzed me and I passed. I stung him for a *copa* of *Torres Diez*. Then he introduced me to the three others at the table. The first, a sandy-haired man in his mid-thirties named Alipino Pérez Tabernero, was the Salamanca *ganadero* who had furnished the bulls for that day's *corrida*; the second was Roberto Espinosa, a former *novillero* who, having finished a career in the ring unscathed, as an impresario received a

231

cornada between nose and right eye when a bull got him cornered during a *sorteo*; and the third was Emilio Muñoz, a celebrated matador who was due to perform in the next day's *corrida*. He wore a horizontal stripe summer shirt, nondescript jeans and no socks. Nobody could have affected less of the glamorous movie-star image normally associated with Spanish bullfighters – Campuzano, for instance – than Muñoz. He stood up to shake hands with me: which he did with an old-fashioned bow from the hips. Terribly thin, he was; and pathetically young-looking despite his experienced, character-ful face. When we sat down I noticed that on his feet he had a pair of those thin pumps, much like a ballet dancer's, which bullfighters habitually wear in the ring.

I was embarrassed, not wanting to appear a bore and a pest and a hanger-on. Bullfighters, like the cult figures of pop music and sport, have to contend constantly with much tedious adulation from all manner of tauromaniac groupies. I indi-cated that I did not wish to interrupt his conversation. Muñoz stuttered over his gracious response, clearly taken aback either by what I had said or by my foreign accent.

'Bullfighters aren't too bright,' Ríos whispered to me as Muñoz resumed his conversation with the other two men. 'I'm fairly new to their inner world, but that's one thing I really have learnt thoroughly. Also, they're most of them cowards at heart, you know.'

'There can't be true valour without some degree of intel-ligence, surely,' I said.

'Some degree. But they only show it in front of the bull. Believe me, I know them. They flinch if they have to have so much as an injection. Outside the ring, they're babies.'

Muñoz was talking to the *ganadero* about the Madrid *afición* at the San Isidro that year. 'Ignorant and prejudiced,' said Muñoz. 'They whistle even before you've made the first pass.' He stood up; struck the formal attitude for inciting a bull, with little twitching movements of the imaginary *muleta*. It was a thrilling moment: a gangling young man in casual clothes – who might just have knocked off work as an office cleaner – was transmogrified by movement into an assured artist. On the pavement opposite the hotel terrace a cluster of young admirers watched with awe. 'As prejudiced and ignorant,' he added, 'as certain journalists in the bullfighting Press.' He sat down, picked up his glass of Coca-Cola and, as though it were champagne, raised it in the direction of Ríos.

'Tell me your opinion of the *Sanfermines*,' I said to Muñoz.

'A barbarity. It does no good for bullfighting's reputation either in Spain or the outside world.'

Señor Tabernero confirmed this. 'I could show you horrific pictures of old ladies impaled on horns. *Una barbaridad.*'

'A good friend of mine,' said Señor Espinosa, 'lost three fingers through no fault of his own when he got wedged in the main entrance to the bullring. He had no chance. Sheer weight of numbers. And most of them are foreigners who come to Pamplona to run with the bulls but without the remotest idea of what they're up to.

'The Americans are the worst,' said our waiter.

'So don't ever go to Pamplona,' Ríos said to me sententiously. 'They're a bunch of drunks and fools. *Borrachos y locos.* You can't mix wine with bulls.'

The *vaquilla* proper began next morning. 'Saturday Sunday and Monday,' ran the *Diario de Teruel* headline, '*Fiesta Sin Descanso*,' 'Festivities Without Let-up.' This may sound naive: cheerfully exuberant words, nothing more than the endearing and understandable exaggeration of a staunchly provincial sub-editor. But *sin descanso*, literally translated 'without rest', proved to be the very truth of it. The *fiesta* was to be remorseless and unremitting, taking no account of mealtimes, or of daylight and dark.

At four o'clock in the afternoon all the *peñas* squashed together into the main square for the garlanding of the *torico*. This year the honour had fallen to the *Ajo*, or Garlic Club. A scaffold of bodies grew high round the little bull's stone column and up it shinned a skinny fellow to tie a neckerchief round the neck of the beast. It was virtually a fertility ritual, the crowning of a monumental phallus. As soon as the *pañuelo* was tied, the vehement and jam-packed crowds uttered a roar the like of which I had never heard before: primitive, lustful, as profane a noise as one imagines may have been uttered in ancient times at a sacrifice. The doe-eyed Festival Queen and her seven Maids of Honour on show in the trailer of a Land Rover now looked less like the twentieth-century sanitized pin-ups they were than white-robed virgins specially picked and prepared and brought to the square for ceremonial rape and throat-slitting.

233

There were upwards of half a dozen *peñas*. Each had its own brass band, or *charanga*, behind which to march. The garlanding was over, it was time for the *Peña del Ajo* band to lead the rest from the Plaza del Torico, noisily up past the chapel containing the long-sleeping Lovers of Teruel and over the lofty viaduct to the bullring for the *corrida*. It was a stirring *pasacalle*. Once part of the procession, you were impelled not so much by the physical pressure of those behind as by the thump of drums and the low, throaty thrum of voices anticipating pleasure. In a bar close to the ring I had a drink of Zoco with an old man who, he told me, came in to Teruel just once every year for the festival. Zoco is a popular brand of *pacharán*, a concoction of sloes and aniseed. 'We have our own little *vaquilla*,' he said. 'On St James's Day. If you ever come to my village, sir, you are welcome to stay in my house. You can't miss it. It's the one right next to the big rose bush. I fought in the Civil War here. I spent three years in prison on account of my beliefs. At last we have a settled democracy and I hope I'm spared for many years to enjoy it. Perhaps you'll be running in the ring yourself later on – like I used to until well past the age you are now. I'll look out for you. I'm over seventy and a bit too old for such things these days! *Vaya con Dios*.'

Close to me in the ring sat an enormously fat man; in fact so big was he that he occupied two seats. When somebody volubly complained about this, he held up two ticket stubs between thumb and forefinger and stared blankly ahead, saying nothing. With him was a provocatively-dressed woman – presumably his mistress – who amused herself by giving the glad eye to a *banderillero*: that is, until her whopping protector noticed what was going on; upon which she began to barrack the poor young man cruelly, shouting, '*Madre de Dios*, Mother of God, how that fellow does play to the gallery!' It was not a memorable *corrida*, otherwise: though a fair *bonne bouche* for what was to follow that night, the next and the next.

From nine o'clock until midnight the *peñas* marched behind their bands. Round and round the streets and squares and alleyways of Teruel they progressed: ceaselessly, the tempo never slackening. Arms aloft and holding hands, ten or a dozen abreast, they advanced gently – more an uncontrolled marking-time than a slow marching forwards – seemingly in

234

a kind of daze, or trance, and drawing upon what must have been a simply vast reservoir of energy. Only one of the clubs – *Los Marineros*, in their sailor-suits – wore a distinctive uniform. The others were in standard *fiesta* rig. You did not have to be a club member in order to tag along; indeed, it was difficult for a bystander not to be roped in by a passing *peña* and bundled to the middle of a file, gripped by both arms and not released until – as though by some intuition similar to that which makes a flock of birds turn in flight as one – the phalanx of club members containing him broke away for a round of drinks in a bar. Now and then some of the instrumentalists would have some respite – trombones, trumpets and saxophones being set aside while bottles and *botas* were passed around; but bass drum, side drum and snare drum would continue the rhythmic beat, as though urging the swift return of plangent brass. Quite often it happened that two *peñas* would come face to face in a constricted street, unable to pass; and the two *charangas* would go on playing their respective tunes loudly, as in a Charles Ives symphony: but there was never the slightest hint of the ugly side of rivalry which elsewhere might lead to unpleasantness and even to violence. One group or the other would graciously give way, the bands and their followers would recede; and the narrow street would be left quiet, even desolate, again.

At midnight, though the marching stopped, the music went on. Each *peña* had its own allocated open space in the centre of town where a stage had been set up for its band and where there was room for dancing and for a few tables and a bar to be set up. In the more staid areas of Teruel – such as that near the cathedral – the dances were suitable for the middle-aged and elderly; whereas in the modern business quarter, where the smart bars were (known as *La Zona* to the young trendies), there was a rock group. The *Peña del Ajo* had its versatile band set up in the Plaza de los Amantes, whose old buildings were rendered suddenly even lovelier, transformed by coloured lights and flares.

By the small hours of that morning, *la madrugada*, the *fiesta* (the result not only of *pacharán* but also the mesmerizing effect of constant drumbeat and incipient exhaustion) became for me less a sequence of events than a kaleidoscope of three nights and two days of simultaneous, inseparable, blindingly vivid impressions. In the bullring ablaze with lights amid the pitch black of night I remember being among the packed crowd of spectators when a little bull, its horns tipped with white spheres about the size of cricket balls, was let loose in the arena. Perhaps fifty or sixty young men and a few girls, some of them armed with rolled newspapers, cavorted and pranced to incite the animal to charge them. When it did charge, what they did was jink or run a few steps until the bull's attention was attracted elsewhere: but on occasion it would not be diverted; and the chase would send the pursued youngster sprinting to the barrier where – if lucky – he or she might nimbly spring across to safety. Sometimes however the little bull caught up with its tormentor. There would be a brief and usually painless scrimmage in the sand; then the bull would be lured away while the fallen runner stood up and dusted himself down, not much the worse for wear. After a while the bull would become bored and tired and it would be removed and replaced and another baiting would begin.

I remember being tempted to try my luck in the ring but, courage failing me, making a craven way back to town, meeting friends, having one or two glasses more of Zoco, seeing an old lady dancing a paso doble by herself, beautifully, elegantly, while a young fellow in the gutter begged for the price of a bed and some food and his bus fare home. I recall the characteristic sound of the streets after the *charangas* had at last stopped playing: the rattle of empty drink cans kicked and ricocheting off echoing alley walls, the rumble of barrow and trolley wheels as their owners went in pursuit of pre-dawn customers for slices of coconut, *turrón*, popcorn, sticks of barley-sugar and *chocolate con churros*. There was an astounding moment, one of those two sunrises, when I happened to be loitering over a beer in the *callejón* behind the ring: the great wooden gate burst open and a bull on a long tether charged past me, closely pursued by a crowd of mad-eyed older men possessed of some antique demon. But I relive more often than any of these those minutes when, back yet again at the bullring and having decided that it was now or never, I found myself in the centre of the arena confronting not a horn-tipped bull but a *toro de fuego*; a bull with two flaming torches in a metal frame contraption round its shoulders; and how I came unintentionally close enough to feel the heat of the flambeaux, see terror in the animal's eye, ward off the flank as, turning within its length, the animal brushed my arm. In my kitchen cupboard I keep the brand-new pair of open-work shoes, their toe-caps scuffed and ruined by my ludicrous scramble up and over the concrete *barrera*.

CHAPTER FOURTEEN

The name of La Mancha derives from an Arabic word, *manxa*, the dry country. Water comes to it artificially these days: they can grow crops as thirsty as spinach; and a characteristic image of the landscape is the lovely, peacock-fan iridescence of ever-turning, far-flung water-jets. For all this, the vast plains are dry in their hearts. They feel, and they sound, dry. Oxen drawing wooden wagons look perennially thirsty; the wheels creak and crack and groan and their high-piled loads of garlic (hundreds of thousands of cloves the purple of boozers' noses) rustle in their desiccated skins at each rut and bump in the road. The first sound heard in La Mancha, though, if you come from Cuenca by way of La Almarcha, is that of the humming and buzzing of lavender fields. Long perspectives of dead straight rows of pin-cushion clumps are thickly encrusted with bees, like billions of chips of topaz or tiger's-eye; but more astonishing is their wings' murmuring: like malcontent voices in a distant town anticipating bother. At Belmonte you see your first windmill. Fugitive lower down, winds are heard whenever you climb the merest knoll hereabouts. Soon you come to innumerable, exhausting acres of cereals and sun-flowers and vines where, if you could not drive away, you feel you could go mad. The barley is funny: so short-stalked that the stubble in the mown fields looks nearly as tall as the standing crop. You stop in the implacable heat to stare and wonder. This is a place, if ever there was one, to be in thrall to: not for conventional beauty (there is little of the picturesque in La Mancha), but for its very soil, pheasant copper-red, to take a handful of and let sift, hot and dry, through your fingers. If you love such landscapes, you will think of people you dislike who would certainly hate them: and this is not the least satisfaction of your travels.

The Spanish National Tourist Board has been doing its best

to popularize this area for visitors, documenting the route of Don Quixote and erecting kitsch metal signs at the edges of villages mentioned in the novel; but La Mancha, thankfully, is likely to remain to the popular tourist trade as *Don Quixote* is to Mills and Boon. There cannot surely be many who take acute pleasure in uncomfortable terrain. On the road between Tomelloso and Pedro Muñoz I stopped for the shade of the only roadside tree for many miles. It was mid-afternoon in Valdepeñas wine country. Here and there among the vines there were pump houses. There were shelters, too, hemispherical, made of flat stones, whitewashed. In the overwhelming heat there was something bizarre about their suggestion of igloos – their whiteness, their tunnel entrances – that ensured that spot a corner for ever in my memory: but a coach-party, one feels, would not necessarily thank you for leading it, for such a reason, to such a place.

The brasher kind of guidebook will assure you that 'when you've seen one windmill you've seen them all' – leaving quite out of account the fact that the similar mills are found in dissimilar places. If Quixote went on a twentieth-century tour of his old haunts, he might feel inclined to tilt less at windmills that at the grain silos and towering cranes that claim his horizons nowadays. Amazed, I discovered they were experimenting with wind power once again for their energy. A German firm has erected an enormous cylindrical tower, painted red and white, to rise from the plain on the way to the village where (some say) Don Quixote was born, Argamasilla de Alba. One to each hillock, with mute irony, lovely old white mills still survey the cereal fields, their sweeps now arthritically stiff. Above Campo de Criptana is a group of restored mills immediately adjacent to the village limits; on one of them is the inscription:

LOS ESCOLARES DE
CAMPO DE CRIPTANA
A
D. MIGUEL DE CERVANTES
18-4-1982

These are pleasant enough, but my favourite group of mills is the eight or nine above Consuegra, in the province of

Toledo. These, too, have been restored of late, but not too over-officiously: already the spars and struts of wood have become ruinous. The cone-topped simple masonries are beautiful but desolate and obviously useless; and they are perched up there as ever they were in a ceaseless wind beyond the equally useless, desolate but beautiful castle. This, the *Cerro Calderico*, is one of the best hilltop sites I know anywhere. While the wind moans through the sail-wires and (although baking hot below) you shiver and shelter in the lee of a mill, you may survey miles of apparently fallow saffron fields (the bulbs are concealed beneath the surface) and observe that La Mancha, far from being flat, is gently undulating, that there is nearly always a mountain range in the far distance. Every so often you will see – just as the Don did – an inverted cone of red dust rising. Perhaps it is a local meteorological phenomenon – a vortex of warm air, a miniature cyclone – but maybe (as in Cervantes' time) it is the dust rising from a flock of sheep on the move or (just as likely) the trail from a Land Rover, or a tractor, or one of those small, dustbin Citroën vans so prized by small farmers. Not far away you can see Madridejos, where, as you drove through, you smelt the hot and pungent reek of the olive oil processing plant. (One of the unforgettable smells of Spain, this: oddly, not as unpleasant as all that, once you get used to it, for it is candid and utterly of its place.) But the land, the land is what your eyes devour: the squares and rectangles of light rose-ochre earth where, in October, the saffron crocus will be in bloom, the dead straight lines of the vineyards, the dark green rows of spinach and onion, the gold of barley and barley straw, also left in lines.

I had the hill to myself for an hour. I could not put from my mind for a long while the tragic feel of it. The sweeps of the mill I crouched under were rough-hewn, slender tree trunks. Some of the wires that had held the cloth sails were dangling down loose and there were bits of smashed batten strewn on the ground: whether vandals or gales had been responsible, there was no knowing; but the sadness was well-nigh palpable. When I drove away from the mills along the rough track, I guessed how I was causing one of those inverted cones of dust for someone many miles away to remark upon.

Down in Consuegra again, having bought some saffron in the *supermercado*, I crossed a bridge and came across a bookshop-cum-stationer's. It was one of those enormous, cavernous shops one so often discovers in Spain behind deceptively small doorways in out of the way corners of unremarkable *pueblos*. Why, I wondered, in a country where bookshops are rare and inadequate, should such a premises – a corner shop at that – not be that of a grocer, a draper, a furniture dealer? The shelves were well stocked with every kind of book from cheap novels to handsome limited editions of *Don Quixote* and the Bible, also with children's games and toys stacked higgledy-piggledy. The conundrum was solved the moment I met the owner: for he was the kind of man who, if he had to live in a sentry-box in the middle of the Gobi Desert, would very soon turn his habitation into a bookshop. His name was Francisco Domínguez Tendero; his headed notepaper bore the Toledan coat of arms and his title: *ACADEMICO CORRESPONDIENTE DE LA REAL ACADEMIA DE BELLAS ARTES Y CIENCIAS HISTORICAS DE TOLEDO.* He was also the official *cronista* of Consuegra. Don Francisco – Paco, he had me call him – had written more newspaper articles and learned essays than he could remember about his town, his province, his region of La Mancha and his ancient kingdom of New Castile. He wrote a regular column for the national daily , *Ya.* From a large back room he brought a pile of his publications – pamphlets, monographs, tearsheets from journals – to show me. He most generously gave me, too, a roll of colourful posters about the October saffron festivals of years gone by. Some of these depicted the mauve-pink crocus flowers in bloom against the crumbly, baked soil before the emergence of the leaf; others, the orangey-yellow stigmas, all but weightless, picked by deft, patient (and, one suspects, underpaid) women's fingers and placed in large, primitive scale pans. Saffron is, by weight, the most expensive foodstuff in the world. In the background of one of the pictures were some items of pottery. I expressed my interest: a piece of pottery is after all a piece of the very earth you can take home and keep as something useful; and I wanted, very much, to own a bit of La Mancha. 'If you want to know about our *manchego* pottery,' said Don Paco, 'you must talk to my son. His name is Francisco, too. He'll be calling in here shortly. He's just gone to see about ordering some pork chops.'

Don Paco Junior shared his father's passion for the folk

culture of La Mancha; but I sensed at once that his interest was less rarified and intellectual, more pragmatic and commercial. He was setting up a ceramics museum in what had been, years ago, a well known, thriving pottery. We drove in convoy, fast, through a maze of dusty streets at the edge of town, to what at first seemed simply four tall, bare walls containing a yard. In a restored and blindingly whitewashed room he had the beginnings of what he intended would become a comprehensive collection. Some of the ware was arty and pretentious, but most pieces were genuine peasant utensils such as pitchers and jugs for water and wine. To raise money for his project he had turned his embryo museum – unlikely as this must sound – into a night club. We went outside into fierce sunlight. When my eyes became accustomed to the glare, I saw that there were indeed stacks of chairs and tables in the yard. There were pieces of Roman columns and masonry lying about, too, old mill wheels, odds and ends of bygone, broken farm implements and blacksmith's tools. It smacked somewhat of that now ubiquitous, bedevilling pseudo-culture which creates a spurious sense of history by assembling and juxtaposing bits and pieces of undoubtedly genuine but undeniably anachronistic items of miscellaneous discarded rubbish of past ages. A workman was laying some bricks to make a dividing wall: another was giving an old wall a coat of limewash. Don Paco issued some peremptory orders; then he showed me his barbeque: he burned old vine roots on it; the old kilns were fired by vine roots too.

'After dark,' he said, 'this place is transformed. Full of people. They come from far and wide. This is fast becoming the place to spend an evening. You, too, must come and see for yourself. But now I must go and collect my order of pork chops. I'm getting behind with my day's chores. Oh, I nearly forgot. Once there were forty potters in Consuegra. Forty. Now there is only one. I'll take you to his pottery. Follow me. I shall speak to him first. Then you'll be able to buy some examples of his work at a discount.' So we drove to the alfarería of Baltasar Moreno. While parleying occurred within, I waited in the street, feeling like a spy in a film. Then, at his urgent bidding, I followed Don Paco through a series of curtained vestibules and past ladies who paused in their chatter until I had passed them. Señor Moreno, rather sleepy and droop-eyed, was in his warehouse, surrounded by almost toppling piles of dusty pots. It would be agreeable to say that the pieces were of good design and quality; but the fact is that they were misshapen and crude and badly glazed. I could scarcely leave without buying something, given that my visit had necessitated so much protocol; so I acquired a jug, a pot and a jar with an ill-fitting lid, 500 pesetas the lot. When I got them back to England all three proved leaky – as I guessed they might. But I like them well. They look dusty and dry as La Mancha; characterful and charming when planted with red pelargoniums, standing at the side of a flagged path in the Spanish manner.

The specialities of La Mancha, apart from her windmills and pottery, are lace, cheese and wine. The area around Consuegra abounds with old ladies sitting at their thresholds of an evening, manipulating the many dozens of spools and pins required to make intricate patterns of white lace; the same fingers that pluck the crocus stigmas in October, perhaps, are the nimble ones required for this fiddling, filigree work. As for the cheese, I have not been anywhere in Spain where *queso manchego* is not available: but it is of course also manufactured elsewhere in the country. In my view even the genuine local article is overpraised and overpriced: I find it a bland, boring, variety, not a patch on the fierce Roncal of the far north or some of the excellent blue goat-milk cheeses kept under oil in tins.

The wines, by contrast with the cheese, have for much too long been under-appreciated both in Spain and abroad – though supermarket chains are at last beginning to popularize the low-alcohol whites in Britain. The vineyards cover an enormous area; their yield is unimaginably large. Some of the reds as well as the common whites are delicious and memorable, yet there are few wine buffs who can talk with authority about the qualities of even the name-brand products of Manzanares and Valdepeñas. As you enter or leave the latter town by the Madrid road, you pass along an avenue of gigantic wine crocks of terracotta, amiable-looking, antique vessels which have long since been superseded in the wineries by concrete vats the size of gasometers. In Valdepeñas I chanced to see something else seldom encountered in Britain: a religious *paso* of a standing saint – Joseph, I think – on the back of a lorry and passing, arms outstretched, through the revolving blue roller-brushes of an automatic car-wash.

Neither of the wine towns was particularly attractive, both of them suffering, through being located on the main trunk road connecting Andalusia with the capital, from constant heavy pounding by traffic. The provincial capital Ciudad Real on the other hand, being isolated and aloof, depends upon neither tourism nor passing trade; it therefore still feels charming and self-sufficient. I found it excellent on statuary (there's a marvellously quirky Don Quixote which is the focal point of the evening *paseo*) but rather poor on accommodation and restaurants. (This is a bitter-sweet situation for the traveller in a parched and dusty land: he desperately needs, on arrival, a plentiful supply of hot and cold running water, a good dinner and a comfortable bed in a clean room, but will resent it bitterly if he then finds the natives putting on a special show for visitors.) In the centre of town I peeped inside a particularly gloomy-looking *hostal* whose dining-room tables looked as though they had been abruptly deserted sometime during the Thirties. The only place to get a sit-down dinner appeared to be an over-hygienic road-house four kilometres out of town. But a central bar served generously-sized *boca-dillos*, and from its terrace I enjoyed the passing show for an hour or two: little girls playing that skip-and-jump game with a giant rubber band; and their older sisters, all in that year's fashionable combination of pink and white and apple-green, struck poses to impress and drive to distraction marauding platoons of young soldiers doing their *mili* in nearby barracks; and, best of all, that *rara avis* in Spain – a public, noisy but good-natured, ambulating drunk.

At the opposite, northern end of New Castile from La Mancha is an area called La Alcarria. This name derives from an Arabic word meaning 'the country of huts'. It is an elevated landscape of flat-topped hills, *páramos*, rising between flat-bottomed valleys. The countryside is abundant and fertile, with plantations growing lush, mixed crops on the precipitous hill-sides. Three good rivers – the Tajo, the Tajuña and the Guadiela – water it. Above the cultivated ground, where fragrant herbs and wild flowers thrive, very frequently the traveller glimpses a line not of little huts but of wooden hives following the contour of a hill. The local honey is superb and superabundant: wherever you stop and listen you are likely to hear the billions of bees at work. Its villages and towns (Cifuentes, Pastrana, Brihuega, Sacedón) are compactly grouped; pleasant, charming, peaceful, but frankly unremarkable. Scarcely ever is it considered worth a mention in the guidebooks or tourist literature; yet it is the subject of one of Spain's best-loved travel books, *Vieje a la Alcarria*, by Camilo José Cela. During the Forties Cela spent a few days walking through the Alcarria, taking a few things in a knapsack and staying in simple *fondas* on the way. His book, written inside a week, is an unpretentious and concise account, mostly without subjective comment, of the people he encountered and the things that he saw in the places he passed through. The book's objectivity – a strange device in a travel book – is increased by its having been written in the third person, Cela alluding to himself throughout (and this can become wearisome) as 'the traveller'.

I now found myself being drawn towards the Alcarria not only by a long-standing affection for the book and its author but also on account of the irritation and frustration of trying, but trying in vain, to track down the ghosts of Cervantes, his contemporaries and his characters of fiction in the Don Quixote country of La Mancha. It is quite fatuous to attempt such a thing, of course: the essential reality and 'truth' of any great novel resides only within its covers and is not guaranteed enhancement by seeking out the actual fabric of places painted from life by the writer, or studying the physical characteristics of their latter-day inhabitants. But my chronic weakness is so to do, and sometimes (as with *Three Men In A Boat*) I have been amply rewarded. In El Toboso, however, home village of the romantic Don's idealized damsel, I found no serving-wench in the bar to remind me even faintly of Dulcinea. In Puerto Lápice I came across her name in an advert for Dulcinea chocolates; in Quintanar de la Orden I saw Quixote paving-slabs on sale; in a road-house three lorry-drivers mauled Sancho roast chickens for lunch. The commercialization of Cervantes in Spain is trifling compared with what happens to the shade of Shakespeare (Cervantes' almost exact contemporary) in Stratford-upon-Avon; but I did find those paving-slabs enough to grate so to speak, and those chocolates to cloy.

245

Cela, I thought, though quite frequently seen and heard jovially expounding upon this and that on television, was not yet an embalmed, classic author to be pillaged and vulgarized, with his works, by advertisers. And perhaps his territory was still something like he had known it forty years before; maybe I would even meet somebody mentioned in this book. So I decided for the next three or four days, to go where he had gone and sleep where he had slept, and I would re-read his little masterpiece as I went.

I began my journey to the Alcarria not as Cela did at Guadalajara but at Alcalá de Henares, not twenty miles east of Madrid. Here his stopping train discharged most of its passengers, including some cavalry soldiers in black-peaked caps. Alcalá has long been a garrison town. In the early morning you are awakened by *diana*, reveille, being blown repeatedly in barrack squares close by the town centre; but when you look from your hotel window what you are likely to see is not a platoon of squaddies assembling on a parade ground but the wonderful façade, crowned by an enormous stork's nest, of the university founded by Cisneros (he who, in all the glory of his cardinal's crimson, led his own troops into Africa). I began here – perversely, having abruptly quit Quixote country – because the town contains the birthplace of Cervantes: contains it twice over, in fact, for claims to this honour are made by two different houses. I went to neither, fearing that both might give as much sense of life as does a stuffed kingfisher under one of those glass domes. But in the *plaza mayor* I was entranced by a truly superb statue of the great man. Life-size, with cloak and sword on a high pedestal, he had been made to come alive not simply through the sculptor's art but by the happy whim of whoever – perhaps a young recruit – had clambered up to tie a length of scarlet ribbon round his right wrist. The ribbon it was that moved, of course, fluttering in the breeze: but its movement created the illusion that the realistic, bearded effigy was about to step down and come among us. 'It's my left wrist you should have tied,' he might have said then: for, as every Spanish schoolboy knows, Miguel de Cervantes, who also had been a soldier, lost his left hand at the battle of Lepanto.

My tour, following Cela's route, was inevitably punctuated with disappointments as well as happy surprises. At the junction of roads near Tendilla the *merendero* where Cela's beer had cooled at the bottom of the well had been replaced by a sanitized establishment still smelling of wet plaster (but I ate satisfactorily, sloppily served by a little fat girl whose build and efficiency would have rated part of a minor clause in anyone's travel book); the *posadas* and *fondas* everywhere had, predictably, lost the picturesque earthiness of a generation before when they accommodated not only drovers but also their horses, mules and asses – often in the same room. Surfaces now were covered with formica rather than dusty chaff and straw, and the smell of fresh dung had given way to the reek of car exhaust fumes. In Tendilla itself it is unlikely that a casual guest these days would wash before meals in the back yard of the inn from a bucket, accompanied by a flock of pigeons, two dozen hens, as many ducks, six or seven peacocks and two geese (one of which gave Cela a vicious peck in the buttocks and all but drew blood!). One is not entitled to regret – certainly not for the sake of nostalgia, that base emotion – the installation of plumbing and telephones and much of the rest of the paraphernalia of hygienic and labour-saving twentieth-century living: but 'progress' in small, provincial Spanish towns has too often meant merely a kind of spurious modernity of style, whereby no longer acceptable old clutter has been replaced by new clutter which not quite everyone yet thinks entirely hideous.

Azulejo tile plaques had been affixed to the walls of lodging houses where Cela had stayed. The one in the tiny village of Casasana (and one feels that Cela would be pleased about this) had been damaged by kids playing *pelota* against it; in his day the *frontón* of the *pelota* court had been the castle wall. Approaching Casasana by way of a small lane winding uphill (known as the *Cerro de la Veleta*, or 'Weathercock Rise') I felt apprehensive: perhaps, in such a remote and unfrequented place, the inhabitants might be cold or unfriendly – even downright hostile. Cela had come over rough terrain from Pareja, on the other side of the hill: a stranger, too, like myself, but bearing a message for a certain Fabián Gabarda, the brother of a married woman he had spoken to in a village called Durón. Their mother, *dueña* of the *posada*, received Cela with a certain reserve: for in villages hereabouts they tended to be wary of a stranger in case he turned out to be a fiscal inspector (this had happened before) pretending to be a beggar but in reality coming to sniff out how a crop of beans was to be disposed of.

The place was no longer a *posada* but a shop-cum-bar; and it was run by Fabián Gabada's wife, a delightful, old but energetic lady with a blooming complexion and a cheery smile, who received me with absolutely no trace of reserve. She explained how things had been in her mother-in-law's time, pacing out the dimensions of what was now little more than a commonplace stores and bar-room. She gesticulated, years slipping from her as she recalled her youth. 'This was the big entrance hall, the *zaguán*, where the muleteers came in. Here's where they washed. Here's where my mother kept her pans and spoons. Here's where they sat down to eat. Oh yes, it was all very different in those days, I can tell you.' Also in the shop was a middle-aged, good-looking woman and her ancient mother, who wore widow's weeds. I asked the three ladies to sign my copy of Cela's book. The old mother, being illiterate, could not; but she was lively and interested in what I was doing and wanted to explain why she could not so much as write her name. 'When I was a child there was no school in Casasana,' she said. 'And besides, there was no need then for girls to be able to read and write. I used to go to Sacedón market with my father every Friday – with the mule, you understand, carrying a load of animal feed. Every Friday, yes.'

Señora Gabarda told me then how the *posada* stopped being a *posada* when the carriers no longer needed somewhere to stay. The availability of modern transport had changed a centuries-old way of life within a decade. 'In his book,' I said, 'Cela wrote that the men of Casasana didn't smoke or drink.' I read aloud the appropriate passage, then drew attention to the fact that I was drinking a *botellín* of beer, bought over the counter. I was smoking a cigarette, too. 'I'm sure these aren't stocked just for you ladies of Casasana,' I said. The old lady laughed and nodded. 'That's true, too,' she said. 'Something else that has changed. Ay! Look at that shelf!' It was piled high with stacks of Ducados cigarettes and many bottles of Martini. 'It was never like that in the old days – no, never!' A fourth woman, middle-aged, by the name of Lucía López Rimón, came in; the other three told her what had been said. She clearly remembered the day – she had been a young girl – when

Cela came into the schoolroom next door to the *posada* and made an unofficial inspection of the class. It was a scene charmingly related in *Viaje a la Alcarria*. I read aloud another passage from the book, of which the following is a rough translation:

The traveller has a bit of a wash at the inn porch while his meal is being prepared. Through a thin wall he can hear schoolgirls singing. The school in Casasana is remarkable, terribly poor, with benches all botched and patched, large damp stains on walls and ceiling and a floor whose tiles are loose and badly fixed. Within – as though to compensate – all is cleanliness, order and light. On the wall hangs a crucifix and a coloured map of Spain: one of those maps at the bottom of which, in little boxes, are the Canary Islands, the Protectorate of Morocco and the colonies of Río do Oro and the Gulf of Guinea . . .

On the teacher's desk are some books, exercise books and two thick glass vases containing yellow, red and lilac-coloured wild flowers. The mistress, who accompanies the traveller on his visit to the school, is a pretty young woman, with something of a city look about her, with painted lips and wearing a very smart cretonne dress. She talks about teaching and tells the traveller that the children of Casasana are good and hard-working and very intelligent. Outside, in silence, and with astonished little eyes, a group of boys and girls looks into the schoolroom. The mistress addresses a boy and a girl.

'Now then, let this gentleman have a look at you. Who discovered America?'

The boy does not hesitate.

'Christopher Columbus.'

The mistress smiles.

'You, now. Which was the best queen of Spain?'

'Isabel the Catholic.'

'Why?'

'Because she fought against feudalism and Islam, brought about the unity of our country and carried our religion and culture beyond the seas.'

The mistress, beaming, explains to the traveller, 'She is my best pupil.'

249

The little girl is very serious, very conscious of her leading role. The traveller gives her a milk-coffee flavour sweet, takes her to one side and asks her:

'What's your name?'

'Rosario González, if you please, sir.'

'Very well. Let's see now, Rosario, do you know what feudalism is?'

'No, sir.'

'And Islam?'

'No, sir. That's not included in the book.'

The girl is confused and the traveller concludes the interrogation.

I looked up from the book and said, 'I wonder what might have become of Rosario?'

'Oh – Rosario, the clever one,' said Señora López. 'She went off to live in Madrid, of course!'

'*Fabián Gabarda no está casa – está en el campo*,' I read: Fabián Gabarda is not at home, he is in the fields. 'I suppose that's where he is still, forty years later?'

'That's right!'

'Cela says that the men of Casasana were so hardworking that they even slept in a squatting position.'

This made all the women laugh and give each other knowing looks.

'Don Camilo came to visit us after the book was a success,' said Señora Gabarda. 'He came with a lady – German, I think she was. He brought me a gift of some lovely handkerchieves. There were journalists here too, writing down everything I said and publishing it all.'

'Don't you think it amazing, *señoras*,' I said, 'that on account of this little book, Casasana is known about all over the world? In my country, for instance, every year a great number of high-school students study it as a set text for their General Certificate of Education.'

The ladies said, politely, that it was amazing, but I do not believe they were much impressed. And I am bound to say that Casasana felt, at that moment, considerably nearer the centre of the universe than, say, London or New York or even Madrid, where Rosario, the *hija preferida* of the village, no doubt was living the sophisticated life of a country girl who has made good.

'Rosario wasn't the last to leave, of course,' said the daughter of the old lady. 'It's worse now than ever before. All the young people have to go off in search of work. There are only thirty *vecinos* in Casasana now. Several of the houses belong to weekenders. Some are empty. See for yourself.'

In the street I could see some widows and a few children.

'Belong to holiday-makers. The school is closed. Shut up for good. Not a school any more.'

The village telephone was at the back of the shop. It was the telephone that brought people in more than the items on sale in the shop. The ladies told me they had thought that I had come in just to use the telephone.

'Not many foreign gentlemen would come to Casasana,' one of them said. 'And there'd be none at all if it wasn't for don Camilo.'

'What was he like?'

Señora Gabarda took a long time answering, leaving me in no doubt that he must have been a real ladies' man, slim and tall, with a good head of hair. Also, we took a long time saying goodbye outside the shop before I drove away. I looked out for Fabián in the fields but saw nobody. What I did see was wheat, barley, rye, oats, beans, chick-peas, *de todo y todo en pequeña cantidad*, something of everything and everything in small amounts, as Cela had written; the trees that would bear the 'very small, very flavoursome olives which the people eat with great relish'.

I had a hankering to see my beloved Cuenca again before I left New Castile; so for a couple of days and a night I interrupted my tour of the Alcarria (some of which extends as *pinar*, pinewoods, into the province of Cuenca) in order to look up old friends in old haunts, and to visit the *Ciudad Encantada*, or enchanted city, an area of fantastical rock formations which, having been without a car, I had not been able to go to during my extended stay some years before.

The area covers twenty square kilometres of high ground, half an hour's drive to the north-east of the city. Twenty square kilometres sounded daunting on an afternoon when, even in the shade, the pine needles burned underfoot and grasshoppers were piercingly strident: but most of the memorably striking formations were, thankfully, within a comfortable hour and a half's walk of the entrance. Wind, rain, snow, ice and subterranean rivers have eroded the exposed rocks into remarkable shapes and patterns: natural sculpting which, without whimsy or fantasy, can remind one variously of a man's face, a Roman bridge, the pointed door of a convent, ships, an elephant, a seal, a toboggan run, streets, a tank, the waves of a choppy sea. The most characteristic shape, both here and elsewhere in the *serranía*, is that of the *tormos*, vast flat-topped masses of rock resembling anvils or giant fungi – chanterelles, milk-caps – whose stalks have been so excessively eroded you think they must topple over at any instant.

In Cuenca, yet more apartment blocks had been built at every approach to the city. There was more evident prosperity and (its ironic concomitant) more evident poverty. There were now considerable numbers of beggars in the streets – so many that the *Diario de Cuenca* devoted a leading article to the problem – but the three brothers who had opened the Trébol bar (I had been one of their first customers) were doing very nicely, with a run of fifty metres of terrace tables and a bar so packed it was a struggle to get to the counter. 'I suppose you three must be multi-millionaires by now,' I said to Angel, jokingly. 'Nearly,' he replied, not jokingly. 'We've earned it. Eighty hours a week. All of us, you know, not to mention our wives in the kitchen, preparing the *tapas*. Come back and talk when we're not so busy. Your drink's on the house. You used to take gin-and-tonic – right?' At my former *hostal*, I disarmed Señor Arias at the reception desk by taking him a packet of British postage stamps to add to his collection; he looked ill; the mustard-coloured suit he had always worn now hung loosely on him and his poor teeth made him appear even more gaunt: I feared for him. At El Bodegón Julio said he was keeping fairly well: he had all but worked himself to death after his wife died, but he was still feeling some benefit from his pancreas operation. Shortly, his daughter was to be married to the barman, José, and that would take some of the pressure off him. I had some pickled carrots, then a *morcilla* and a *zarajo*, as in the old days. 'You Spaniards grind yourselves into the dust with work,' I said. 'Those three brothers at El Trébol will be the next to break their health.' Julio shrugged, as though to suggest that nothing could be more normal or inevitable. I went to my usual *quiosco* for a

252

paper and a chat with the old dear who spent twelve hours a day, six days a week in her cramped, dark, uncomfortable little cabin all through the year: in the furnace-heat of summer and the glacial cold of winter. 'My sister and I are having two weeks in Scandinavia soon,' she said. 'We've been everywhere, my sister and I. London, Scotland, Russia, Hungary. It's worth being cooped up in here if you can fly like a dove once a year!' The woman at the station tobacco stall had a similar tale to tell. Anybody, it seemed, who had a job or owned a little business worked extraordinarily hard – too hard, usually – not only to make a success for the financial rewards that work brought but because, well, work was what you did in order to fill the days. I finished the evening at the Cantábrico bar where I used to go a couple of times a week for a nightcap. The owner, Julián, was incapable of relaxing for even a second, delighting in doing three or four things at once: wiping down the bar with one hand, filling *cañas* of beer with the other, punting a bottle-top, shouting an order. It was marvellous to watch him dodging and weaving, pouring and mopping, dispensing *tapas*, finding things for himself to do whenever everything necessary to do had been done. He remembered who I was the moment I entered the bar, telling me my name and what I did for a living. He gave me a glass of beer and a hard-boiled egg; and when I had drunk the beer and eaten the egg he refilled my glass and gave me a large prawn and would not let me pay a single peseta. 'I'm famous all over Europe for not keeping still,' he boasted. 'People come from all over just to see me move.' He danced out to his kitchen and brought back trays of little live crabs which his customers fell upon and cracked like nuts between their molars. 'You surely have to be still sometimes,' I said. Julián jigged past me, bearing a *tapa* of Russian salad and a *ración* of anchovies. 'I like to go fishing,' he said. 'You know the bridge over the Madrid Road?' It was a wonderful fantasy for him to weave: Julián patiently fishing, enjoying the stillness and tranquillity, was as plausible as a rabbi cornering the market in pigs' trotters. I was enjoying myself and would have stayed longer, had not the *Hofkriegsrath* of *Fuerza Nueva* not come in, to be given a hearty welcome by Julián.

CHAPTER FIFTEEN

You can always be terrified by Spanish landscape. You begin
to feel accustomed to it – comfortable even – and then you
turn a corner and what you see makes you gulp and shiver.
You check your fuel gauge, recalling Richard Ford's frequent
injunction, before embarking upon certain laps of a journey,
'attend to the provend'. You would not want to be stranded
in this rugged wilderness. I allude of course not to run-of-the-
mill mountains – particularly not to ones with pointed peaks
– but to the kind of vast basin you have to cross north-
east of Huete in the province of Cuenca. This is terrain of
indescribable grandeur, the colours of the rock masses and the
land varying from deep maroon, through all gradations of
ochre, to the reds, the tangerines and pomegranates, the greys,
the milky whites. You come to a small town like Canaveras.
Far from feeling reassured by the presence of human beings,
you worry about what kind of folk would choose to remain
on that scraped-bare little hill all pitted with caves which, one
supposes, must now be store-houses but which, behind those
stout-looking doors, might yet be human dwellings. The
bisecting road was not surfaced: just a strip of bare earth, all
ruts and boulders. It was the *pueblo* of José the barman at El
Bodegón, who was soon to marry Julio's daughter. I pictured
him as he might have been some years before, a wide-eyed
adolescent bumping down that barbarous hill on a noisy two-
stroke and revving away to seek a starched white shirt, a
fortune and a wife in the provincial capital.

At Priego you are briefly in the Alcarria again. They make
baskets from osiers cultivated in *huertas* near shaded streams
and rivers. The cut osiers are dried in stooks a deep wine-red.
Despite the wildness of the countryside around, briefly if
irrationally you feel safer. But then you come to a savage
gorge, with a village like Bateta perched up on its rock spike,

and uneasiness sets in again. You leave the Alcarria and its beehives behind definitively. The pinewoods are lonely; you long for a little company. In Villaneuva de Alcorón there was only an empty bar. Outside, I asked the postman whether there was anywhere I could get a meal. He had a word in the ear of the bar proprietor and I was led to an apparently secret *comedor* in a crowded, small back room. As soon as I entered (a real exotic, I must have been, what with a foreign accent and a car with right-hand drive and a *matriculación* hardly ever seen in those parts) all conversation ceased. In a sweat of embarrassment, sharing a table with three deeply suspicious and utterly mute young farm workers, I ate a plate of green beans, some loin of pork with chips and two luscious pears which, with bread and three bottles of beer, cost considerably less than two pounds. As soon as I left, talk erupted behind me in an excited, half-angry uproar, like a radio turned on loud in the middle of a play.

You cross the Tagus by way of a deep, leafy hollow in the gorge and soon you reach the last town in New Castile: Molina de Aragón, so named because its castle – and the remains of Moorish ramparts and stupendous walls striding down the hillside – once defended the frontier. Then, heading north, beyond Campillo you reach the river Piedra, where Aragon begins in earnest. The first few miles of this arid land bring a surprise, the Monasterio de Piedra and its delectably watered park: a series of pools, cascades and streams – and of caves, tunnels, fissures, outcrops of rock – on various levels within and around a ravine. This beautiful, refreshing, tree-shaded and highly unlikely oasis might be in the Isle of Wight, so strongly does it suggest the Victorian romanticism of that island's chines – in particular its combination of the artifice of Man with the works of Nature, the hallmark of English landscape gardening. The waterfalls are enchanting, their configurations reminiscent of horses' tails, a girl's head of hair, a terrace of weeping willows. There is a grove of plane trees at the bottom of one flight of rustic steps where the cool seems palpable; and it is cool, too, in a grotto whose entrance is curtained with a lace of perpetually falling water through which elegant pigeons fly hither and thither from their nests. Misty vapour occasionally touches your cheeks in here, a welcome balm. Everywhere there is the sound of water either dripping or flowing, inviting you to dabble your fingers and slap a cupped handful on your nape. There is a trout farm at the lower end of the walk, with graduated fish – from fry up to whoppers – to gaze at, teeming in tanks on different levels and all, in time, to be consumed by the residents of the Monasterio Hotel. Then, by the Mirror Lake, you see the orange and dark green of the Devil's Rock so reflected that it looks just as Rouault might have painted it: black bold lines separating passages of bright, sun-washed stone like strips of lead between pieces of stained glass. After this, returning to your starting point, you come to yet more waterfalls, some of them strangely ominous: one cascade had run almost dry, leaving only flanges of viridian moss over its rock; another had long since failed altogether: its moss had blackened, and died.

Out again into the heat I pressed on towards Calatayud, the Moorish city Kalat Ayub, whose very name had always sounded magical to me. Nowhere I know looks so strange, so utterly improbable, glimpsed from afar. To its west the bare, whitish, folded, dry hills look like a brain exposed within the skull, or a bowl piled high with blanched soft cod's roes. Beneath, the dusty old buildings clamber and cluster and scramble and huddle, more African than European, with a mosque complete with minaret, Mudéjar towers, belfries, roofs of glazed tiles and a general air of exhaustion and despair. When you enter the town, all you want to do is stand on a bridge and stare at the swift-flowing, rusty river Jalón – as, presumably, the sharp-tongued poet Martial once did. He was born in the Roman city of Bibilis, just east of Calatayud, about seven years after Christ was crucified; and retired to it, his 'city of gold and iron', after his years in Rome. He would turn a nice, malicious epigram, I think, had he to return from the dead and stay in the hotel I was obliged to occupy, close to the site of his villa on the hellish main road to Zaragoza.

Next morning I arrived in Soria, the capital of its province in Old Castile, in time to witness a 'right-to-work' march by the unemployed. It moved off along the avenue beside the park. The procession was made up of 140 families whose breadwinners were out of work. There was concerted chanting and brandishing of banners as the march passed the post office and the public administration offices, whose employees (and, who knows, perhaps some of their bosses) leaned out of upper windows to watch. I overheard a snatch of conversation as I walked along the pavement. 'They'll not get jobs while there's socialism,' said one old man. 'They'll not get jobs till there is,' answered another. This seemed to me a neat summing-up of Felipe González' brand of left-wing politics, which, at the time, satisfied nobody too radical but which was gaining steadily in support from the middle ground. Whether or not Soria's admiration for its best known poet Antonio Machado was whole-hearted or grudging it is hard to judge. In the Plaza del Vergel there is a most extraordinarily funny, huge head of the great man on a stupidly small-proportioned plinth of rough hewn stone. Literally a head: no neck; a Humpty-Dumpty. The lower lip protrudes like that of a petulant child, the mouth is set in a glum curve, two deep lines frame his funny little moustache and his popping eyes seem to complain, as well they might. Most odd.

But not as odd as what I came across in Ólvega, a small town off the main road to the east. It was a very peculiar and unsettling place indeed, comprising several widely-spaced and oversized recent buildings, some of a distinctly eccentric design, arbitrarily scattered about and wholly ignoring the crumbling remnants of the nice little original village they almost encircled. By far the biggest building – covering the area of two football pitches – was the Revilla sausage factory. The next biggest were the great apartment-block slabs for the workers, facing the rear of the factory over some waste ground. Some architecture in Ólvega was decent, with good, clean lines; the factory itself and the school were fine. But much of it was idiosyncratic to the point of plain and maddening idiocy, the self-indulgent whimsy of one who presumably will not have to live in the place: the churchy-looking library with window-sills apparently melting like Dali watches; the absurdly canted roofs of the *hostal* and some of the privately-owned detached houses. It all had the feel of a one-man show, a megalomaniac's dream creation made real by the connivance of an opportunist, meretricious architect, possibly a relation.

I took a pine-panelled, sauna-like room in the *hostal*, opposite the entrance to the sausage factory, whose tremendous dimensions I was now better able to appreciate: eight storeys high;

a great gate to admit lorry-loads of porkers one end and a similar one to release lorry-loads of hundreds of thousands of *chorizos* at the other. It was a bizarre site for an hotel.

However I found the meals to be uncommonly good. For lunch I had *pisto madrileño* (potato, onion and tomato hash with roundels of potato to cap it, like a Lancashire hotpot), followed by pork liver no doubt from across the road, and good, Navarrese red wine. For dinner there was a Spanish omelette as big and round as a tea plate and thick as a bread board, followed by three bits of sirloin, tender as marsh-mallow. I stayed three days, both fascinated and repulsed by Ólvega. At each meal there was a long table occupied by thirteen youngish men who, I guessed, were white-collar executives, employees of the Revilla factory. Had I been a painter, I should have wanted to do them as a Last Supper. You could have put a name to each of them: Judas in one corner, not saying much; Thomas, looking hard at his plate; Christ in the middle, bearded, exactly the right age, nattering about how to get an old clapped-out car to start. They behaved with much courtesy towards each other, sharing an enormous salad placed in the centre and making a ritual *Agape* of breaking bread, pouring wine and adding oil and vinegar to a neighbour's salad while he was saying something to the waiter. And, after the meal, how *culto* was their taking of coffee, a generous *copa* of brandy and a good cigar, before they rose, wished me *buen aproveche* and went back to work.

The doomed pigs reached their place of execution at dead of night, as political prisoners, *desaparecidos*, do. I would be awakened by a wailing siren – the gate alarm operated by the arriving lorry-driver. Someone within would open the huge, grille-like factory gates (which now reminded me of those of maximum security gaols). Soon there would be a terrific and terrible cacophony, prompted by what sounded like a steel scaffold pole being dropped repeatedly, followed by a horrible, panic-stricken squealing. I am convinced it is true that pigs can smell death: it was not just the squealing and grunting you would expect from pigs being chivvied off a lorry; rather, a cavernous roar like the echoing of a rush of water in a roomy culvert. After all this would come the slamming shut of the lorry's tail-gates and the banging tight again of the factory gate. Sometimes I would look from my window and see the driver in the street, stretching his arms, lighting a cigarette. He would look up at the factory, the half-moon in the sky; then take a deep breath of air, get in his cab, start his motor, rev it more than necessary, move off. And then it would not be long before the next load arrived.

At breakfast I talked to the *dueño* of the hotel, Pepe, the son of the owner. He was one of four brothers who alternated between Ólvega and Barcelona, his birthplace. Casually, I mentioned the town's individual style of architecture.

'It's a knock-out!' he said. 'Glad you've noticed it!'

'Who's the architect?'

'A cousin of mine, actually. Mariano Delso. From Tudela, in Navarre. He did all of it. Well, nearly all. You couldn't mistake his style, could you?'

'No, I suppose you couldn't.'

'And you should have seen how much concrete got tipped under this place: *Madre de Dios!* And have you seen the *Ayuntamiento* yet – and the new school?'

'Yes. And I've seen the old ones, too. Dating from what – about 1926?'

'Those awful old-fashioned buildings! If you like, I'll take you downstairs to see our wine-cellars. Talk about concrete! No amount of atom bombs or earthquakes could shift this place!'

'I don't doubt it. Tell me, what's the factory over the road like inside?'

'You could eat your dinner off the floor. You can go and see for yourself, you know, if you present yourself at Reception. There's a conducted tour every morning at ten thirty.'

Go I did. A fidgety man in an immaculate white coat met me. I was the only one in his party and he was not best pleased. Passing at breakneck speed from department to department, floor to floor, we took a bare twenty minutes to complete what was a lengthy tour. Everyone I saw, once the offices were left behind, was dressed entirely in pristine white. All was spotless; my attention was constantly drawn to this proof of exemplary hygiene. The workers all moved at the speed of my guide. I shall never again be able to eat a slice of *chorizo* without recalling that pell-mell inspection.

When the pigs arrive, they are put in a pen. Each weighs eighty kilos. At seven-thirty am (if they have arrived by night)

259

they are electrocuted, have their throats cut and are hung, like coats, on hooks. One hundred and fifty beasts an hour are processed on the production line. Without delay, their cleaning and dismemberment begins. They are scoured with high-velocity water jets, scalded in a steam-house, passed through vast, cylindrical wire brushes to remove their bristles; then scalded and washed again. By now they are ghostly white cadavers. As you move from one area to another on the tour, the carcases sway past, and sometimes they lurch disconcertingly towards you, like punch-bags in a gymnasium: you must dance like a butterfly if you are not to be knocked flying. The line now reaches a row of butchers on a raised platform. One of them, all day every day, has the job of swinging a felling axe to rip each pig open from throat to belly. The others remove, with cleavers, choppers and knives, the legs, head and tail. In an adjacent room, several dozen specialist butchers, in teams of four, at tables beside the production line, carve off their particular bits and then cut these bits into smaller bits still. Meanwhile, other workers are arriving from the scalding steam plant with yet more and more white, plastic open-work crates to be filled with chunks, joints, off-cuts of pork. You are enjoined to inspect the machines that produce the steam and to comment – favourably – upon the company's cleanliness. (There are a few spots of blood on the floor – but no more than a meticulously careful murderer might leave behind and far, far less in the way of messy slops than you will habitually see on floors of English motorway cafeterias.)

From here on the tour becomes, as a pornographer might express it, stronger stuff: so at this point visitors (and readers) of a delicate disposition are advised to quit. For it is the thorough-going mincing process we must next witness; and, after that, the enormous tympani of cauldrons. Once these have been noted, we shall be obliged to pass rows and rows of churning mixers – very similar to the ones that mix cement on building sites – wherein is glimpsed tumbling, newly-chopped, newly-cooked meat, lean and fat, blended with the rust-red spicy sauce which will soon be staining lips and fingers of countless consumers of *tapas* and *entremeses* and *bocadillos*. The odour is powerful; not the appetizing whiff of the new-cut slice placed beside your beer with a cube of

260

bread and an olive, but a slamming pungency that will cling to your clothes and your hair. Perhaps you are about to blench, remembering in fine detail what you had for breakfast. Dazed, the white-clad workers look at you without compassion. By now you are somewhere in the centre of the factory; the quickest way to the exit is by enduring the rest of the tour. You continue to a department where some poor devils have to separate sausage skins while others attach labels to them. After this comes a process as obscenely suggestive as anything I have ever come across in real life: a worker (he, too, regarding you dispassionately) fits a sausage skin like a massive condom on to a steel penis which at once spasms and ejaculates orange-red into the instantly erect skin. A side-show like this could make somebody a fortune in Amsterdam. Upstairs you are whisked in a lift to ramble through ever so many silent and spacious drying-rooms, in which the thousands upon thousands of chorizos hang (most are still, some slightly sway) from poles. They look like giant church candles dangling by their uncut wicks from sections of chimney-sweep's brush handles. You are invited to gaze outside: which you most willingly do, for the window is open a little way and you can smell the blessed wind off the sierra and see the fresh-smelling, unhygienic earth off which, thank God, you would not dream of eating your dinner and to which, mercifully, you will be returning soon. What you are supposed to be looking at is the original factory building; you are expected to express surprise and admiration that Revilla has grown so amazingly. But alas! there is no time to struggle for words now. You must run and skip to keep up: glance in at this rest room, note the medical centre (with a doll-like nurse ever in attendance), nod an acknowledgement to the packing department proud of its sell-by date-stamps, boxes and crates, and then, phew, suddenly, finally, after yet more ascending and descending by lift, here you are back in Reception with a shirt-sleeved army of clerks still pounding their key-boards – and the visit is as near as not over. All that is left to come is the *presto furioso* handshake from the fidgety guide and the free-sample kilo of chorizo which he then smacks into your palm . . . And lo! you are out in the sunshine.

At lunchtime, after a long walk and much deep breathing, I quizzed Pepe in the bar about the Managing Director of the firm, Emilio Revilla. 'You'll probably see him walk in here before long,' said Pepe. 'He belongs here, born and bred in Ólvega. Spends two days with us and the rest of the week in Madrid. He started up with his father from nothing. He's into all kinds of commodities and businesses. Refrigeration though, mostly. Buys up meat when it's cheap, freezes it, sells it when the price starts going up. See that chap over there? That's the brother.'

I had seen the brother scoop the fruit machine's jackpot the evening before, his cupped hands overflowing with *duros*. Now he was looking out of the window, rattling his keys. After half an hour the Great Man arrived; and the bar-room suddenly was full of his scent: by which I don't imply that he smelt malodorously of his simmering vats across the road but that he was redolent – sweetly, rarely, complexly – of subtle after-shave, new clothes, soft leather shoes, Havana leaf: the effects, in short, of the money the contents of those vats had earned him. His shirt cuffs were unbuttoned, negligently folded back between wrist and elbow; he wore a plaited gold bracelet and lunks of gold suspended from a chain round his neck. It was the *de rigeur* style of colour-supplement trendies. I thought of the slogan painted on all his lorries: *Revilla, un sabor que maravilla* (the neat jingle means 'a flavour that astounds'), and wondered whether he had thought it up himself. He was on the telephone straightaway, with his brother and the hotel staff buzzing about in attendance like courtiers, with pencils and scribbling pads and time-tables. I had the briefest exchange with him over lunch. I told him how I had made a tour of his factory. He told me that the following morning – Sunday – was when they made the vivid orange sauce which gave his sausage its astounding *sabor*. But I had much better not even contemplate trying to enter the factory gates on a Sunday because nobody – but nobody – was ever allowed to see the process: for like Coca-Cola, his *chorizo* contained a secret ingredient. Never mind, I said: actually, I should be leaving early next day – and probably before breakfast, before the vats were warming up.

Four regions meet not far to the north of Ólvega: Old Castile, Rioja, Navarre and Aragon. I made for upper Aragon, to the north-east. After a long stretch of undistinguished countryside,

I came to the *pueblo* of Ayerbe; and from here I took a cul-de-sac some miles up towards the higher ground in order to look at a castle. I am not especially enamoured of castles; besides, all the great castles in Spain – Segovia, Coca, Peñafiel and the rest – have been documented and described so often that they must be eroding by description and photography by now, no less than by tourist footfall: but I found myself bewitched not just by the fabric but by this one's palpable atmosphere and very remoteness.

You drive up between almond orchards and past a comically makeshift football pitch. At first, you think you are on your way to the castle you spy diagonally to your left: but the Castillo de Loarre, the one you want, is diagonally to your right – what you had mistakenly thought was a rocky out-crop on the mountainside. As you approach, losing and regaining sight of it as you hairpin upwards, paradoxically it becomes ever more, not less, entrancing, and impossibly romantic. In my experience distant prospects of castles are usually more tempting than the close-up, boring reality of ten-foot thick walls, but not so here. Perched so very high up, inaccessible as a gold eagle's nest, Loarre must have been absolutely impregnable to any attack; its walls and turrets stride down precipitous slopes which smell of juniper and pine and which had such a feel of wildness that you would not be surprised if you saw a bear or a pack of wolves emerge. I thought I had the place to myself: but I shared it with a Dutch girl in something of a bikini – until she gathered up her things, slammed the door of her Mini and furiously drove away. At once I understood her petulance. The enormous, panoramic view over the valley of the Ebro is one you would sooner have to yourself for a few minutes. The presence of one other person divides its effect by two.

'Roseate' is a word to wrest back from amateur lady poets in order to describe the colour of the puddingstone cliffs at nearby Riglos. This is as vulnerable-looking a settlement as could be imagined; dwellings cower under eroded *mallos*, sugar-loaf rocks, one of which is hand-shaped; a mitten, a face-flannel glove with the traces of fingers and a thumb beneath. High up, in pock-marks and deeper hollows, are the haunts of countless birds: most noticeably, eyries of birds of prey but also nests of their smaller brethren such as jackdaws and swifts. Long, grey stains of excrement – looking, at first glance, like snagged pages of newsprint – soil the cliff-face. A wonderful place for birdwatchers, this: the great, noble, predatory birds launch, ride their thermals a while, then wheel in to their ledges; and each time you half-expect their heavily taloned feet to send a *mallo* toppling over to crush everything below. At the entrance to Riglos are plaques commemorating mountaineers who have fallen to their death – not just in this part of Spain but in climbing centres all over Europe, such as the Eiger.

What one needs, after so many unsettling images in so short a space of time, is a rest in some solid, respectable (if dull) resort. I went to Jaca therefore, a kind of Cheltenham of the Pyrenean foothills, where I put up, like a retired gentleperson, in a decayed hotel running to bathtubs on claw feet. The town was full of summer visitors at language schools: some of them were the usual, cloned, footloose young of Nordic countries; but many were the kind of middle-aged and elderly women who drape their hips in beige, ill-fitting slacks: sad-faced, blue-rinsed British and American widows and spinsters thumbing inadequate dictionaries at terrace tables and shaking their heads. There was nobody much to talk to apart from the hotel porter. He told me how his home-made *pacharán* was much better than the shop-bought, brand-name stuff like Zoco; he gathered sloes up in the mountains nearby and used them to flavour ordinary *anís*. His word for sloes was not the usual word in Castilian, *endrinas*, but one from a local dialect of ancient Aragonese, in which they were called *arañones*.

Jaca was not the kind of place I find congenial: ubiquitous disco music after dark, miniature wooden paddles with which to stir your coffee, innumerate waitresses in tiger-stripe minipants and other, miscellaneous, non-Spanish horrors to grate nerves and shock sensibilities. I drove away towards higher ground, through stand-offish villages that looked like spoil-heaps of waste shale, from Anso in Aragon to the Roncal valley in Navarre, where mountains wore their summer snow like epaulettes.

This was the eastern edge of the Basque country: for Euskadi – the Basque nation, their language and their culture – is not confined to the Vascongadas provinces of Vizcaya, Guipúzcoa and Alava, but extends across much of Navarre and over the national frontier into France. Here one begins to see separatist graffiti which will continue westwards to as far as where the province of Santander begins.

It seemed perverse to be leaving Spain on her national day – the festival of Santiago, St James – but I did so in order to re-enter, within a few hours, by the classic pilgrims' route to Santiago de Compostela, at Roncesvalles. The approach to France was impressive enough: the mountain peaks were grand, jagged, rather frightening at times. There were wild horses (as there had been in Andorra, but these were prancing or cantering about), and cows, wearing tonk-tonking bells, that stared you out, unwilling to move aside, slap-bang in the middle of the road. That stretch of no man's land was several miles long and not much used, it seemed, even in high summer. You kept crossing and re-crossing the frontier, concrete posts marked F or E keeping you apprised of which side you were on. I covered the French ground as quickly as I could – Aramits, Tardets, St Jean Pied de Port: all very pleasant, no doubt, but too bland for an Hispanophile's taste – and scuttled for the frontier post at Valcarlos. Here, the French and Spanish border officials were *en fiestas*, none of them wanting to suspend drinking in order to check documents or ask questions. I was waved through, raucous laughter emanating from their riotous sentry-box; and for some miles I was uncertain whether I was in France, Spain or the limbo in between.

Before long, I was no more in doubt. Dozens of Spanish families were out for the afternoon along the pilgrims' way, enjoying a twentieth-century style *romería*. I too, having brought provisions for an al fresco meal, found a spot on a roadside strip of meadow just before Roncesvalles. It was next to a modern chapel; a sign invited the traveller to enter and say a prayer: but on this, the very day of Santiago, the door was firmly locked. I peeped in the window. There were some of last autumn's leaves on the floor. The site, I presumed, was a holy one; one at any rate much associated with centuries of piety, given that so many hundreds of thousands of weary pilgrims must have halted here for a final breather before the crest. Groups of families and friends made flotillas of vehicles, up to nine or ten cars, vans and trucks to draw up in rings, like latter-day wagon-trains. A good-humoured party of left-on-the-shelf old maids and widows and younger, attractive,

265

career women – all obviously colleagues from the same firm – teased each other with merciless, loud good humour about their remaining prospects of marriage with the boss. A lorryload of boy scouts arrived, played the kind of roustabout, hurly-burly game that scouts play and, after ten minutes, got back in their lorry and departed. An old couple took a card table from the boot of their little Seat and played a genteel game of *mus* before opening a bottle of *gaseosa* with which to toast their national patron saint, and then a lone young racing cyclist stopped, took off a helmet like a pound of loose sausages, wiped his brow and, oblivious to the rest of us, drank gratefully from the water bottle fixed to his machine. It was a happy interim. The city of Santiago de Compostela, more than 800 kilometres to the west, where I intended to go before the summer was out, was as though linked to that spot by a chain of similar parties of picnickers the entire length of the route. There was, for those few minutes, the illusion of universal peace and calm.

CHAPTER SIXTEEN

The basque language looks as if it would feel in the mouth like bits of Brazil nut shell: *Establezimendu honetan bezero jaunek badituzte beren esku 'Erreklamazio orriak'. Legezkoak dira eta dohainlk*, says the notice on the bedroom door. With the possible exception of the first word, the message is not to be unravelled. There are no overlappings with any of one's assorted fragments of linguistic knowledge; nowhere to grab hold of it and grapple for meaning. Like Finnish and Hungarian, *Euskerra* is not one of the Indo-European family of tongues. Some graffiti are easy enough to understand: *Amnistia, sozialismoa, Independentzia* (but you might assume, unless someone puts you right, that Herri Batasuna is the name of the candidate rather than that of the party: 'People's Unity' – the political wing of ETA). South of San Sebastián – *Donostia* in Basque – it was a hitchhiker who put me right. His name was Ramuntcho and he was on his way to work. He was about forty, with a florid face and skin as smooth as a baby's. He tried to teach me some simple, common words and phrases: numbers one to ten, 'There's a pelota match tomorrow,' 'Thank you very much', and so on; but it was every bit as jaw-breaking and tooth-spitting a language as it looked; and, immediately forgetting all he taught me, I apologized for being a slow pupil.

'No matter,' he said, his Castilian full of fishbones and guttural laughter, 'you're not the first foreigner to give up after just one lesson.'

I asked him what he thought about separatism.

'There's only about fifteen per cent of Basques in favour of *Euskadi ta azkatasuna*, complete independence and a Basque homeland spreading over into Navarre and France,' he said. 'And only about six per cent who would go the whole hog and support Herri Batasuna. And they're all mad – and I mean really mad. They've killed about five hundred people since ETA was formed at the end of the Fifties. Nonetheless, we *are* a different people from the rest of Spain. We *do* resent our taxes going to Madrid. We get so little back in exchange for them. We don't like the way ETA goes about things but that doesn't stop us being in favour of most of the things they stand for.'

We were going past some extensive road works which I indicated.

'Oh yes, there is something to show, I won't deny it, and Felipe González has kept some of his promises to us. Since the Statute of Guernica we've had Euskadi set up as an autonomous – ha-ha, more or less! – state with our own regional government in Vitoria, for example. But there's still far too much unemployment. Take me. I've got a job, sure, but my brothers haven't and nor has my father and nor have my two eldest boys just out of school. I have all those mouths to feed from one wage packet. Now, we're a hardworking lot round here. We know how to organize and plan. There's no doubt that we could do something about it if we had an even greater degree of autonomy. Not through supporting Herri Batasuna though – crazy extremists blowing up banks and killing even our own policemen.'

I dropped him off right next to a traffic policeman, who looked particularly vulnerable as mammoth container trucks on their way to Bilbao rumbled close past him, belching black fumes.

Basque policemen, products of British SAS training, are terribly conspicuous. They wear bright scarlet berets and blue jerseys such as you might buy in Marks and Spencer's: a uniform that strikes one as provocative and foolhardy in such a violent and volatile region. But it is a characteristic of the Basques to over-emphasize their difference from other Spaniards – much as the lunatic fringe groups of the British Celtic communities will proclaim, with sound and fury, their distinctiveness from the English. And these small nations have much more in common than the speaking of a barbaric language and the sour, simmering rancour of the long-since defeated. The Basques, like the Scots, set great store by grotesque exhibitions of brute strength; their furious log-chopping, stone-dragging, weight-lifting (of strange, square, heavy boxes) and tug-of-war competitions recall the atavism of the Highland games. Their rowing races on the open sea, in double-banked whaling boats, echo pagan Cornish regattas. ETA/Herri Batasuna is (very roughly) paralleled by IRA/Sinn Fein in Northern Ireland. The obliterating or altering of Castilian-language road signs reminds one of the green paint activites of Plaid Cymru: though the over-painting is neat in Guipúzcoa as it seldom is in Gwent; and there is nothing of the half-cock whining, effete Cardiff saloon bar rhetoric about nationalistic talk as heard in the streets of Durango and the tough bars, *txokos*, used by the tenement cliff-dwellers of Rentería. Basque separatism wells up not from a soft, sentimental or pretentious heart like Taffy's: it rises from somewhere much deeper, an evil bile secreted by some primitive, bestial organ only criminals and true fanatics are born with. There is something very frightening about the meticulousness of Herri Batasuna's multi-coloured, murderous graffiti. It looks as though it is effected not in a hurry, at night, by clumsy yobs wielding spray-cans but with care and much patience, by trained assassin sign-writers using the correct tools of the trade and exact measurements. It has the obsession with symmetry of the disturbed child. The Basque national flag, the *ikurriña* – a white cross on a red background with green diagonals – is painted with the reverence due to a holy image. Basque 'official' lettering – that of shop fascias, advertising and such – is vaguely oriental, with peculiar, vertical serifs and uprights shaped like scimitars: the upper-case A looks like a little pagoda.

The countryside – mountainous, but on a small scale, more like pointed hills, often thickly planted with pines – is oddly unsettling: undeniably lovely, yet curiously jagged and untidy, with small copses, hedgerows and building developments arbitrarily placed as though by persons without much of an eye for balance or proportion. The houses, often of wood, have walls painted white, off-white or cream, with maroon window-frames and doors, under steeply sloping orange roofs and overhanging eaves. Between rows of suburban houses – with well made pavements and little patches of front garden – there may be a small patch of runner beans or maize, or a hay meadow of diminutive sugar-loaf haycocks, each with its little plastic rain hat; or – just as likely – there could be a small mill, factory or workshop next to some ponies out to grass. And, striding through everything, taking no notice of either landscape or townscape, come those curious electric pylons so frequently seen in Spain: like monstrous wire maquettes for models of two gymnasts or tumblers holding each other round the waist and leaning backwards, braced ready to give a third one a leg-up on to their shoulders.

Away from the coast, Euskadi does not concern itself very much with catering to the needs of tourism. You come across far fewer bars and hotels here than in other regions; you sense that the inhabitants – a tight-lipped and serious lot, on the whole – are far too busy with grave matters such as working and making a profit to be bothered with frivolity and frittering time away in idle chatter. The Basques are a rather coarse people, not celebrated for such social refinements as leisurely drinking: however, they do know how to eat. In San Sebastián there are well known eating clubs, exclusively for men; and good roadside restaurants, *caseríos*, abound – in which the service at table is provided exclusively by women: rare, this, in Spain. Some of the best English translation howlers in my considerable collection come from Euskadi. One hilarious menu alone provided *weelsteek, chikeled rost, rabshit in garli, shrimp chops* and *cramfish*; and a list of puddings which included *ice cream fart, solid custard, custard*, and *solid custard with custard*. For all this, the general standard of Basque gastronomy – for both gourmand and gourmet – is probably the best in Spain.

The ubiquitous and lingering flavour of Euskadi, though, is that of incipient violence. On the cliff road near Lequeito I had a flat tyre. While changing the wheel, my attention was attracted by a motorcyclist waving an arm up and down as he approached. He was warning me, I guessed, of a police radar trap ahead. I was soon on my way again. After a few kilometres, I reached a lay-by where three carloads of young men had been stopped by a police patrol. At the point of machine-guns they were being searched and their vehicles ransacked. Whether or not they were terrorists I was not able to ascertain, as I was motioned (also at gun-point) to continue without delay; but the headlines in the next day's newspaper were about a policeman having been murdered in cold blood quite near that spot. On a wall at the edge of Guernica there

270

was a slogan obligingly written in Castilian. Its message was: *Because that which has been begun cannot now be stopped.* The feelings engendered by this is one of fatalism, then of despair. I visited Guernica, that tragic little town, to see the ancient oak tree – the *Guernikako Arbola* – under which, in ancient days, Basque parliaments met and had their *fueros*, chartered rights and privileges, guaranteed by successive new rulers. There is a young tree, grown from an acorn off the old one, flourishing now. The night before my visit, a violent storm had blown down a bunch of leaves and twigs; I took some of the withering leaves to press and put in a frame at home to remind me of the place. You look up at the sky and so easily imagine how it looked, full of the Junkers and Heinkels of the Condor Legion which Hitler had provided for Franco to obliterate the town and, with it, the gritty determination of the Basques ultimately to achieve self-government. Guernica itself was not a military target. There was a munitions factory outside the town, but that was left untouched by a raid which, *The Times* reported, was 'unparalleled in military history'. When the Civil War was over, Franco banned the use of the Basque language and instituted such draconian measures of oppression that, by the time he was dead, what had been an understandable, reasonable yearning for nationhood had become something else: something altogether grotesque and distorted. You get the impression that, even if Herri Batasuna were granted every last one of its demands by the central government in Madrid (which it certainly will not be), the terror would continue: for terror has become, as in Belfast, a way of life, an integral part of the very culture and expectation of a section of the people; in short, as the slogan has it, that which has been begun cannot now be stopped. From the main street in the rebuilt Guernica I climbed a flight of steps towards the Casa de Juntas. The staircase widened, forming an auditorium; and behind this there was a noisy five-a-side soccer tournament for youngsters in progress, the players cheered on by an audience of doting parents unaware, it seemed, of bombers still coming for ever. I needed to get out for a while, to feel safe once more.

In Old Castile – but no distance from the border with the Basque province of Alava – I came to the charming small town of Villarcayo. Far from having escaped the company of Basques, I now found myself surrounded by them, Villarcayo being a favourite summer resort for the inhabitants of Bilbao as, say, Aberystwyth is for Brummies.

The place was exactly what I needed for a few days' rest: a quiet community grouped round a *plaza mayor* graced with a V and an L of pleached plane trees. I found a genteel, early nineteenth-century residential hotel whose Reception was full not of plastic and formica but of somebody's nice old rugs and treasured trophies and swords and such; and the house had high ceilings, decent rooms of an ample size, but efficient plumbing, old fashioned beds and furnishings. At the windows there were some antique wooden shutters with massive iron bars to secure them. There was a garden, too, which was a benison: plenty of grass to sit on, swings (for elderly guests to enjoy, never mind the children for once), a couple of enormous cherry trees shedding their fruit, some apple trees with cats running up and down their trunks, an acacia or two for dappled shade, a pergola of Russian vines, a miniature bullring and a pelota court which, when not in use, served as a carpark. And beyond the garden there were cereal fields.

The *dueño* was a former bullfighter called Platillerito – or Plati for short – who spent most of his days in the *conserjería*, writing articles for the bullfighting Press while supping endless bottles of beer. A volatile man, large-nosed, short, hectic in the face, he was easily moved to anger by his staff, who knew how to manage him, and his flinching wife, who did not. When I filled out the *ficha* for him upon my arrival, he paid scant attention to me: he was nursing an anger about some trivial matter to be loudly indulged later on, invisibly but most audibly, within the confines of the kitchen.

The guests were a varied bunch, good-humouredly tolerant of Plati and his moods. There was a group of five elderly ladies who loved to be paid small compliments or to be the recipients of an old-fashioned act of gallantry or some simple, bygone courtesy. Entering the *comedor*, I would usually find them already installed in their straight-backed cane chairs; I would bow to them from the hips, kiss their hands, remark upon their frocks or their beads, and when they stood up to leave on their side of the room, I would stand up on mine and bow from the neck – as though that was what was still habitually done,

272

if not by the English *afición fubolística*, whom we all agreed to tut-tut about, then certainly by respectable *caballeros* from the Home Counties on a touring study of Spain. During my stay, and to my initial embarrassment, the ladies were to encounter the real thing: a silver-haired, slightly built, distinguished-looking English ex-public school amateur lepidopterist, who had homes both in Tonbridge and the Dordogne. His manners were exquisite: precisely those of one who needs formality and ritual to protect him from emotional involvement with people. I was not surprised to learn that he had been a military doctor, a specialist in malaria who had served many years in the Middle East and India. Spending his retirement chasing about Europe in pursuit of butterflies, he had come to Villarcayo because there had been sighted, near kilometre 312 on a certain nearby highway, a species found nowhere else.

I asked him to identify a moth which I had found dead, stuck to the molten tarmac of a road in Navarre and which I had carried about since in a matchbox. He did so: a Fox Moth, he said. But later, back in England, I was to receive a letter:

Villarcayo is a delightful and lingering memory. Sadly, while there I was running a slight temperature and was clearly disoriented. This, certainly, is my only excuse for the misidentification of your moth. I am very familiar with the species, which was, of course, the Oak Eggar, *Lasiocampa quercus*; not in the least like the 'Fox!' Actually I woke in the small hours of next morning with my mistake leaping into my sleep; I then forgot to pass on the corrections to you before we parted company next morning.

That day I had a very successful couple of hours collecting on a torrid ridge in the Sierra de la Magdalena, near Castrobarte. There, *inter alia* I took the first recorded Meleager's Blue from NW Spain. Pushing on through a day of truly infernal heat . . . shade temperature of 94°F . . .

The five old ladies (I never told him this) were utterly charmed by his presence in the hotel and thought I was merely teasing them flirtatiously when I described how, with his net, he ran in the tall heat of the afternoon over the rock-strewn heights in literally hot pursuit of insects. They refused to believe me;

for butterflies were inedible and had no commercial value, they said. Doña Carmen (a retired schoolmistress) said that I had displayed a commendably lively imagination. This at once prompted me to the innocent mischief of inventing, for the ladies' amusement and mine, some scandalous and outlandish Münchhausen yarns about how the former medic filled his days. He spoke no Spanish and they no English: no embarrassment could possibly come of it. Or so I thought.

However, the ploy turned out unexpectedly: for they did credit some of the things I invented: and I was much alarmed to realize that they were inclined to believe anything I made up about his secret life in the doubtful quarters of Singapore and Madras. At dinner and lunch the poor man would be standing me bottles of wine while every teaspoon and tumbler in the *comedor* vibrated with tittle-tattle about him from the geriatric *tertulia* in the far corner. I despaired of trying to put matters right. Everything I said only served to make matters worse. He, of course, with much colonial gallantry, would return their smiles and parry their knowing looks with a broad grin; and they would simulate collective shock and store it up to relish individually in private later. The evening after he left, after dinner I tried to render a few lines of Coward's *Mad Dogs And Englishmen* into Spanish for them: but the ironic self-mockery of the English – which is in truth nothing less than a powerful affirmation of unshakeable belief in their superiority – is not a concept easily conveyed to a people whose own dignity and pride depends upon taking themselves not just seriously but solemnly: the song lost, rather, in translation. Barely able to suppress laughter at myself for having attempted a task as far-fetched – nay, impossible – as explaining the rules of cricket to Venusians, I made my last attempt. 'Doña Ana, doña Rosario, doña Inés, doña Carmen, doña María,' I said, 'you must excuse me for weaving all those fantastic fictions about the *caballero*. It is preposterous to suppose that you would ever believe my good fellow-countryman capable of such bizarre behaviour. *Venga! Les beso la mano*, I kiss your hands, *señoras y señoritas*, and thank you for being such good sports and indulging my silly joke.' But they had indelibly believed what they wanted to believe; and I can only hope the wretched fellow never goes back there.

Butterfly-hunting may seem unbelievably eccentric to the

Spaniard; but, in a meadow not far from the town, I came by chance across an old chap whose behaviour might well seem bizarre in England. I was strolling under the alders beside a beautiful, teeming but overhung and virtually unfishable trout stream, admiring the abundant wild flowers and the dragon-flies, when I spotted a bald head bobbing just above a gorse bush. By now, I had approached so close that it would have been embarrassing not to pass the time of day. But the man was deeply engrossed in what he was doing and had not seen me. I must have startled him: he dropped a bunch of reed stems he was holding. His jaw sagged.

'*Hola*,' he said, guiltily, like a Peeping Tom caught in the act. 'This is only to pass a little time, you understand.'

He was liming for birds. Here and there among the gorse he had placed cramped, home-made wooden cages, each containing a pair of exquisite, sweetly-singing goldfinches, *jilgueros*.

'I'm sorry,' I said. 'I've disturbed you. I'll go.'

'Not at all. I had scarcely begun. As I said, it's only to pass an hour or two.'

He picked up his reed stems. I watched him anoint them with sticky goo and set them out. The treacherous couples of decoy goldfinches twittered and then sang their hearts out as though enchanted, enraptured: they were indeed a lovely charm of goldfinches.

'I don't want to get in your way,' I said. 'But I must say, I'm curious. I've never seen this done before. In my country it's illegal.'

He scanned the far field edges, cocked an ear as though to detect any policemen crawling up on him through the acres of alfalfa beyond.

'Illegal here too,' he muttered. 'You understand, it's only to while away the time. Not for the money. I'm from Bilbao. I own a factory, I'm well off and well known. I love trapping birds, see? The only time I'm really happy is on holiday here. My father taught me. Every summer I come back. My wife says, "Why can't we go to the Canary Islands for a change?" *Canaries!* I ask you! Well, I suppose I could trap canaries. But I prefer the plumage of the *jilguero* to that of the *canaria*, I tell her. But more than that, though, I like it here. Can you English husbands still do the things you want? I love this place.

Every day for one week every year I come. Only to pass an hour or two. I don't catch many birds. I let go any I do catch. There are no goldfinches in Bilbao.'

His last sentence sounded to me like an excellent title for a novel: *Jilgueros no hay en Bilbao*.

Back at the hotel I next made the acquaintance of don Benedicto, another industrialist Basque from smoky, over-crowded Bilbao spending summer holidays, as he had as a boy, in daily pursuit of natural things. Mushrooms and other edible fungi were his quarry. He would be up well before dawn every day in order to drive to some moist and shady woods whose whereabouts (not that I asked him to disclose them) he repeatedly insisted he would steadfastly refuse to disclose. He was a steel and electrical engineer, he told me; and his career had taken him to Manchester and London as well as to the United States: so perhaps I would not mind if he practised his English on me. It was very awful English. Also, don Benedicto was very ugly. He wore pebble lenses in front of the kind of glistening, piggy eyes that make their unfortunate owners look untrustworthy, distasteful, megalomaniac. And don Benedicto did have his disagreeable side; sometimes he could be a bumptious little braggart you would want to set banana skins for: but he was also generous and full of loving care for his wife who, not long out of hospital, was suffering with jaundice and had a complexion the chemical colour of Bilbao's septic river Nervión. You would see him at odd times of the day bringing her a peach or an apple. Solicitously, he would persuade her to sit beside him in the garden and, after he had peeled the fruit with his penknife, one by one she would take the slivers he offered her and nibble them daintily until all was gone.

One night after dinner he took me for a *café completo* to one of the thronged cafés in the *plaza mayor*. The bar room was full of Basque women playing cards and board games. He gave his few, mildewed English phrases an airing; but soon he reverted to Castilian, having urgent things to tell me.

'My son might be coming on Sunday,' he said. 'My son is working in Galicia. He likes to go collecting *percebes* on the shore among the rocks. I taught him that. So on Sunday, if we are lucky, we shall have mushrooms and *percebes* at din-ner.' (Later, I looked up *percebe* in my inadequate dictionary.

276

The meaning it gave was 'barnacle'. Shortly after, in Galacia, I was to try a *ración* of *percebes*. They looked appalling – black and pointed, like devil's toenails – and it was difficult to guess how to eat them without crunching the shells for the small juice they yielded.) 'Nature is what keeps us sane, don Eduardo,' he continued. 'I gather *setas* in the lonely woods. My son gathers *percebes* on the lonely coast.'

I told him about the bird limer in the lonely gorse meadow.

'I like to shoot a few thrushes when I'm here on holiday. They fly into the hotel garden from the fields of oats. There were no *setas* to pick this morning. Nor yesterday. It has been too cool. We need another day of warmth. But I have to go back to my desk next week. Another year to wait before I can go mushrooming again. And my wife is ill. She lost a lot of weight and is low in spirits. But my son might come from Galicia on Sunday and that will cheer her up. Maybe he'll be having more luck with the *percebes* than I've been having with the *setas*. Not one – no, not one – have I found in the woods this year, don Eduardo.'

We walked back to the hotel and paused at the gate. He plucked at my elbow and, behind the chunky lenses, his hugely magnified little eyes were beseeching.

'Come and listen to some *jotas*,' he said.

We sat in his Japanese car in the pelota court next to the toy bullring and he put a cheap cassette into his Japanese recorder.

'From Navarre,' he said.

Jotas, I find, are very boring songs; no doubt of very great importance culturally and folkloristically to the Navarrese and the Aragonese; but monotonous to the English ear. But I could not find it in my heart to disappoint the sad, ugly, failed mushroom-hunter. I sat through both sides of the tape, enjoying my cigar and the dusty, dry smell on the breeze from the oats where the thrushes flew. That morning, a few miles away beyond the cereal fields, I had counted forty vultures along a cliff-top high above a lonely road. I would have told don Benedicto this when the second side finished; but he pressed the eject button with disgust, got out of the car and said, 'No good. Nothing's any good any more. See you in the morning, when I'm back.'

I thought that out of despair he might one day put a bullet

through his head when he went to the woods. In Spain you could die in a remote place and not be found for years. His orange-skinned wife would call in the police and feel foolish, unable to say quite where he had gone, and his son, the interior of his car faintly redolent of rotting seaweed, would know in the instant how much or how little he had loved the piggy-eyed dad who, after years of family holidays by the seaside, had ratted and reverted to the mouldy, pathless forests where there was never a clean, brisk wind to breathe. I went to bed full of concern for doomed don Benedicto.

But in the morning his pathos had evaporated and he was full of himself. He had brought back a bag of *setas* big enough to feed everyone in the hotel, he bragged. We leaned against the wall of the little bullring. The son of the *dueño*, a haughty young man insufferably officious towards old Pablo, the jack-of-all-trades servant, was giving a riding lesson to a boy of about fifteen. I liked Pablo. He was a diminutive, bandy-legged little man with cross eyes who was able to absorb all the abuse and contempt the *señorito* could hand out without for one moment appearing to be subservient or short of *pundonor*. The pony was lively. Round and round the perimeter he trotted like a circus horse, obviously knowing more about teaching a lad to ride than Platillerito's son ever would. When the lesson was over and instructor and pupil had gone, don Benedicto surprised me by mounting the pony and saying he intended to demonstrate to Pablo and me what a good seat he had. He held the animal on the shortest possible of reins so that it would prance a bit like the spirited horses of *rejoneadores*. In his town clothes, with his hunched shoulders, he succeeded only in looking ridiculous. After a few minutes he dismounted and complained to Pablo that the cinch was loose. Pablo tightened it; then got on himself and rode superbly, one-handed, making circles to the left, to the right, to the left again. The pony was transformed. Unfortunately for Pablo, however, the *señorito* then unexpectedly came back. Immediately seeing how the old fellow was giving us, in his unostentatious fashion, a dazzling display, he started to rant. He ordered Pablo to dismount. He found fault with the way he used the curry-comb, how he doled out the feed and did a dozen other chores round the place. I twigged that most of this was for my benefit: so, to save Pablo unnecessary tongue-lashing, I sidled off.

Don Benedicto stayed though, long after everyone else had gone. I could see him from my window while I packed my bags, feeling the time had come to leave. In Basque, the town of Bilbao is Bilbo; and the adjective from Bilbo is *bilboko*. Don Benedicto was a *Bilboko*. I had a final look at him. Round and round he was trotting, slump-shouldered and ignominious on the tired little pony, almost certainly unaware that he was the kind of man people keep feeling sorry for and wondering why they do.

CHAPTER SEVENTEEN

Bears' ears and sleepyheads are children's names for cow-slips and wild daffodils, high in the snow meadows of the Picos de Europa. Three months before, in early May, I had stopped my car at the top of one of the passes connecting Old Castile with Asturias. For about half an hour I had shivered, watching a shepherd – with a donkey and a dog with a bell round its neck – lead his flock up to the snow-line and further onwards still to exposed rock between deep drifts where there was new green just showing. The man and his animals took no notice of me, or of the road. They were bound for a place not many would know: a place that perhaps had no name for cartographers. A few kilometres down the other side of the pass I came upon the spring flowers. They were there in multitudes as I rounded a bend; so improbably many, they made me gasp: the ten thousand daffodils of Words-worth's poem would have been lost in a small corner of the host I saw. The snows had not long begun to melt in the year's strengthening sun; the golden flowers the children called sleepyheads had stirred only a matter of days before. When I walked among them in that mountain prairie I saw many which had actually opened beneath a transparent glaze of ice formed from snow that had all but thawed and then frozen again and filmed the blooms over by night. They looked like delicate Victorian paintings on glass. I have seldom seen anything so beautiful, and not a week passes but I think of those daffodils. However, 'This,' I remember stupidly telling myself at the time, 'is not the True Spain I've come in search of.' And after I had stamped warmth back into my feet, I turned the car round, drove back to the summit of the pass and down once more into the province of Palencia in Castile: which was still my narrow version of what 'true' Spain was. Since then, I had been in every one of the regions except for

Asturias and Galicia: and I had learned that nothing (or, more wisely perhaps, *everything*) I had seen anywhere in Spain had to be considered typical, characteristic and true of the country: a discovery neither profound nor original, but one every traveller must make for himself.

But in the north-western provinces of La Coruña, Lugo, Pontevedra, Orense and Oviedo, the discovery is harder to believe in than anywhere else: harder, even, than in Euskadi.

In Galicia, the people are Celts. Unlike other Spaniards, *Gallegos* are a squat, thick-set, lumpish, physically unattractive race. None of the older women seems of average size: a group of black widows divides, comically, between the very tall and scraggy, and the short and monstrously fat. The men are dark, flat-headed, latently aggressive. He who waits on your table looks as though he could play prop forward for Redruth. When off-duty, he will not be slow to make gleeful (or sour and peevish) remarks about his oppressors, the Castilians, just as some of the Welsh will about the English. If he thinks he can bully you, he will stridently insist upon the fact of his nationhood in the way the Basques insist upon theirs. Beneath this superficial, weak, whingeing and whining manner he is often even more sour than you think from his looks. He can be slily resentful rather than openly hostile, to the extent of displaying a muted churlishness and sullen inhospitality (what schoolmasters used to call 'dumb insolence') that is rare in Spain. And he is not given to easy laughter like the south Welsh, or to violent action like the Basques.

The *Asturianos*, their neighbours, are utterly unlike them, even down to their physical characteristics, often being fair-haired and blue-eyed. The only people not to have been defeated by the Moors – and the reconquest having actually begun with the legendary battle of Covadonga, within the borders of the ancient principality – *Asturianos* seem to have an inherited, indefinable sense of assurance, as though feeling themselves independent to the marrow, no matter what any latter-day Constitutionalists or governments may say. Many of them, like the *Gallegos*, are farming or fishing folk; but many others are workers in mining and heavy industry. They live – amid the perpetual dampness of the ever-falling

281

orbayu, or drizzle of the sea – in valleys of once lovely, now laid-waste, terrain. Theirs is a toughness, a real grittiness, to be reckoned with if ever they get riled. One is forever reminded of what their dynamiting pitmen could be all too capable of, both before and during the Civil War. The *Asturianos*, being their own men, have the gift of self-mockery. *Qui va un Asturiano. Pasa algo?* they like to say to you in their dialect: Here comes an Asturiano. What's going on? They drink splendid cider, *xidrra* (Villaviciosa is the 'cider capital' of Spain), and they eat mountainous meals of *fabada*, an explosively windy mess of different sausages, beans and *serrano* ham. *If you've got beans and cider, you're never short of gas* runs the jingle of the car rear-window stickers: *Con fabes y sidrina non fai falta gasolina*. Perhaps the surest clue to the *Asturiano's* sturdiness of spirit lies in the great mountain ranges that hem him into his remote fastness, despite the immensely long tunnels like the 4,102-metre Túnel de Negrón connecting him with the outside world. The Picos de Europa, his bastions, are grand mountains; mountains to honour and respect far more than the mighty Pyrenees, the Gredos, the Sierra Nevada, the Guadarramas and the rest. When you are driving dizzily high up in Asturias, along a stony road that feels like less than the width of a kitchen shelf, sometimes you might look across at a neighbouring cliff seeming close enough to reach out and touch; until, that is, you dare to look down into the chasm separating you from it, which would take unthinkable time, energy and courage to descend into and climb up from; and which in any case you probably would not be able to do unless you were shod with those colossally chunky, three-pointed clogs – the size of diminutive milk-maids' stools – which the local people still wear, *zuecos*.

In Galicia there is scarcely any heavy industry. If you are a male *Gallego* you may fish or work the land or, more probably, go far away to seek your fortune. Argentina is where most of your relatives and ancestors used to exile themselves to: in Argentina there have been so many of your kinsfolk that down there the word *gallego* has come to mean 'Spanish' rather than 'Galician'. These days you are just as likely to make for Madrid or Barcelona, or to the Common Market countries. I met a man with a grocer's shop in La

Coruña who had worked half a lifetime in up-market hotels in Edinburgh and Leamington; another, with a café, who had been seventeen years in Bristol and London. But whether or not you do make your fortune, the chances are that you will come back to your homeland before you die. Maybe you will open your bar, or a little store; or else (if it was indeed Argentina you went to) you might want to impress them in your village by providing them with a *churrasquería*, in which you will nightly preside, serving up those immense portions of chops and entire rib-cages that so bemused you when you first arrived in Buenos Aires. In your beautifully lyrical language, which looks and sounds closer to Portuguese than to Spanish, there is an emotive word, *morriña*, which means that kind of searing homesickness which the Welsh call *hiraeth*. Other Spaniards have the word, too, but when they speak of it, the yearning they experience is nothing like as powerful an emotion as yours: when *Extremeño* explorers made off for foreign parts, discovering new lands, conquering their peoples and exploiting their natural resources, they had neither the leisure not the imagination to languish upon the drawn-out sighs, the sadness and longing, that you so enjoy. For *morriña* is that self-indulgent, deeply depressive, Gothic side of nostalgia, the blues that, deep down, you relish and need – for the same reasons as your Portuguese cousins need their *fado*. You cannot avoid it and nor would you want to, because belly-aching is in your curdled blood and all your joy is in being abject.

The peasant womenfolk in Galicia are extraordinary. Little seems to have changed for them since the Middle Ages. It is they who look after the miniature smallholdings while the men are away; they whom you see with one cow or a goat or two on a frayed piece of rope, progressing along a deserted beach or standing stock-still and gazing into space on a patch of grass the size of a suburban living-room; they who carry improbable loads on their heads, no-hands, of laundry, corn cobs, firewood, bracken and bedstraw for the animals, cans of butane, vile green plastic buckets, loose cabbage leaves done up like a swatch of cured tobacco, a large Spar grocer's box containing one turnip-top, a bundle of prepared timber, a fifty-kilo sack of cement; they who will carry on their vacant heads, lacking other burdens, a twisted-up towel or a musty old black woolly cardigan. Along they plod at all hours stoically in their barred clogs or wellingtons through the mauve-tinted veils of misty rain, maybe with a scythe or an ace-of-spades-shaped hoe over their shoulder, bound for a few square yards of hay to cut or turnips to weed. Or perhaps they will own a wheelbarrow: in Galicia you are nobody if you do not own a wheelbarrow. All day long women are wheeling barrows along the main roads from somewhere to somewhere else; and as often as not the barrows are quite empty: it is almost as though they are being given an outing for no other purpose than that their drivers would feel undressed or bereft without them. You see wheelbarrows parked outside shops, outside cottages where perhaps their owners have gone visiting. In the middle of a main road you will come across an unattended barrow containing nothing but a trowel or string. The ubiquitous barrow is fast taking the place of the traditional Galician ox-cart: though there are still many of these two-wheeled, loudly creaking wooden vehicles about, with a pointed front like the prow of a boat, drawn as often by yoked cows as by oxen. They cross busy highways, their drivers oblivious of modern traffic, to plough some minuscule piece of ground; it is a woman who normally leads the team while grandfather guides the share. And it is the women who tend the garden plots, every one of which seems to contain a patch of a species of kale or cabbage which grows up to eight feet in height and provides the dark green foundation of *caldo gallego*, a filling, dispiriting soup appearing on every menu in Galicia.

It is small wonder that the Galician countrywoman is seldom seen to smile. The grimness of her solitary lot, a dour, louring climate that dampens and fusts and mildews all she owns, the terrible, stodgy monotony of her diet, a self-perpetuating and 'natural' poverty, the tyranny of her inescapable traditions: how could she ever think that life might be enjoyable? Yet at the Tuesday market in Redondela you may see her in a rare, vivacious mood, up to town for the day with a bunch of something misshapen and with muddy roots to sell; or perhaps, for a change, wanting something to buy. I saw one young woman in a funny yellow hat leading three young lambs on bits of string; another wearing a hobbled and struggling piglet round her neck like a fat stole.

They were buying maize bread in great, heavy slabs that looked like whalemeat steaks. I tried some. 'It's lovely with fried eggs or baked sardines,' the stall-holder assured me. It was the most ponderous foodstuff I had ever eaten; a tinrib dog I offered the rest of my piece to barked at me and ran off. In the market what they sold most, after livestock, eggs and fruit and vegetables, was the much-reinforced, beige-coloured and enormous corsetry with which, it would seem, all the womenfolk of Galicia guard their chastity and gird up their unimaginable loins.

Home from market, the Galician women will have chores to attend to: bellows to fill with DDT dust to puff at the young cabbages that must stand through winter; rye to thresh outside her door, beating the sheaves on stools or with sticks; an upright granite post to replace in her vine pergola; her woody-stemmed pelargoniums, red and pink and purple and maroon, to take cuttings from and dead-head; the dog (of the local fancy, like a cross between a Peke and a Jack Russell) to feed; and if she lives (as she is bound to in the north-west) not far from mountains, she will offer a prayer that wolves come not down by darkness and take her few sheep. In the provincial newspaper, La Voz de Galicia, there has been a report that thirty were taken in one afternoon near the Sierra Meira, adding to the many millions of pesetas' worth of livestock lost every year to the wolves. And finally, perhaps fretting about her absent husband, she must be sure to bolt the door of the hórreo.

Hórreos are small raised barns, granaries, or drying sheds: ubiquitious; and by far the most idiosyncratic feature of Galician architecture. There are tens of thousands of them, and though each one is of the same basic pattern their variety is astonishing: an elongated oblong box made of granite, anything from eight to fifty feet long and up to six feet wide, with a ridged roof of granite tiles and finials at the gable ends, the walls provided with rows of vertical slits for ventilation and the whole resting upon mushroom-shaped steddles to prevent rats from entering. They are often situated immediately adjacent to houses, but just as often well away from human habitation: a single one, perhaps, in isolation in a field, or several in a line along the foreshore. You find them in the middle of towns, this one humped up against a church, that

285

one cantankerously standing its ground next to a new supermarket. Sometimes they are placed at arbitrary angles to boundary walls of upright, tombstone-like slabs; and sometimes they are parellelogram in plan, or inclined to the horizontal. Before you learn what they are, they are likely to disturb you: they may make you think of sepulchres or sarcophagi, of chest tombs with fancy roofs; of something sinister, at any rate: something religious or – worse – quasi-religious, something to do with the mumbo-jumbo of death, or arcane, sacerdotal practices pertaining maybe to black magic. Are they family vaults? Maryan shrines? Are sacrifices made in them? Asturian *hórreos* are far less numinous, being squarer, taller, often thatched and with wooden walls and balconies that give them a comforting, domestic, less 'other' appearance. Galician *hórreos* are not buildings I should willingly bed down in – or near – for the night. At Corcubión, near Cabo Finisterre, I stayed in a motel called El Hórreo. It was characterless, bland and anonymous as such places always are; but near its entrance stood its long-disused, eponymous little barn, faintly ecclesiastical with its crucifix finial but also, being an ancient artefact juxtaposed to a modern institution, strongly suggestive of the properties of a Hammer horror production. I was constantly aware of its proximity. After dinner, try as I might to concentrate hard upon the lovely sight of ships' lights moving across the still, black waters of the *ría* below, I wondered what horrors involving chicken gizzards they might get up to, out of season, up in the padlocked *hórreo*.

At Cabo Finisterre, the westernmost tip of Spain and the very edge of the known medieval world, you gaze out towards the Americas and sense what so many must have felt who have stood on that spot before you. You have come by way of a beautiful route through close, glossy woods, the road gradually rising until it became a *corniche* looking over a wide bay towards three massive sierras. You reached some scattered cottages, and the lighthouse, and some storm-battered memorials and commemorative plaques in a small car park which was as far as you could go. There, you left the car and impatiently scrambled as far as you could over the rocks, ever westwards, westwards, checking your directions by the position of the hazy sun. Now, some hundreds of feet below, there are perhaps two dozen brightly painted boats, prow to the cliff, jiggling for squid. They look vulnerable as toy boats; a violent storm could blow up within minutes along this exposed stretch of coast. Precisely where you sit, hundreds of thousands of the most pious and energetic pilgrims once used to come, scallop shells in their hats and thanksgiving prayers in their hearts, after successfully completing their long and hazardous journey to the holy shrine of Santiago de Compostela; and these are the same rocks that still make the local men curse their luck and make up their minds to go in search of better things an enormously long way west by south. On an abrupt slope under the lighthouse there were three old women and an old man swapping down with bill-hooks such as there was of fodder: the short, thin, yellowy grass of August, tough bents, raggety willow-herb. A false step could have had them tumbling and bouncing down off the boulders among the squid-boats; but they had no option but to labour on, as their parents had laboured on, because every leaf, every blade was needed to conserve in the family *hórreo*, to see beasts through until the next warm weather.

'What's it like here in winter?' I asked the old man.

'Waves fifteen metres high,' he said in *gallego*. 'Nobody comes here after October. We're here on our own in winter.'

I bent to drink from a tap beside the path.

'Better if you drink from the spring higher up,' he said. 'It has good salts in it. The water from the lighthouse tap is drinkable enough, it'll quench your thirst – but it's got no goodness in it. The other water prevents the arthritis, you see. It's all we ever drink, it's good water.' This was all he had to say, needing to get on with his work. All three of the old ladies wore their cardigans on their heads, shaped into toques with hairgrips. It was much of the sum of all their wisdom to drink correct water so that they could live to a great age and be sure-footed, without arthritis on the perilous slopes. And all through the year, even in high summer, they had to keep in the warm. Their light was pearl. Sunshine seldom pierced the sea-fret here. Though it felt warm in the lee of the lighthouse, you could tell it would not take long for you to suffer from exposure. The old people, though working ener-getically despite their uncomfortable stance on the cliff-side, were swathed in black against the bad evening cold soon to come. Yet such is the contrary nature of Galicia, in the hinterlands of these shores that the Gulf Stream washes, you can be astounded by sub-tropical vegetation: not five miles away from this bleakness are palms, aloes, cacti, Madonna lilies, lemon trees, vivid-flowered succulents.

The entire shoreline of Galicia – from Ribadeo, through the *rías altas* round the corner past Cabo Finisterre to the *rías bajas* and Vigo, north of the Portuguese border – is uncompromising and dramatic and for the most part unspoiled. The ravening beast of cynical and all-out commercial tourism on the lines of the Mediterranean *costas* has not yet sunk its pyorrhoeaed teeth in, probably because the sun here is at best fugitive; and bathing in cold Atlantic waters from such uncomfortable, granite-grey, inconvenient and inaccessible beaches (for all that they are incomparably lovely) is not likely to become an attractive prospect. Some development has gone on – in particular at O Grove and La Toja Island, on the estuary west of Pontevedra – but this is of a kind more likely to appeal to Spaniards wanting to avoid the implacable heat they are normally subjected to, than to Nordic sybarites wanting to fry even before their time.

I liked O Grove, finding it was one of those old-fashioned and wayward seaside resorts containing far more than at first meets the eye. Those in search of sporting activities – golf, tennis, shooting and such-like tomfoolery – can cross by the causeway to La Toja, a pine-covered island the restorative property of whose waters was apparently discovered when a sick donkey regained its health by drinking it. There is little point in either humans or donkeys these days going to La Toja to take the waters, the wonderful springs having long since run dry; therefore it seems far preferable to stay in a humble *pensión* on the very waterfront of O Grove to sample the local seafood, which is considered by many gourmets to be, with the possible exception of that of Newfoundland, the best in the world. How could this not be so, given that throughout the region they hold annual octopus and eel festivals and that octopus distribution centres abound?

Here, as elsewhere in Galicia, the variety and abundance of shell-fish is astounding and bewildering. Just as an Eskimo has a large vocabulary of nouns for the infinite forms of snow which fall on him, house him, or which he drinks or tramples underfoot, so the Gallego has coined an impressively stout lexicon of nouns not only for those crustacea which are little known outside his region (like the *percebes*, the goose barnacles I had sampled), but also for all the gradations in size or colour of those which are known elsewhere, but by only one name. For the outsider, the problem is further complicated by the fact that even fat Spanish/English dictionaries are of little help to him when he scans the menu in a *marisquería*: most of the items have *gallego* names, or Castilian names which prove to be local variations yet unknown to scholars. The commonest word in Spain for mussel is *mejillón*: but hereabouts you will just as likely find *morcillón*, *macillón*, *musclo*, *muskullón*, *muskullo*, *mocejón*, *mazajón*, *mojarón*, *miquillón*, *mexillón*, *músculo*, *mojojón* and, for every foodie-snob insisting upon a word not starting with m, *linguerón*. If fourteen words for one mollusc seems excessive, then what will the diner make of the twenty-four recipes for mussels listed by the Amegrove collective of 300 families who, in their pamphlet, declare that they are 'daily dedicated to the cultivation of the mussel'? Even a non-specialist restaurant is likely to have as many as twenty different fish and shell-fish on offer, from the massive lobster known as *buey*, or ox, to the smallest shrimp, or *camarón*; from the whopping crab, *centolla*, to small spider-crabs, *nécoras*; there will be all sizes of prawn and crayfish, with familiar names, *gamba*, *langostino* and *langostín*; there will be octopus, cuttlefish and squid – like *chipirones*, small squid fried in breadcrumbs; also, all gradations of clams and scallops; and then sea-bream and grouper, turbot and angler-fish and hake and eels. By the time you have reached this section of the menu, perhaps you will have discovered that *bagavante*, which usually means 'the stroke oar in the racing eight', is yet another type of lobster. But there are other words which must remain a mystery, like the powerfully lickerous *lubrigante*, which sounds considerably more of an effective aphrodisiac than your workaday *ostra*, or oyster. What can one do, to overcome one's ignorance, in the face of so multitudinous a choice? Not much one *can* do except sigh pleasurably and find out by gradually eating one's way through the entire list as the days go by. However, it is not as though your difficulties are confined to the fish section of the menu. If fruits of the sea bring you out in hives, or you opt for meat for a change, you may yet be put out by discovering that the contents of that simply enormous, rectangular pie on the counter, *empanada gallega*, might well be fish: so next you will wonder what might constitute a Moaña chop, or precisely how 'shoulder of pork with turnip-tops' will go down, or whether the *churrasco* is indeed likely to be (as you have heard) a lump of meat from the barbecue so big as to cover entirely the wooden platter it comes on. Then there is pudding to contemplate. Can one with confidence take on a portion of *brazo de gitano*, or 'gipsy's arm'? (One can: it is nothing more exotic than a kind of Swiss Roll enclosing not jam but custard.) The fresh local white wines to go with your seafood are acceptable; but eaters of red meat in the vicinity of La Coruña should be wary of a certain liquid, red and fizzy, served in a kind of white, porcelain crucible more apt for the preparation of copper sulphate crystals than the drinking of wine.

The waterfront of La Coruña, the Avenida de la Marina, is one of the most spectacular streets in the whole of Spain. The quaysides, with fishing vessels, cargo boats and warships moored cheek by jowl, are full enough of lively interest: but it is the wonderfully long, continuous row of tall, glass-fronted buildings standing back behind their broad avenue which claim the attention and a niche in the grateful memory. The glazed balconies, *solanas*, are purely functional. They trap and make the most of every ray of rare, warm sunlight, and they exclude the perpetual gustiness off the Atlantic. As with airliners, pure function has great beauty as its inevitable by-product: the hundreds of rows of white-painted window-bars on different levels, the broad white horizontal strips separating floors and vertical ones separating properties, impart to the slightly curving architectural cliff an utter freedom from monotony which might with profit be studied by designers of glass-faced tower blocks. The buildings of La Coruña (and similar ones elsewhere in the north-west) exude a sense of correctness and civilized behaviour. Vandalism is unthinkable in flats built along lines such as these.

The port has a fascination for blinkered English patriots. Here, four hundred years ago, the invincible Armada set sail, to be vanquished no less by foul weather than by Drake, Hawkins and their handier ships. Here, two and a half centuries later, the English commander against Napoleon's troops, Sir John Moore – after a rapid retreat across mountainous terrain – lost his life in a battle he might have won but for a fiasco of embarkation: two events which those cynical of Britain's much-vaunted naval and military power could cite to demonstrate the fortuitousness of her notable successes and the amateurish bungling of her notorious failures. Having done his damnedest, however, good Sir John was immortalized in the celebrated poem. His memory is also kept alive in a shabby *hostal* in which I stayed in Lugo, by a plaque of the fourth Battalion of the Royal Green Jackets. It was presented by a commissioned descendant of Sir John who stayed there while retracing the remarkably fast scuttling of his ancestor from Villafranca del Bierzo: very touching, very English, infinitely sad.

I did not want to go to Santiago de Compostela: not yet, I mean. Some stopping places along the way in one's travels are simply halts in which to spend the night; others (predictably or not) are remarkable and worth going to for their own sakes; and some (few) others are definitive destinations so massively impressive they impart a sense that not until you have been home, unpacked, reacclimatized and started again from scratch will there be anywhere for you to go without disappointment and anti-climax. Santiago would be one such. Though not a Catholic and unable to find it possible to believe that St James travelled to that obscure and rainy corner of Galicia, I knew how to compensate for lack of faith with a superabundance of imagination. The place was bound to enthrall me if only because I was following in the sore and weary footsteps of so many, over so many centuries. Already I knew what Santiago would look like: almost as many words had described it as pilgrims had ever arrived there.

So, for a spell, while still heading for Santiago de Compostela, paradoxically I journeyed away from it, first staying in small, quiet, remote cities of the region of León like Zamora and Ciudad Rodrigo: unspoiled, tranquil, old-fashioned, where the convent schoolgirls still wore boaters and correct brown uniforms and the sounds of private music lessons escaped from upper windows in the early evening. In the *plaza mayor* of Ciudad Rodrigo there was a bull-crazy bar with the unlikely name of Sanatario, its walls entirely covered with splendidly stirring, large black and white framed photographs of the annual *encierro*. In the quiet hour in the last of the afternoon heat, an old, noble-looking gentleman cantered past on an immense black stallion, filling the temporarily deserted and echoing square with a metallic clatter of hooves such as the town had known for a thousand years or more. In Zamora there was, in an enclave of peacefulness even within the city's general quietness, a cathedral whose Byzantine cupola roof tiles made it look like a hunched-up pangolin; and I came to a heart-rending view from the ancient city walls of the Duero and a landscape that, ever afterwards, I would yearn to see again. My idea of Spain, I thought in that instant: I could stay there for ever . . . Unless I continued to Salamanca, the lovely sandstone city I had visited before, on a tour of the great cities of the *meseta*. Yes, and I wanted to go back some day to Toledo, to Ávila, where the *hostal* porter wore the frock-coat his great-grandfather had worn, and to Sigüenza, where there grew the Indian bean tree with the longest pods in all Spain; and I wanted to see Burgos again, if only to walk under the city's matchelss *alameda* of linked plane trees to where the mounted statue of El Cid, his cloak like the bristling frill of an angry dinosaur and his sword extended mightily, is always set to charge full pelt across the river. And oh, I wanted to spend another night in the hotel in Segovia whose balconies look towards the great aqueduct and its long evening shadows; and after the last of the sun to eat hugely of *cochinillo asado* and then mount the hill to stroke the sphinxes that in the dark had so frightened Jan Morris (an exactly duplicate pair adorns the gate-posts of a tame new house in Sussex). I wanted to return to El Escorial and the Valley of the Fallen, which bear massive, continuing witness to the folly of grandiosity and pomp. Go back I would: even if disabled, an old man doctors confined to bed or chair. My head was crammed full of images that would not deteriorate or die, as photographs do.

In the provinces of Salamanca and Zamora, on the way back to Santiago, I kept stopping for the wildlife and vegetation as I had done earlier in the year. Then the wilderness had been strewn with tall broom shrubs, white and old gold; with lavender, crimson common peonies and lupins such as we cultivate in English gardens. May blossom and poppies had startled the eye among patches of young wheat, as did butter-cups in their millions studding the meadows. I had counted twenty bee-eaters in a field at the edge of a rock chaos, beside a pond. They had perched, all gloss and shot-silkiness, on fence-posts or barbed wire, or hawked and momentarily hovered for bees along dry stone walls of delta-shaped boulders. Now the plains had reverted to the kites and eagles, harriers and buzzards. The grass was old, brown as coconut matting. I was feeling tired out; but, after each short and frequent halt, with an incomparable sense of refreshment that comes from knowing the end of a journey close, I felt exultation gathering: a pleasurable ache across the shoulder-blades which grew more and more intense and which would not tauten, burst and subside until, unworthy motor-car pilgrim that I was, I locked my little Fiat, and climbed the great staircase to the Obradoiro and placed my fingertips in the wonderfully deep, touch-eroded holes of the stone Tree of Jesse.

GLOSSARY

(N.B. Ch and Ll are separate letters of the alphabet.)

A LA PLANCHA, fried

ABAJO, below; down; under; downhill

ABRAZO, hug, embrace

ACTIVIDAD, activity

ACTO, event; PROGRAMA DE ACTOS, programme of events

ADELANTE, forward, onward

AFICIÓN, support, following, fan-club (for football team, bull-fighter, pop star, etc.)

AJILLO, chopped, fresh or young garlic

AJO, garlic

ALAMEDA, formal avenue of trees

ALCALDE, mayor

ALCAZABA, citadel

ALCÁZAR, fortress

ALFARERÍA, pottery (i.e. potter's workshop)

ALGUACIL, mounted constable who leads the ceremonial procession at the beginning of the bullfight

ALIANZA POPULAR, Popular Alliance (Conservative Party)

ALIMENTACIÓN, food; provisions; grocer's shop

ALTO, tall; high

AMANTE, lover

AMBULANTE, walking, strolling, travelling; VENTA AMBULANTE, walking salesman, hawker

ANDALUZ, Andalusian

ANDALUZ, person from Andalusia

APPROVECHAR, to benefit from; QUE APROVECHE, *Bon appétit!*

ARRASTRE, the dragging out of the dead bull at the bullfight

ARRIBA, up; upper; above

ARROYO, course of a stream

ARTE, art
ASTURIANO, Asturian, from Asturias
AUTOPISTA, motorway
AYUNTAMIENTO, town hall
AZULEJO, glazed (ornamental) tile

BAJADA, descent, slope
BANCO, bank
BANDERILLA, barbed, paper-decorated dart used in bullfighting
BANDERILLERO, the bullfighter who places the *banderillas*
BANDOLERO, bandit, highwayman
BAÑO, bath
BAÑO COMPLETO, bathroom with bathtub, shower, bidet, hand-basin and WC
BARBARIDAD, barbarity, barbarism; ¡QUÉ BARBARIDAD! How ghastly! What an awful thing!
BARÇA, (*fam.*) Barcelona Football Club
BARRA, loaf of bread
BARRERA, barrier fence in bullring
BARRIO, quarter of town or city
BARRIO CHINO, (literally) Chinese quarter: the red-light district of Barcelona
BARRIO GÓTICO, the Gothic quarter (of Barcelona)
BARRITA, small loaf, or large roll, of bread
BECERRADA, bullfight with bull calves
BECERRO, calf, bullock
BELLAS ARTES, fine arts
BOCADILLO, sandwich
BODEGA, wine cellar or warehouse
BODEGÓN, cheap eating-house
BOLA(S), bowl(s)
BOLLERÍA, assorted pastries; pastry shop
BONITO, tunny, tuna-fish
BOQUERÓN, anchovy
BORRACHO, drunk; drunkard
BOTA, boot; wineskin
BOTE, pool or communal *tronc* of waiters' tips
BOTELLÍN, small bottle (of beer)
BRIGADA, brigade

BUEN TÍO, good chap
BUEN VIAJE, *Bon voyage!*
BUEY, OX, large lobster

CABALLERO, gentleman
CACAR, (taboo) to shit; CACA EN EL PANTALÓN, He shits his
  trousers
CAFÉ COMPLETO, black coffee, a brandy and a cigar
CAFÉ CON LECHE, white coffee; CAFÉ-COÑAC, coffee and brandy;
  CAFÉ CORTADO, coffee with dash of milk,; CAFÉ DESCA-
  FEINADO, decaffeinated coffee; CAFÉ SOLO, black coffee
CALLE, street
CALLE MAYOR, main street; high street
CALLEJÓN, alleyway; the passage between the inner and outer
  barriers of the bullring
CAMARERO, waiter
CAMARÍN, dressing-room
CAMINO, way; road; path; track
CAMINO DEL REY, the King's Path
CAMPANITA, little bell
CAMPESINO, peasant; SOMBRERO DE CAMPESINO, straw hat
CAMPIÑA, cultivated, open farmland or countryside
CANARIA, canary
CANARIAS, Canary Islands
CANGREJO, crab
CANTE HONDO, deep song; Andalusian flamenco gipsy singing
CANTIDAD, quantity
CANTIMPLORA, water bottle
CAÑA, small glass tumbler
CAÑADA, drover's road; gulley
CAPA, cloak, cape
CARINOSO, loving, warm, affectionate
CARMEN, (In Granada) villa outside the city; country
  house
CARTEL, poster, placard; bullfight advertising bill
CASA, house; ¡MI CASA, SU CASA! Make yourself at home!
CASA COLGADA, (In Cuenca) clifftop (literally, hanging) house
CASA DE JUNTAS, (In Guernica) Town Hall
CASA REAL, Royal House

CASA SEÑORIAL, house of nobility family, often bearing stone-carved coat of arms on façade

CASERÍO, country house; (In Basque Provinces) high-class road-house restaurant

CASINO, club

CASO, case; ¡NO HAGA CASO! Don't worry! Take no notice!

CASTELLANO, Castilian; POTAJE CASTELLANO, Castilian stew

CASTELLANO, Spanish (language)

CASTILLO, castle

CATALÁN, Catalonian, Catalan; the Catalan language

CATALUNYA, (Catalan form of Cataluña) Catalonia

CATALUÑA, Catalonia

CATÓLICO, Catholic

CÉNTIMO, cent

CENTRO NUCLEAR, Nuclear Plant

CERILLO, small hill, hillock, incline, slope

CERRO, hill

CIENCIA, science

CIUDAD, city

CIUDAD ANTIGUA, Ancient City

CIUDAD ENCANTADA, Enchanted City

CLARO, obvious, clear; ¡SÍ, CLARO! Yes, of course!

COCKTEL, cocktail

COCKTEL DE MARISCOS, seafood cocktail

COLGADO, hanging, suspended

COLUMBICULTURA, pigeon-fancying

COMBATIENTE, combatant, soldier

COMEDIA, play; comedy

COMEDOR, dining-room

COMENDADOR, knight commander (of military order)

COMPLETO, full; complete; CAFÉ COMPLETO, black coffee, a brandy and a cigar

COMUNIÓN TRADICIONALISTA, Traditional Communion (a political and religious conservative movement)

CON, with

CONDE, count, earl

CONQUENSE, to do with Cuenca

CONQUENSE, inhabitant of Cuenca

CONQUISTADOR, conqueror

CONSERJE, porter, caretaker, doorman

CONSERJERÍA, porter's office

CONTRABARRERA, bullfight seats near the ring itself
COÑAC, brandy
COPA, (brandy) glass
COPITA, small brandy glass
CORDOBÉS, Cordovan; belonging to Córdoba
CORDOBÉS, inhabitant of Córdoba
CORNADA, goring
CORO, choir, chancel
CORREO, mail
CORREOS, mail; post office
CORRESPONDIENTE, correspondent
CORRIDA (DE TOROS), bullfight
CORRIENTE, ordinary; VINO CORRIENTE, table wine
CORTADO, cut off; CAFÉ CORTADO, coffee with a dash of milk
CORTES, the Spanish Parliament
CORTIJO, (In Andalusia) farmhouse
CORTO, short; TRAJE CORTO, outfit worn by country bullfighters
COSA, thing
COSTA, coast
CRISTO, Christ; CRISTO ES AMOR; Christ is love
CRONISTA, local historian; chronicler; local correspondent
CUADRILLA, a matador's squad
CUANDOQUIERA, whenever
CUCHILLERÍA, cutlery; a cutler's shop
CUCHILLERO, cutler
CULTO, cultured, refined, educated, well brought-up

CHARANGA, brass band
CHATO, small wine glass
CHAVAL, lad, youth
CHICO, boy, boy friend
CHINO, Chinese
CHISTE, joke; cartoon
CHORIZO, type of spicy pork sausage
CHUMBA, HIGUERA CHUMBA, prickly pear
CHURRASCO, barbecued meat; large cut of meat
CHURRASQUERÍA, barbecued meat shop or restaurant
CHURRERÍA, stall or café selling CHURROS, q.v.
CHURRO, fritter

DESAPARECIDO, disappeared; LOS DESAPARECIDOS, the vanished ones (of Argentina)

DESCAFEINADO, decaffeinated

DESCANSO, rest; DÍA DE DESCANSO, day off; SIN DESCANSO, no let-up, without stopping

DESGARBADO, slovenly, sloppy, untidy, ungroomed, uncouth

DÍA, day; DÍA DE FIESTA, holiday

DIARIO, daily (newspaper)

¡DÍGAME! (title of BBC Spanish language TV course) Tell me!

DIOS, God; VAYA or VATE CON DIOS, Goodbye (literally, Go with God)

DIRECCIÓN, management. DIRECCIÓN GENERAL DE EMPRESAS Y ACTIVIDADES TURÍSTICAS, State (or Regional) Tourist Enterprise Board

DISCOTECA, disco

DOBLE, double

DON, (Courtesy title used before Christian name, the equivalent of Esquire)

DONDEQUIERA, wherever

DOÑA, (Feminine equivalent of DON, above)

DUCADOS, Ducats (brand-name of cigarettes)

DUEÑA, lady of the house; proprietress; landlady

DUEÑO, owner; proprietor; landlord; the boss

DURO, five-peseta coin

ELOCUENCIA, eloquence

EMPRESA, enterprise; company

ENCANTADO, enchanted; LA CIUDAD ENCANTADA, The Enchanted City

ENCIERRO, corral; the penning, or corralling, of animals

ENTREMESES, *hors d'oeuvres*

ESCUELA, school; ESCUELA TAURINA, school of bullfighting

ESPADA, sword; matador

ESTOQUE, short sword used for despatching dying bull

ESTRAPERLO, black market

ESTUDIO, study

EUROPA, Europe

EXMO, (= EXCELENTÍSIMO) most excellent

EXTREMEÑO, from, or pertaining to, Extremadura

FABES, (Asturian dialect) beans
FADO, (Galician and Portuguese) type of sad folk song
FAENA, the extended performance of the matador
FALANGE, phalanx; FALANGE ESPAÑOLA, Fascist Party of Spain
FERIAL, pertaining to the fair; TERRENO FERIAL, fairground
FERM, (Catalan) road surface
FICHA, form; chit; record card
FIESTA, festival, festivities, celebration, public rejoicing
FINCA, property; parcel of developed land outside town
FINO, fine, excellent; (of people) cultured
FINO, dry sherry
FLAMENCO, gipsy dancing and singing in Andalusia
FONDA, humble tavern providing accommodation and
    meals
FORTUNA, fortune, luck; FORTUNA, (brand of cigarettes)
FRONTÓN, front wall of pelota court
FRUTERÍA, fruiterer's shop
FUEGO, fire; light (e.g. for cigarette); TORO DE FUEGO, bull
    bearing lighted flambeaux
FUERZA, force, strength, might; FUERZA NUEVA, New Power
    (political movement)
FULMINANTE, fulminating; exploding; gushing (blood)

GALLEGO, Galician
GALLEGO, A Galician; (In Argentina, any Spaniard)
GANADERO, stockbreeder
GASEOSA, fizzy drink
GASOLINA, petrol
GAZPACHO, Andalusian cold soup
GENERALÍSIMO, Field Marshal
GENERALITAT (DE CATALUNYA), (Catalan) Autonomous Govern-
    ment of Catalonia
GOLPISTA, one taking part in a coup
GRANIZADO, iced drink
GRUPO, group; circle
GUARDIA, policeman (of the Civil Guard)
GUÍA, guide; directory; handbook; GUÍA DE HOTELES, Hotel
    Guide
GÜISQUERÍA, whisky bar

HAY, there is, there are
HERMANO, brother
HIDALGO, noble(man)
HIJA, daughter; HIJA PREDILECTA, favourite daughter (of a town, etc.)
HIJO, son; HIJO PREDILECTO, favourite son (of a town, etc.)
HOLA, hello! hi!
HOMBRE, man; ¡hombre! good heavens!
HOSPEDERÍA, hostelry, hospice
HOSTAL, hotel
HOTELERO, hotel proprietor
HOZ, gorge
HUERTA, vegetable garden (In Valencia and Murcia) large, irrigated, fertile area under constant cultivation
HUERTO, kitchen garden; private garden; HUERTO DEL CURA, (in Elche) The Priest's Garden
HUÉSPED, guest, lodger; host, landlord

IMPERECEDERO, imperishable; IMPERECEDERA MEMORIA, everlasting memory
IMPORTAR, to matter; NO IMPORTA, It doesn't matter
INFANTA, Princess
INGLÉS, English
INGLÉS, Englishman

JAMÓN, ham; JAMÓN DE YORK, York ham. JAMÓN SERRANO, country-cured ham
JARA, cistus flower
JEFE, chief; boss
JOTA, type of dance – and the music for this – in Aragon
JUNTA, committee; assembly

LEVANTE, east wind
LOCO, mad
LUZ, light; VIRGEN DE LA LUZ, The Virgin of Light

MADALENA (ALSO MAGDALENA), plain small cake; *madeleine*

MADRE, mother; MADRE DE DIOS, Mother of God

MADRIGAL, madrigal; (Arch.) bramble or briar patch

MADRILEÑO, inhabitant of Madrid

MADRUGADA, the very early morning

MAGDALENA (also MADALENA), small cake; *madeleine*

MAHONESA (also MAYONESA), mayonnaise

MALVINAS, Falkland Islands

MANCHEGO, pertaining to La Mancha

MANSO, a tame (sometimes castrated) bull used to accompany a bad or mutilated fighting bull from the ring

MANTILLA, mantilla; head covering, usually of black or white lace

MARAVILLAR, to amaze; UN SABOR QUE MARAVILLA, a flavour that astonishes

MARGARITA, daisy; (also, almost any small flower)

MARICÓN, (*fam.*) queer, poofter

MARINERO, sailor

MARISCOS, shellfish; also seafood in general

MARISQUERÍA, seafood restaurant, bar or stall

MASINO, pertaining to Mas. GRUPO DE ESTUDIOS MASINOS, The Mas Study Circle

MAYOR, main, bigger; PLAZA MAYOR; Main Square; CALLE MAYOR, High Street

MERENDERO, picnic area, usually with bar, shade, tables etc.

MESETA, tableland, plateau; MESETA, the central plateau of Spain

MESÓN, inn and restaurant with 'traditional' décor

MI, my; MI CASA, SU CASA, my house, your house; 'make yourself at home'

MILI, (*fam.*) military service

MIRE (from MIRAR) look!

MOJE, type of *hors d'oeuvre* from MURCIA

MOLINO, mill

MORCILLA, black pudding

MORENO, dark (of hair, complexion)

MORTERUELO, (dim. of MORTERO, mortar) a kind of meat hash, a local speciality of Cuenca

MOSTO must (unfermented grape-juice)

MULETA, the matador's red cloth and stick

MUNICIPAL, municipal; POLICIÁ MUNICIPAL, urban police

MUS, mouse (a card-game)
MÚSICA, music

NADA, nothing; NADA DE NADA, Not a bit of it! Who cares!
NADIE, nobody
NATURAL, 'natural' pass in bullfighting
NAVAJA, penknife
NEGOCIO, business; shop
NOCHE, night
NORTEAMERICANO, North American; from the USA
NOVIA, girlfriend, sweetheart, fiancée, bride
NOVILLADA, bullfight with young bulls and novice bullfighters
NOVIO, boyfriend, sweetheart, fiancé, bridegroom
NUCLEAR, nuclear; CENTRO NUCLEAR, Nuclear Plant
NUEVO, new

OCHO, eight
OLOROSO, fragrant, sweet-smelling; sweet sherry
OLLA, pot; stew
ONDULACIÓN, (Catalan) bump
ÓPTICA, optics
ÓPTICO, optician
ORDEN, order

PAELLA, dish of rice, fish, shellfish and white meat
PAÍS, nation; locality; VINO DEL PAÍS, local wine
PALO, stick
PAN, bread; a loaf of bread
PANTALÓN, trousers
PAÑUELO, (piece of) cloth; handkerchief
PARADOR, hotel (run by the Spanish government)
PAREJA, (married) couple; (fam.) pair of Civil Guards
PASACALLE, march, parade led by brass band; the music for this
PASADO, the past; LO PASADO PASADO, what's past is done
PASEO, walk, stroll (i.e. promenade), outing; boulevard
PASO, religious float; step, pace; PASO DOBLE, a fast dance
PAZ, peace; VIVA EN PAZ, Live in peace
PECADO, sin; SANTA MARÍA LA SIN PECADO, Holy Mary, she
  without sin

PELOTA, ball; the game of pelota
PENSÍON, boarding-house; guest-house
PEÑA, rock, crag; club, society, group
PEQUE, (fam. form of pequeño, small), kiddy, little 'un
PEQUEÑO, small; PEQUEÑA CANTIDAD, small quantity
PERCEBE, type of edible barnacle
PERIODISTA, journalist, newspaperman
PESETA, peseta (the Spanish unit of currency)
PICADOR, mounted bullfighter
PICO, (mountain-) peak; corner (of hat); small amount; (fam. nickname) Titch
PINAR, pinewoods; pine forest or plantation
PLAZA, square; PLAZA DE TOROS, bullring
PLAZUELA, small square
POLICÍA, police force
POLICÍA, policeman; POLICÍA MUNICIPAL, urban policeman
POLLO, chicken; POLLO AL AJILLO, chicken pieces deep-fried with garlic
PONIENTE, westerly wind
PORRÓN, wine vessel with long spout
POSADA, lodging house; simple inn
PREDILECTO, favourite
PREFERIDO, preferred; favourite
PRENSA, press
PROGRAMA, programme; list; PROGRAMA DE ACTOS, programme of events
PROVINCIA, province; EN PROVINCIA, in the provinces
PÚBLICO, public, PLAZA PÚBLICA, The Public Square (local var. of Plaza Mayor)
PUEBLO, small town
PUNDONOR, honour, self-respect

QUE, (followed by various words or phrases) What a—! How—! Also introduces imperative or command
¡QUE APROVECHE! (from APROVECHAR, to benefit from), v.i. Bon appétit! Eat well!
¡QUE BARBARIDAD! How awful! What a terrible thing!
¡QUE NADIE SE ENGAÑE! Let no one deceive himself!
¡QUE RARO! How extraordinary!
¿QUE TAL? How are you? ¿QUE TAL LA SEÑORA? How's the wife?

QUESO, cheese; QUESO MANCHEGO, La Mancha cheese; QUESO
DE RONCAL, Roncal cheese
QUITE, manoeuvre in bullfighting in which the bull is dis-
tracted and drawn away from an injured man

RACIÓN, portion
RAMBLA, dried-up river bed; RAMBLA, (in Catalonia) wide
boulevard or avenue with central reservation for pedestrians
RARO, uncommon, strange, extraordinary, odd
REAL, royal
REDOBLE, drumroll; EL REDOBLE, The Drumbeat (patriotic song)
REFORÇAMENT, (Catalan) strengthening, reinforcement
REJONEADOR, mounted bullfighter who fights with a REJÓN, or
lance. (N.B. not to be confused with PICADOR)
REJONEO, the art of fighting bulls on horseback
REPARACIÓN, repair; EN REPARACIÓN, under repair
RESOLÍ, local liquor from Cuenca
REY, king; sovereign; LOS REYES CATÓLICOS, the Catholic King
and Queen Ferdinand and Isobel
RÍA, estuary
RÍO, river
RIOJANO, pertaining to Rioja
ROMERÍA, pilgrimage; excursion; trip
RUBIO, fair, blond

SABOR, taste, flavour, aroma
SAGRADO, sacred, holy; SAGRADA FAMILIA, The Holy Family
SALA, hall, meeting-room
SALCHICHÓN, sausage (of salami variety)
SALÓN, hall, salon; SALÓN DE MÚSICA, concert room
SALUD, health, ¡SALUD! Cheers!
SAN, (Short form of SANTO), saint
SANFERMINES, the Madrid bullfight festival of San Fermín
SARAPE, (in S. America) blanket
SECO, dry
SEÑOR, gentleman; sir; Mr
SEÑORA, lady; madam; Mrs

306

SEÑORES, gentlemen, ladies and gentlemen; sirs
SEÑORITA, miss; young lady
SERRANÍA, range of mountains; hilly or mountainous country
SERRANO, of the country; rustic; JAMÓN SERRANO, country
   cured ham
SERVICIO, service; toilets; SERVICIOS DE PRENSA, Press facilities
SETA, mushroom
SEVILLANA, gipsy dance of Andalusia
SEVILLANA, woman or girl from Seville
SEVILLANO, pertaining to Seville
SEVILLANO, man or boy from Seville
SIERRA, mountain range
SIESTA, nap; snooze; afternoon rest period
SIN, without; SIN VERGÜENZA, without shame; shameless
SIN, (trade name of beer) Without (i.e. without alcohol)
SOL, sun; SOL Y SOMBRA, sun and shade (seating in bullring)
SOMBRA, shade
SOMBRERO, hat; SOMBRERO DE CAMPESINO, peasant's (straw) hat
SORTEO, draw; drawing of lots; toss-up
SOTANILLO, small cellar (dim. of SÓTANO)
SUIZO, type of flaky pastry
SUPERMERCADO, supermarket

TABERNA, tavern, inn
TACONEO, the art of dancing with stamping of the heels
TAL, such; ¿QUE TAL? How are you? How are things?
TALGO (= Tren Articulado Ligero) Articulated, lightweight,
   highspeed train
TAPA, hors d'oeuvre; snack
TAURINO, pertaining to bullfighting; ESCUELA TAURINA, school
   of bullfighting
TAXISTA, taxi driver
TEATRO, theatre
TERNASCO, lamb; TERNASCO AL HORNO, roast lamb
TERRENO, ground; extent of land; TERRENO FERIAL, fairground
TERTULIA, social gathering; café circle; SALA DE TERTULIAS,
   clubroom
TIERRA, land; earth
TINTO, (stained) red; VINO TINTO, red wine

307

TÍO, uncle; chap, fellow
TÍPICO, 'typical' i.e. (usually bogus) traditional
TIRADOR, marksman; shot
TODO, all, everything
TONTERÍA, a piece of nonsense or foolishness
TORERA, female bullfighter
TORERO, bullfighter
TORICO, small bull
TORIL, bull pen
TORO, bull; TORO BRAVO, fierce, spirited bull
TORRÀ, (Valencian *dial.*) barbecue
TORRE, tower
TORTILLA, omelette, usually with potato filling
TOSTADA, toast; piece of toast
TRAJE, suit; TRAJE DE LUCES, suit of lights; TRAJE CORTO, outfit
  worn by bullfighters at small country bullfights
TRANQUILO, quiet, peaceful
TRASVESTIA, transvestite
TURÍSTICO, pertaining to tourism; touristic
TUROLENSE, pertaining to Teruel
TURRÓN, type of nougat made from almonds and honey

VALENCIANO, pertaining to Valencia; Valencian
VALENCIANO, inhabitant of Valencia
VAQUILLA, amateur bullfight
VATE CON DIOS, goodbye (literally Go with God)
¡VAYA! well! there! come now!
VECINO, neighbour, resident
VEGA, stretch of fertile land; plantation
VENGA, come; come along
VENTA, roadside inn; VENTA AMBULANTE, strolling salesman
VERBENA, open-air festivities; local fair and dance
VERGÜENZA, shame; SIN VERGÜENZA, shameless
VERÓNICA, type of pass in bullfighting
VIAJE, journey
VINO, wine
¡VIVA! ¡VIVAN! Long live! ¡VIVA ESPAÑA! Up with Spain! VIVA
  EN PAZ, Live in peace
VOLUNTAD, wish, desire; (of contributions) whatever you like

VOZ, voice
VUELTA, turn; stroll; lap of honour for bullfighter

XORIÇO (Valencian dialect) CHORIZO, a type of sausage

Y, and
YA, already, now, at once, at last

ZARAJO, (local delicacy of Cuenca) strong-flavoured strips of
  lamb or kid wound on twigs
ZONA, (combat) zone; (*fam.*) applied to entertainment or
  nightlife centre of city
ZURRA, fruit-cup (similar to sangría) in Cuenca

INDEX

LINKWORD LANGUAGE SYSTEM

The fastest, the easiest, the most enjoyable way to learn a language!

Pick up 400 words and basic grammar in just 12 hours with LINKWORD.

* Travelling
* Eating Out
* Telling the Time
* Emergencies
* At the Hotel
* Going Shopping
* Numbers
* Clothes
* Family
* On the Beach

Ideal for holidays, business travel, schoolwork.

'Unforgettable memory joggers'
The Sunday Times

'It took 12 hours to teach a regime that normally takes 40 hours'
Training Manager, Thomson Holidays

'It works and it's fun'
The Guardian

Available for the following languages:
0 552 13053 2 **FRENCH**   0 552 13054 0 **GERMAN**
0 552 13055 9 **SPANISH**   0 552 13056 7 **ITALIAN**

All priced at £3.95

IN SOUTHERN LIGHT
by Alex Shoumatoff

As a travel writer, Alex Shoumatoff is drawn to places beyond the frontiers of Western civilisation. IN SOUTHERN LIGHT describes two such places – the dense, rich jungle of the Amazon and the lush, exotic rain forest of Zaire.

His fascinating journey into the Amazon describes his ascent of the Nhamunda River, a little known tributary. To go up this river is to go back in time. The fabled Amazon women are said to have lived there. Homesteaders living in the era of Daniel Boone are also to be found. In contrast, at one place, Michael Jackson is the rage with jeans and message T-shirts worn, and a passion for TV soaps and breakdancing.

In Zaire, Shoumatoff treks into the heart of the Ituri Forest, the land of the BaMbuti and Efe pygmies, visiting villages where white people have seldom, if ever, been encountered. Here is a country that is more an anarchic collection of tribes, a land of corruption and promiscuity, but also one where warmth and joy radiate even from settings of stark deprivation.

Both journeys are fascinating, vivid and excitingly exotic. Some of the adventures are terrifying in their potential danger of disease and natural hazards, and the social conditions described are often eye-opening to the pampered Westerner. Without romanticizing or patronising the people he meets, Alex Shoumatoff brings to the reader an accurate, compelling portrait of so-called primitive societies that helps us better understand our own beginnings.

'This is transportation by literature. An exotic and wonderful book'
Tracy Kidder

0 552 13329 9

THE HOUSE BY THE DVINA
A RUSSIAN CHILDHOOD
by Eugenie Fraser

'Eugenie Fraser has a wonderous tale to tell and she tells it very well. There is no other autobiography quite like it'
Molly Tibbs, The Contemporary Review

A unique and moving account of life in Russia before, during and immediately after the Revolution, THE HOUSE BY THE DVINA is the fascinating story of two families, separated in culture and geography, but bound together by a Russian-Scottish marriage. It includes episodes as romantic and dramatic as any in fiction: the purchase by the author's greatgrandfather of a peasant girl with whom he had fallen in love; the desperate journey by sledge in the depths of winter made by her grandmother to intercede with Tsar Aleksandr II for her husband; the extraordinary courtship of her parents; and her Scottish granny being caught up in the abortive revolution of 1905.

Eugenie Fraser herself was brought up in Russia but was taken on visits to Scotland. She marvellously evokes the reactions of a child to two totally different environments, sets of customs and family backgrounds. The characters on both sides are beautifully drawn and splendidly memorable.

With the events of 1914 to 1920 – the war with Germany, the Revolution, the murder of the Tsar, the withdrawal of the Allied Intervention in the north – came the disintegration of the country and of family life. The stark realities of hunger, deprivation and fear are sharply contrasted with the day-to-day experiences, joys, frustrations and adventures of childhood. The reader shares the family's suspense and concern about the fates of its members and relives with Eugenie her final escape to Scotland.

'A wholly delightful account'
Elizabeth Sutherland, The Scots Magazine

0 552 12833 3

THE PAST IS MYSELF
by Christabel Bielenberg

'It would be difficult to overpraise this book. Mrs Bielenberg's
experience was unique and her honesty, intelligence and
compassion makes her account of it moving beyond words'
The Economist

Christabel Bielenberg, a niece of Lord Northcliffe, married
a German lawyer in 1934. She lived through the war in
Germany, as a German citizen, under the horrors of Nazi rule
and Allied bombings. *The Past is Myself* is her story of that
experience, an unforgettable portrait of an evil time.

'This autobiography is of exceptional distinction and importance. It deserves recognition as a magnificent contribution
to international understanding and as a document of how the
human spirit can triumph in the midst of evil and persecution'
The Economist

'Marvellously written'
The Observer

'Nothing but superlatives will do for this book. It tells its story
magnificently and every page of its story is worth telling'
Irish Press

'Intensely moving'
Yorkshire Evening News

0 552 99065 5

A SELECTED LIST OF BIOGRAPHY TITLES
AVAILABLE FROM CORGI BOOKS

THE PRICES SHOWN BELOW WERE CORRECT AT THE TIME OF GOING TO PRESS. HOWEVER TRANSWORLD PUBLISHERS RESERVE THE RIGHT TO SHOW NEW RETAIL PRICES ON COVERS WHICH MAY DIFFER FROM THOSE PREVIOUSLY ADVERTISED IN THE TEXT OR ELSEWHERE.

☐	99315 8	**NO TIME FOR ROMANCE**	*Lucilla Andrews*	£3.95
☐	99065 5	**THE PAST IS MYSELF**	*Christabel Bielenberg*	£3.95
☐	99271 2	**MY HAPPY DAYS IN HELL**	*George Faludy*	£4.95
☐	99314 X	**A VOYAGER OUT**	*Katherine Frank*	£4.95
☐	12833 3	**THE HOUSE BY THE DVINA**	*Eugenie Fraser*	£3.95
☐	12863 5	**THE LONG JOURNEY HOME**	*Flora Leipman*	£3.95
☐	99247 X	**THE FORD OF HEAVEN**	*Brian Power*	£3.50
☐	99293 3	**THE PUPPET EMPEROR**	*Brian Power*	£3.95
☐	99305 0	**HELEN OF BURMA**	*Helen Rodriguez*	£4.50
☐	13329 9	**IN SOUTHERN LIGHT**	*Alex Shoumatoff*	£3.95

All Corgi/Bantam Books are available at your bookshop or newsagent, or can be ordered from the following address:

Corgi/Bantam Books,
Cash Sales Department, P.O. Box 11, Falmouth, Cornwall TR10 9EN

Please send a cheque or postal order (no currency) and allow 60p for postage and packing for the first book plus 25p for the second book and 15p for each additional book ordered up to a maximum charge of £1.90 in UK.

B.F.P.O. customers please allow 60p for the first book, 25p for the second book plus 15p per copy for the next 7 books, thereafter 9p per book.

Overseas customers, including Eire, please allow £1.25 for postage and packing for the first book, 75p for the second book, and 28p for each subsequent title ordered.